# HowExpert to Bodyguarding

## 101 Tips to Learn How to Bodyguard, Improve, and Succeed as an Executive Protection Agent

**HowExpert with Cody Blocker**

**For more tips related to this topic, visit HowExpert.com/bodyguard.**

# Recommended Resources

- HowExpert.com – Quick 'How To' Guides on All Topics from A to Z by Everyday Experts.
- HowExpert.com/free – Free HowExpert Email Newsletter.
- HowExpert.com/books – HowExpert Books
- HowExpert.com/courses – HowExpert Courses
- HowExpert.com/clothing – HowExpert Clothing
- HowExpert.com/membership – HowExpert Membership Site
- HowExpert.com/affiliates – HowExpert Affiliate Program
- HowExpert.com/jobs – HowExpert Jobs
- HowExpert.com/writers – Write About Your #1 Passion/Knowledge/Expertise & Become a HowExpert Author.
- HowExpert.com/resources – Additional HowExpert Recommended Resources
- YouTube.com/HowExpert – Subscribe to HowExpert YouTube.
- Instagram.com/HowExpert – Follow HowExpert on Instagram.
- Facebook.com/HowExpert – Follow HowExpert on Facebook.
- TikTok.com/@HowExpert – Follow HowExpert on TikTok.

# Publisher's Foreword

Dear HowExpert Reader,

HowExpert publishes quick 'how to' guides on all topics from A to Z by everyday experts.

At HowExpert, our mission is to discover, empower, and maximize everyday people's talents to ultimately make a positive impact in the world for all topics from A to Z...one everyday expert at a time!

All of our HowExpert guides are written by everyday people just like you and me, who have a passion, knowledge, and expertise for a specific topic.

We take great pride in selecting everyday experts who have a passion, real-life experience in a topic, and excellent writing skills to teach you about the topic you are also passionate about and eager to learn.

We hope you get a lot of value from our HowExpert guides, and it can make a positive impact on your life in some way. All of our readers, including you, help us continue living our mission of positively impacting the world for all spheres of influences from A to Z.

If you enjoyed one of our HowExpert guides, then please take a moment to send us your feedback from wherever you got this book.

Thank you, and we wish you all the best in all aspects of life.

Sincerely,

BJ Min
Founder & Publisher of HowExpert
HowExpert.com

PS...If you are also interested in becoming a HowExpert author, then please visit our website at HowExpert.com/writers. Thank you & again, all the best!

# Table of Contents

# Introduction

The field of bodyguarding, executive protection, and private security can be complex and challenging. Yet, in the rapidly changing world, we find ourselves in today, safety and security are essential. Celebrities, wealthy individuals, business owners, high-profile people, politicians, and others need to protect themselves. More and more of these clients are becoming aware of the safety hazards and risks that exist every day. These risks can come from stalking, assassinations, kidnapping, domestic violence, workplace violence, lawsuits, targeted violence, active shooter, terrorism, embarrassing incidents, assaults, or common crimes.

The profession of bodyguarding and executive protection is primarily focused on crimes against people. Yes, a bodyguard is always in charge of everything from personal safety, medical conditions, public safety, fire evacuation, safe driving, logistics, and slip, trip, falls. But the primary function of a bodyguard is to protect one person from another person. Threats can come from anyone. It can be an estranged spouse, an obsessed fan, angry stockholder, disgruntled employee, unwanted pursuer, insulted client, anyone with a grievance, or someone looking to make a statement in the news.

Protecting people has never been more critical than it is today. The men and women out there who chose to make their living defending others have a high calling and a difficult mission to accomplish. This book will highlight the most important tips and concepts that one needs to succeed in this profession. These concepts come from over a decade in this field of study and from situations I have learned first-hand.

Throughout this book I will use the terms 'Bodyguard/Executive Protection Agent/Protector' interchangeably. This book focuses on the title 'Bodyguard' but people may refer to this role with these different terms. For the person being protected, I will also use the terms 'Client/Protectee' interchangeably for the same reason.

# Chapter 1: A Bodyguard's Mind

## Part A: Mindset

### Tip # 1: Professionalism

A bodyguard or an executive protection agent can be described as two different roles, but they largely overlap. Some may have different definitions of the two titles, but at the end of the day, they are both professionals who are making their living protecting others.

A bodyguard has to be professional. And I don't just mean something one does to earn a paycheck. A professional is someone who takes their role and their chosen profession seriously. A professional is someone who strives to get better at what they do. They constantly improve and never settle for "just good enough." A professional strives for mastery over proficiency. A bodyguard will regularly find themselves in situations where they hear personal details, financial issues, sensitive information, medical conditions, or private information that should not be repeated. A client needs to know that their bodyguard is someone they can trust not to repeat confidential information. It takes a great deal of character, trust, and personal discipline to be a professional bodyguard.

The value of protection must be the basis of every security job. This value must be kept front and center at all times. All problems, decisions, and actions can be filtered through the value of protection. If you are in a security role, your primary job is to protect someone or something. All life is precious. You should guard a person because their life and well-being are worth saving. That is what you are hired to do. You should want to protect someone because it is the right thing to do ethically, and you are trained and equipped to do it. You should not decline to guard someone just because they are different than you. You should not protect someone because of the status or recognition you believe it may give you. You should not save someone because you want to gain their favor.

## Tip # 2: Situational Awareness

If your primary job is to protect someone, you have to have good situational awareness. Situational awareness is the ability to be aware of your environment and know what is going on around you that could affect the safety of yourself or your client. It is a good, healthy, common sense awareness of what's going on. It does not mean panic, paranoia, or constantly looking over your shoulder; that will waste energy and quickly wear you out. It is a healthy, calm awareness that can be maintained all day. You need to have a strong mental capability to notice little details and constantly assess information. The more aware you are of the situation, the less likely you will be caught off guard.

Situational awareness is a mindset that can be practiced, and it is something you can get better at if you want to. For example, good situational awareness is knowing how long it will take to drive across town. It's looking both ways before you cross the street, knowing where the nearest fire extinguisher is; it's looking in the windows before you go in and looking out the windows before you go out. It's being aware of the fact that an unknown person could be a threat. Depending on the situation, it's being ready to block a punch while simultaneously being prepared to shake hands.

Good situational awareness can be practiced on a large scale or small scale. On a large scale, it could be knowing the weather outlook for the day, knowing where the nearest ER is, and knowing if your client has any specific active threats. On a small scale, it could be recognizing that your client has pasta sauce on his tie and is about to meet an important client. You may want to let him know so he can remove it before the meeting. Or it may be discerning the height, weight, hair color, and gender of the person who is threatening your client and noticing anyone who matches the description within conversations distance of your client.

## Tip # 3: Ethical and Religious Issues of Violence and Use of Force

Suppose you are in the business of protecting someone from violence, then you must be aware of the possibility that part of your job may include the responsibility of using force in self-defense. If you are not prepared to use force, then you need to get ready to do so. In addition, you must become comfortable with using force in such a way that it does not violate your own personal ethical, religious, or philosophical values.

Because when violence happens, it happens fast, and you will not have a lot of time to debate the religious or ethical issues of using violence. You must know ahead of time what you are willing to do. So that when the time comes, you will be less likely to hesitate and will be able to respond quickly and correctly. You must become familiar with violence, so you know what it looks like, how to identify it, how to defend from it, and how to avoid it.

## Tip # 4: Combat Mindset

If you are working in a role that may require you to use force against someone else, you have to have the appropriate Combat Mindset. Combat Mindset can be defined as the willingness to use the proper degree of force against a threat. For example, suppose a threat attacks you violently and aggressively. In that case, you will need to defend and counter-attack with controlled aggression to stop the danger as quickly as possible. Each use of force in a situation is unique, and you must have the knowledge, training, and discretion of lawful use of force that would be required to protect yourself or your client.

Having a proper combat mindset will help you respond quickly and appropriately. In addition, a good combat mindset will help prevent you from stalling, hesitating, getting caught off guard, or going into shock if you are confronted with violence.

A good Security Agent will have a healthy and appropriate Combat Mindset. It is the mindset that will help give you the courage to act when your skills are needed. A healthy Combat Mindset will help you be able to take a life to save a life if needed. A good Combat Mindset also means you will be able to fight through stress, hardship, and pain to accomplish your mission. It will allow you to screen out distractions to focus on the task you need to perform. All life is precious, and we must do what we are trained to do to protect it. We must come to terms with our mortality and be okay with the possible adverse outcomes, injuries, pain, and even death that can happen with our chosen profession.

### Tip # 5: Combat Breathing

Combat breathing is the discipline of focusing on your breathing before, during, and after a high-stress situation. Combat breathing can be done prior to a bad thing happening. For example, you can sit and control your breathing every morning before you go to work or right before you are going to walk into a big crowd where a potential threat may be. If you cannot control your breathing in a normal, low-stress environment, you'll be less likely to maintain it in a violent, high-stress environment. Combat breathing can be done during an attack. For instance, if a threat starts to attack your client with a punch, you may have to block, control, and restrain that person until help arrives. Controlling your breathing will help you not to over-exert yourself and get lost in an adrenaline dump. Controlling your breathing can help you calm down after a violent event occurs.

In high-stress situations, it is easy to get overwhelmed and freeze. Being able to control your breathing is a way to mitigate problems that can come with too much adrenaline. There are many different schools of thought on what type of breathing method should be practiced and why. But the overall goal is to become aware of your breathing and how it affects your motor skills when responding to a threat. If you focus on your breathing, you can control it, and if you can manage it, it will help you remain calm and remember your training. Conversely, having a good foundation will help you stay calm.

## Tip # 6: Combat Planning

Combat planning is the ability to know your plan and what you will do if a bad thing happens and understand what you're going to do if your plan fails. Combat planning is having a good plan A, plan B, plan C, and plan D, E, F, and so on. You have to have a plan. But what are you going to do if your plan doesn't work? A good acronym to remember for planning is the word PACE. It stands for your Primary plan, Alternate plan, Contingency plan, and Emergency plan.

A good bodyguard will not hesitate if plan A doesn't work. For example, let's say your plan is to drive your client across town to attend a meeting. What if the fastest route is blocked due to construction? What will be the next shortest route you can take? If you have a backup route already planned, you'll be able to re-route faster. The more time you take thinking through possible routes, the more likely your client will arrive late for his meeting, and the more exposed your client will be to potential danger out on a busy street. Having backup plans is quicker and safer.

### Tip # 7: Stress Management and PTSD Awareness

Bodyguard work can often be stressful because you may have to regularly be involved with violence, threats, medical emergencies, little sleep, and a very fast-paced daily schedule. You may constantly be around crowds of people and always be thinking about all the bad things that could happen. You may have to work a very long and stressful day, stay up late typing reports and get up extremely early the next day; you will have to find time to exercise and practice skills like defensive tactics or shooting firearms. In addition, you may have to do all of this while managing your family life.

Your days may be filled with dealing with angry people, yelling insults at you. You may have to deal with violence regularly, and you may have to do this for days, weeks, or years.

You have to be able to complete your job without getting overwhelmed mentally and emotionally. Having good friends, family, mental professionals, and/or team members around you to help you through difficult times can be incredibly powerful. Dealing with violence and bad things for prolonged periods can be stressful. It is your job to keep yourself mentally and emotionally healthy so you can complete your job and keep your clients safe. It is your job as a professional to know what specific stress relievers you need in your life. It is your job to know your limits and know when to say "no." It is your job to train, prepare and remain mentally strong, so things do not stress you out. A professional and appropriate combat mindset will help you with this.

In the business of security, you may come into contact with violence, assault, physical or emotional trauma, medical emergencies, or life and death situations. You will likely be exposed to things you never thought possible. Your client may be a member of a community or culture that is vastly different than what you are used to or that can seem abnormal to you. You will likely be expected to work very long hours or travel away from your family for long periods. These are all things that may add stress to your life. You must be aware of this before you go into the profession of being a Security Agent. You cannot allow pressure from your job to affect your job performance negatively. Know things like Post Traumatic Stress Disorder and Post Shooting Trauma are real and can impact you physically, emotionally, and sociologically. Know that everyone processes stress and trauma differently. What stresses one person out may not necessarily stress you out, and vice versa. Do not try and compare your stress or trauma to someone else. If you are aware of this before a traumatic event happens to you, you will respond better in the moment of trauma, and you will be more likely to process the trauma afterward. Also, remember there is a difference between "managing the stress in your life" and "allowing things to stress you out." It means you have a large amount of control over what you let stress you out or not. Proper mental preparation, education, combat mindset, stress inoculation, and training will help you manage stress and not let things stress you out.

## Tip # 8: Humor

A human can be an important component to help you from getting stressed out. Having a sense of humor can help you get through a rough day. It can help you deal with things that are difficult at the moment and can help relieve stress. Humor can be a powerful tool when you are dealing with multiple people on a team. It doesn't mean you need to be making annoying jokes to everyone constantly. But having a good sense of humor can help you be a more enjoyable team member to be around. A good sense of humor can also be a great tool when dealing with clients. It can make you more approachable and pleasant to be around. If you cannot make light of problems or a stressful situation, you are probably not cut out to be a bodyguard.

In the security industry, you have to have a sense of humor. You have to enjoy life and enjoy your work. If you complain about your job, get a different job or do something to fix it. Having a good sense of humor will help with things like team morale and team building. Humor can break down barriers and break the tension between people. Humor can help you develop rapport quickly with your client or someone you are protecting. As a Security Agent, you may see things, hear things or learn of things that are not pleasant; having a good sense of humor can help you process these negatives issues.

## Tip # 9: Maturity

A good Security Agent must be mature enough to disagree without getting offended respectfully. It is important to remember that you will not agree with everyone, and that is okay. However, it is crucial to be able to disagree respectfully. People are different, and you may have to work with someone on a security detail that has a belief or moral you disagree with. You should still be able to work together and communicate professionally, regardless if you disagree with someone. If you respect other people and their beliefs, you will be less likely to take things personally. Know that not everyone is going to agree with you.

## Tip # 10: Positive Attitude

A good Security Agent has to be able to have a positive attitude. A positive attitude will attract people to you. It will inspire team members to want to follow you. Having a positive attitude will help you be solution-oriented and will help you to solve problems faster. Having a positive attitude does not mean that you are blind to the bad things in life. In fact, it is just the opposite. Because I know there are bad things in life and work, I choose to have a positive attitude because I know I cannot control everything. Accepting that you do not have control over all things allows you the freedom to step back, relax and crack a joke at how ridiculous things can get.

## Part B: Mental Capabilities

## Tip # 11: Flexibility

Someone who is entrusted with the role of protecting another human being must have certain mental capabilities. A bodyguard has to be flexible and adaptable to any given situation because circumstances and plans change. No matter how good of a plan you have, there will always come a time when an unforeseen obstacle gets in your way and forces you to deviate from your original plan. These changes can be as small as the client changing an appointment time at the last minute. For instance, you are told to be ready to leave at 6:00 AM, and you arrive at 5:15 AM to be early. Then the client tells you they have changed their mind and you will not be leaving until 9:00 AM. These types of simple details can change all of the time. However, changes can be more extensive in scope. For instance, you are told you will be protecting one client, and no threat is present. Then, when you arrive, you find out you need to protect the client, their four family members, and a credible threat is present. This type of last-minute change will require an entirely new plan and strategy.

A person who is frustrated with change and especially last-minute changes will not do well as a bodyguard. A good protector needs to understand that changes will happen. A good protector shouldn't be surprised by this or caught off guard. If you set up the expectation that things will change, you will be able to respond to them more effectively. Do not allow frustration or annoyance to creep into your head, or it will negatively affect how you are to do your job.

The value of having an open mind is crucial because it allows you to learn new things. An open mind is what makes you able to listen to criticism and improve at your job. An open-minded person knows they do not know everything, and they know they can get better. An open-minded person knows techniques, procedures, laws, and technology changes, and they need to learn to always keep up with these changes. An open mind will help you remember that people are different and have different experiences, mindsets, beliefs, worldviews, and expectations. You do not know everything, and you never will. Be open to learning various points of view.

### Tip # 12: Working Under Pressure

Being able to work under pressure is vital. Remember, there are different levels of pressure. It doesn't mean you will always have to execute mission goals while under fire. Yes, pressure could mean something serious like dealing with an emergency medical situation or using self-defense against an assault. However, this concept will more likely come into play with regular logistical types of work. It can come in many forms, but working as a bodyguard is a type of job where you are required to have a physical body in a physical place to accomplish the work or fulfill the contract. You need to have people. It is not like other jobs where if John calls in sick, he can pick up the workload tomorrow. In this line of work, if John calls in sick, you need to replace John with someone else immediately. How will you respond if you are required to have three people on your team and one calls in sick one hour before start time? Who will you call? What will you tell the client if you don't have a third person? There will be times when you are expected to perform many duties in a short amount of time. Due to a change in the client's schedule, you may be asked to rent a car, get a carwash, stock the car with drinking water, pick up an AED, and pick someone up at the airport who is going to meet the client in less than an hour. You will never have enough time, intelligence, resources, or sleep.

## Tip # 13: Working with Military and Law Enforcement Personnel

Working as a bodyguard or other private security fields, you are likely to work with members who are current or formal military or law enforcement. You do not need a background in one of these two fields to work as a bodyguard, even though some people say you do. Having prior military or law enforcement experience may be a great help to you as a bodyguard, but it is not always a guarantee. Just because someone wore a certain colored uniform for a couple of years means very little when it comes to the present job. The character, humility, mindset, and work ethic of the individual are always more important than the resume. Generally speaking, a law enforcement individual may be used to chasing criminals, apprehending suspects, and solving crimes. Generally speaking, a military individual may be used to going on the offensive and attacking. These are not bad in and of themselves; it is just what they were trained to do. However, working as a bodyguard can have a seemingly counter mission to these. A bodyguard's primary mission is to keep their protectee alive, not automatically chase the criminal who attacked them, and not automatically counter-attack. Both of these things may be doable if you have a large enough team and the circumstances are right. But it is highly unlikely you will be doing either of these if you are a one-person team and do not have the resources to do three things simultaneously. It should also be considered with other people you may be teamed up with last-minute who have years of different training and experiences. A paramedic, for instance, may feel an urge to treat someone who is injured instead of evacuating them to safety. As a bodyguard, your primary mission is to protect and probably move the protectee to a safe space.

You may consider this and communicate on your primary mission i you show up on a team with four people, where one is a military soldier, one is a police officer, one is a bodyguard, and one is a paramedic. What if the four of you are protecting someone and are attacked by someone trying to assault your protectee, and a bystander is injured? What if the soldier wants to fight back immediately? What if the police officer wants to chase after them? What if the paramedic wants to stop and help the injured bystander? What if the bodyguard intends to evacuate the protectee safely but can no longer do that because he has lost his three teammates. Make sure you are on the same page with your primary mission and what the expectations are for all team members.

## Tip # 14: Don't Get Distracted by the Celebrity

When performing bodyguard work, your protectee could likely be a celebrity or a high-profile person who others recognize. It can be complicated in the instance where your protectee is someone you look up to or admire. In this instance, you have to differentiate between your professional role as a protector and a typical fan. You cannot be both. The relationship between the bodyguard and the protectee must be grounded in professionalism and maturity. It would be unethical of you to use your position as a bodyguard to gain access to the celebrity as a fan. For instance, a bodyguard should never ask the protectee for an autograph or to take a picture with them. You can also cross the line if you talk to them as a fan. Your role as their protector cannot be done as a fan. If you are thinking about how to obtain an autograph, you are no longer focused on protection. It also includes autographs or pictures for a friend or a family member.

It is unprofessional for you to use your position as a bodyguard way to meet your idol. One of the values you can add to your bodyguard service is allowing the protectee time to relax and not talk to fans. Word travels fast in this industry, and if word gets out that you took pictures with or asked the protectee for a favor, you will likely have a short bodyguarding career. Not only is this unethical, but it is tactically poor as well. If you are constantly looking at your idol, you will not be looking outward at the crowd of people who may be a threat.

## *Tip # 15: Leadership and People*

To be a successful team member on a team of other bodyguards, you will have to exercise a high level of personal leadership. It can be formal and informal. A traditional leadership role could be something like you are appointed as the Team Leader for an assignment. You will probably be expected to execute record keeping, time tracking, group communication, and conflict resolution tasks. These are all duties that require confidence and competence. You have to have the confidence to step up and take charge at the moment, but you must also have the humility to step down and take orders from someone else when needed. The situation may change rapidly.

Not only do you have to lead your team under you, but you also need to lead the people above you in the chain of command and your client. The client/bodyguard relationship is a constant dynamic of leading and following. The client is usually the one who signs your check, so in one case, they are in charge. However, you are the one in command of their safety and security, that's your specialty, and that's what they hired you for. But what happens when their goal disagrees with your goals. For instance, what if the client wants to attend a public event last minute. And you have no time to do the proper advanced work or get team members in place. Are you going to tell the client he cannot go? Leading your client is not about just telling them what to do. It is about developing a relationship with them and developing trust, so when a conversation comes up where you have conflicting goals, you will have the credibility to bring this up to your client.

# Tip # 16: Management and Logistics

To be a successful team member, you will have to be able to manage systems and logistics. Much of the work a bodyguard does involves administration and logistics. You will have to help coordinate schedules, shift changes, keep posts filled while not allowing overtime. You will have to account for simple things like meals. When will your team eat if you are all working during your client's lunch meeting? How will you get all team members from point A to point B? It sounds easy when everyone is working at one physical location, but how will transport work if you visit five different sites throughout the city in one day? Working as a bodyguard often requires long shifts and long days. You may have to plan things out in advance and then have a backup plan ready when your initial plan does not work. You will have to have the ability to track your team's time cards, work schedules, equipment checkout, radio batteries, client's itineraries, emergency contact info, daily intelligence briefings, threat assessment reports and make sure the client's care is full of gas and is spotlessly clean from the previous day. And all of this does not account for the logistical problems when something goes wrong; the car breaks down, a team member gets sick, schedule changes, or a new meeting pops up. The ability to manage, organize and plan is critical to any bodyguard.

# Tip # 17 Command Post Operations

The Command Post (or CP) is typically needed in an extensive bodyguard detail involving one or more teams. The CP is one location that monitors and distributes information and intelligence to the team(s). It can be a location that is operated 24/7, stores radios and equipment, charges batteries, stores vehicle keys, etc. How big or how extensive the CP should be depends on your overall mission and budget. A traditional CP is usually not needed for smaller or shorter details. However, if you have larger teams with multiple shifts and many bodies coming in and out over a long period, an organized CP can be beneficial. It can be as simple as a designated room or even a closet located in the client's house or place of work. It can be a simple check-in point for team members to gear up and get the latest intel. You can also partner with the existing security rooms of Security Operations Centers. For instance, say you are assigned to protect a CEO at his residence and office, and the office already has security guards working out of a security room 24/7. You can partner with them as they will have security cameras, access control, and contact points at the office. Partnering with existing security can be highly beneficial for each party to complete their missions.

### Tip # 18: Problem Solving and Putting Square Pegs into Round Holes

A bodyguard must be ready and capable of solving problems at a moment's notice. The very nature of bodyguard work is that plans change, and issues arise. Schedules change, team members get sick, intel is wrong, meetings are added or canceled, equipment breaks, the client changes their mind, etc. Bodyguard work is about physically being present wherever the client is or needs to be. It comes down to logistics. And logistics is one of the things that break down first. What if you end up with a team of six people at one location, and two of you rode in the client's car. Then the client runs into an old friend, and they decide to go out to another impromptu location but now has no room for two bodyguards in his car because he wants to travel with his friend. You now only have one car that fits only four people. Do you leave two behind? Which two? Do you get the two there some other way? However difficult it is, you must still solve the problem. Responses like "I can't" or "I don't know" are unacceptable.

A solution-oriented person knows they have to be flexible and adaptable to dynamic situations and problems. As a Security Agent, you need to be able to put square pegs into round holes. In the security business, you will often be expected to complete tasks with less than adequate resources, money, intel, time, and/or sleep. You will have to be creative and resourceful to find a fast solution. A solution-oriented person focuses on solutions and does not focus on problems. You should not go to your supervisor, boss, or client and complain about your dilemma and expect them to fix it for you. If you have a problem, you should figure out how to solve it and then, if you have to, go to your supervisor and say, "Here is the problem and this is how I plan to fix it."

## Tip # 19: Honesty and Integrity with Personal Information

As a bodyguard, you will be in places and situations where ordinary people are not. You may find yourself overhearing specific phone calls, business meetings, trade secrets, and personal conversations that have nothing to do with you or your job. However, being a bodyguard may require you to be in certain places where you are trusted to hear certain things. You must have the mental discipline to keep up with certain boundaries when you find yourself in certain situations. You must be worthy of confidence and trust and be able to screen out distractions and certain "news" you overhear. If you struggle with wanting to know and share the latest gossip or the latest news, then being a bodyguard is not for you. The clients who need our protection do not need another person in their life who they need to be suspicious of. Our job is to make their life easier, not harder.

# Part C: Ego and Humility

### Tip # 20: Ego: You Can't Be in it for the Spotlight

Leave your ego behind. Your ego is your biggest enemy. If someone is in a bodyguard, executive protection, or security role because they think wearing a uniform or having a position of "authority" will make them feel better about themselves, they are wrong. It means their priorities are out of place, and they are insecure. Many people who work in the executive protection business are trying to compensate for their lack of self-esteem. These people lack confidence in their self-identity, and they are searching for something to give them confidence. These are the worst type of people to have in any position of authority. You should only be in this role because you have the talent and desire to protect others and serve them. If you are in this line of work because others will think you're special just because you get to stand next to the celebrity, then you're wrong.

### Tip # 21: Ego: You Can't be in it Because You Get to Carry a Gun

If you already lack confidence and have self-identity issues and think that carrying a gun will make you feel "cool" or look "cool," then you're wrong. You may be at a point in life where you need to figure other things out first, instead of a new job. Any new job, especially one where you carry a gun, will not help you and will, in fact, make your life more difficult, as well as endangering those you're supposed to protect. If you need to carry a gun to feel better about yourself, then stop carrying a weapon and figure out what needs to be fixed in your life to get your identity and self-confidence back on track. Carrying a firearm will not help and will only get you

26

in trouble. A firearm is a safety device. It is a tool that you can use to save yourself or another. A firearm is not a status symbol or a magical amulet that makes you safe all of a sudden. It is one specific tool for a particular job, and that job is the protection of the innocent. If you treat your firearm as anything more than that, then you will have problems.

## Tip # 22: Ego: You Can't be in it Because You get Authority

People usually attach authority to a firearm. So, when people carry a gun, they feel like they have more control than they do. A weapon does give a person power; this is why a firearm can be such an effective self-defense tool. However, if this is why you take the job, you are doing it for the wrong reasons. People also attach authority to other things, uniforms, radios, positions of power, even physical positioning in a room. Again these are all things that can be attached to a bodyguard, and they may help you do your job. However, if you need to get authority from something or someone else to feel better about yourself, the protection profession is not for you. So, before you begin on the journey of protection, think about it and make sure you are doing it for the right reasons. You have skills, mindsets, talents, experiences, and abilities that make you good at protecting others.

## Tip # 23: A Service-Oriented Mindset and Humility

A truly humble Security Agent will not get defensive or angry when confronted with criticism. A humble person will listen to critique and see how it can apply to their life to make it better. If you are humble, you will be more self-aware of what you need to improve on. You must have a humble desire to serve the person you are protecting. You must have a service-oriented mindset, raising others above yourself. It is not about you; it is about your team, your job, your boss, your subordinates, and your client. Humility comes from confidence. Confidence comes from competence, and competence comes from humility. When you are humble, you learn more. When you know more, you get better at a skill. When you are good at a craft, you become confident. The reverse is also true. People who are not humble lack confidence.

## Tip # 24: Leading and Following

A good Security Agent will have the confidence to step up, speak up, and lead when leadership is needed. A good Security Agent will also have the awareness and humility to step back, shut up and follow when needed. You do not always have to be the leader, and you do not always have to be the follower. But you have to have the capacity to do both. A good Security Agent will know when it is time to be either one. And you may have to switch back and forth between these two mindsets multiple times a day or several times within a single conversation.

## Tip # 25: Teamwork and Alone Work

You have to have the self-discipline to work alone. On a security detail, there will be many times when you have to be alone with no one to talk to for many hours at a time. Extroverts may have difficulty with this. You have to have the mental discipline not to get distracted and get bored. Your job is not to get bored. If you have to stand in an empty hallway guarding a door for five hours, figure out something to do that is productive and keeps your mind alert.

Count light bulbs, ceiling tiles, count doors or lines in the carpet. Count how many paces it is to the end of the hall. Memorize the address of the building you are at or the intel that is in your documents. Continuously think of "what if" scenarios in your head. Think about what you would do if your client had a heart attack? What if an attacker walks in with a gun? What if the battery in your radio goes dead? What if?

Conversely, you also may have to work and live with a team constantly. You may frequently be sleeping in a room with four team members or continuously eating and driving with other people. You may always be in and around large crowds and noise. Introverts may have difficulty with this.

# Chapter 2: A Bodyguard's Body

## Part A: Diet

### Tip # 26: Food and Nutrition

There are many parts to the bodyguard or protection profession that you will not officially see in a formal job description. One of these elements is your physical health. By the simple definition of the job, you will be protecting someone else. What are you protecting them from? One of the primary things you are defending them from is physical assault or violence. There are many tools that a good bodyguard can use to complete this mission, but when physical force comes down to its very basic form, it is one person using unlawful force against another. And again, getting forced down to its basic form, it is physically overpowering another individual. Your physical body, heart, lungs, and muscles are what you have with you at all times to protect your client. Part of the bodyguard's job is to keep your body strong, healthy, and in shape. Eating healthy and eating for fuel is literally part of your job. You must keep your body strong and healthy. Diet is crucial to this. You must eat for energy to grow and maintain your strength. There are numerous diet programs and schools of thought on nutrition. Don't worry; you do not have to discover the long-lost secret; you just have to find a diet and nutrition lifestyle that works for you, your body, and your job. There is no one secret way, no matter what the advertisements tell you. There are many right ways to go about nutrition. Your job is to find what works for you and which one is sustainable for you. Here are a few concepts to start with: 1. Drink more water; you're not getting enough. 2. Eat more fiber; you're not getting enough. 3. Eat less sugar; you don't need it. 4. Stop drinking soda; you don't need it. 5. Eat more real food from the produce and meat department, eat less "fake food" out of bags or boxes.

# Part B: Physical Fitness

## Tip # 27: Functional Exercise and Workouts

Part of a bodyguard's job is to remain healthy and strong. Your job may require you to use force to protect yourself or your client. The stronger you are, the more likely you will succeed and the less likely you will injure another person. The stronger you are, the more physical and mental stress you will be able to overcome. The more in shape you are, the more you will be able to last throughout the day and succeed during long shifts. For example, if you have a twelve-hour stint of standing and walking and your legs and feet are not up for it, you will begin to get tired, and your feet with ache. The more your feet ache, the more you will be focused on that, and the less focused you will be on your job. Fast-forward several more hours, and your feet may be in such pain that all you want to do is sit down, and before you know it, you are focusing on the end of your shift, and you are no longer focusing on your job at the moment. A distracted bodyguard is a liability to their client. How much do you train? How hard do you practice? Remember that you can't prepare enough for a job that could kill you or your client. The more in shape you are, the more hours you can work in a day. The more in shape you are, the more hours you can train. The more hours you can work and practice, the more days you can work and train. The more days you can work and train, the more years you can work and train. Just like a nutrition program, there are a variety of exercise programs you can follow. Your job is to find which one works for you, your job, and that is sustainable. Your exercise should be built around a foundation of functionality for your job. As a bodyguard, you have two primary goals with training: 1. Protecting yourself. 2. Protecting someone else. Everything else should be a means to an end with these two goals.

### Tip # 28: Training and Working While Being Injured

Regularly working out not only facilitates your two primary goals but also helps prevent you from getting injured. If you injure yourself while working out, you're doing it wrong. If you get injured during the job, you will lose workdays, lose crucial strength that you have built up, and most importantly, your client's routine or level of protection may drop if someone has to come in and replace you. It's simple, the more you work out, the less likely you will get injured. However, being in a physical job, and if you are in this job long enough, you may get hurt; it's just part of the job. Don't complain about it. Accept it, fix it, and move on. This injury could happen on the clock or in training. Just because you are injured doesn't mean you can't work. There is a difference between being merely "hurt" or being "injured." There will be many times as a bodyguard you will have to work while hurt. You will have to have the mental discipline and physical pain tolerance to work through this. There will be times when you are expected to perform while not feeling one-hundred percent. You must know your limits and be smart enough not further to injure yourself, but you also must know your limits and know how far you can push through something. Know your limits on both ends.

# Part C: Discipline

### Tip # 29: Discipline

Overall, the most powerful concept is discipline. You must have the self-discipline never to give up and never lose a fight. When faced with an attacker, opponent, an obstacle, or a problem, you must have a rock-solid, firm, and concrete foundation for why you are doing what you are doing and why you should survive, win, and prevail in a fight. What is your motivation for life? What duty do you have to your friends and family, your morals and code, yourself, your mission, or your team to live? You must know what this is before the fight because you will not have time to think about it when the fighting starts. You must have the self-discipline to keep yourself accountable and make sure you are better than you were yesterday. From using the previous values, "self-awareness leads to self-honesty, and self-honesty leads to self-discipline." The world owes you nothing, and you should not complain about something that is difficult. You will need mental and emotional resiliency from small things and big things. A small thing could be you have been working for 24 hours straight, and you are tired. A big thing could be you have to push through seven years of daily, chronic pain. Or a big thing could be having chronic nightmares about a traumatic incident that took place ten years ago. In all of these situations, you must have the discipline to continue your mission and complete your job.

### Tip # 30: Focus

A good Security Agent needs to be focused. When you are on the job, you need to focus on your primary mission, which is to protect someone. You cannot get distracted by your client if they are a celebrity. You cannot get distracted by them if they are someone you look up to or are a fan of. This issue gets a lot of Security Agents in trouble. If you are a fan of the person, you must focus on your mission and treat the client or celebrity professionally. You are their protector, not their fan. You cannot get distracted by the media or camera flashes that are trying to get your attention. You cannot get distracted by other fans and swarms of people who may want to stop you because they know you are associated with the client. You cannot get distracted because you are bored because your client is giving a speech that is going really long. It doesn't matter. You cannot get distracted from your mission of protection. You must be aware of and work with an extreme mental focus on your job to protect. When you are working as a Security Agent, and you are guarding a client, do not ask for their autograph, do not ask for a picture with them, do not give them a gift, or do anything that would associate you as a fan. Once you are a fan of them, you are no longer trusted with their safety and personal information.

## Tip # 31: Sleep Deprivation and Rest

Rest and sleep are just as important as your exercise. Adequate rest not only helps you become physically stronger but helps you stay mentally sharp and helps strengthen your immune system. As a bodyguard, your life must be structured around the long term. The job is a marathon, not a sprint. Getting adequate sleep takes discipline. A bodyguard usually will have to get up extremely early in the morning, work very late at night, and do this for days on end. Let's say your client is the CEO of a major company. Someone of that caliber is likely to arrive at the office very early in the morning.

Let's say your CEO client needs to arrive at his office at 0600, and your job is to pick him up at his house and drive him to the office. From his home to the office, it takes 30 minutes. You can't leave at 0530. You should plan to depart at 0515, giving yourself an extra 15 minutes. Remember, if you're five minutes early, you're late. That means you should arrive at his house at least by 0500. Maybe it is another thirty minutes from your house to his home. So, you must leave your house at 0415 if you plan for extra time. So, if that is your basic schedule in the morning, when will you wake up? How much time will you need in the morning to get dressed and geared up? And when will you go to sleep the previous night to make sure you are not tired in the morning. Remember, the day starts the night before, so plan your life accordingly. The more rest and sleep you get, the better you will work through those days when you cannot sleep. It is very common on a detail or especially during travel that you will not get adequate sleep. But the healthier you are and the more rested you are going into one of these trips will help you.

## Tip # 32: Dependency on Crutches

A good bodyguard or protector will be able to work and operate for long periods without crutches. A crutch can be any sort of substance or habit that you need to function at one-hundred percent. Crutches can be things like addiction to nicotine, caffeine, alcohol, or even gum. It can be anything, but the point is if you need it to get through the day, then what are you going to do during that long day when you don't have it? What if you are addicted to chewing gum, but the client forbids anyone chewing gum in his presence because he doesn't like the look of it? If you need caffeine just to make it through a typical day and "wake up" in the morning, what will you do when you are exhausted from not getting sleep the night before? Caffeine, coffee, energy drinks, or even gum can be great tools to help you through those extra challenging shifts or jet-lag times. But save those tools for those needed times. If every morning is extra challenging, then you probably have another problem.

## Tip # 33: Dedication to Continual Ongoing Training

A good Security Agent will always know they have to train to sharpen their skills continually. They understand that technical skills and motor functions can get lost over time. A person who is dedicated to constantly increasing their skills does not rely on what they were able to do yesterday. A good Security Agent will only focus on what they can do right now. Just because they could do it yesterday does not guarantee they can do it today. Just because one did it safely yesterday does not guarantee one can do it safely tomorrow. You have to focus on today and train hard today. Train like your life depends on it because it does. A good Security Agent knows they are never good enough. They can always be better, quicker, stronger, smarter, and more efficient.

# Chapter 3: A Bodyguard's Thinking Skills

## Part A: Operational

### Tip # 34: Surveillance

When working as a bodyguard, one must have several operational skill sets they are proficient in. Surveillance is the skill of watching other people, places, or things to gather tactical intelligence. For instance, maybe you know the identity and location of a person who is threatening your client. Depending on the situation, you may need to watch this threat to make sure they do not come in contact with your client. A surveillance role will mainly place you away from the client. You can still be a bodyguard without standing next to the client. Like any team, there are different roles to play, and you have to be ready and able to fulfill whatever task needs to be done. Surveillance can also be performed low profile or high profile. Low profile means you are working in a capacity where you do not want the threat to see you, and you want to "blend in" to the crowd. High profile means you are working in a capacity where you don't care who sees you, or you may even want the threat to see you specifically for strategic reasons. Surveillance work can be extremely beneficial to the mission by gathering a lot of strategic information. A surveillance agent can also be the key part of communication about the movement of the threat. It can be long, slow, and tedious, and it can include something like sitting in a vehicle and not leaving for 18 hours straight while you watch the threat's residence. You may have to do this without getting bored, without losing focus, and report any movement in or around the home. Surveillance takes a tremendous amount of patience and mental focus.

## Tip # 35: Surveillance Detection

Surveillance detection is your ability to notice when others are watching you. You need to be able to detect any abnormal behavior. There can be many times when you know you are being watched, but you don't know by whom or by how many people. Remember that the bad guy is not always a guy. It can be a female, a couple, tall, short, young, old, or even children. Bad guys may need to watch your protectee to launch an attack. Your job as a bodyguard is to notice when anyone else is watching you or your client. It can be challenging if your client is a high-profile person or a celebrity when it is natural for people to watch them. To do effective surveillance detection, you have to be constantly "looking outward" by paying attention to who is watching you. If you are always "looking inward" and only focusing on your client, then you can miss crucial information or pre-attack behavior.

## Tip # 36: Counter-Surveillance

Counter-surveillance is the skill of watching for threats who are surveilling you or your client. It is watching others who are watching you. Counter-surveillance can be formal and informal. Formal counter-surveillance is when you are specifically dedicated to the task of observing others to see if a bad guy is watching you. Sometimes, the mission requires there to be specific roles like this. Informal counter-surveillance is when you are looking for surveillance while you are doing any other position. Most of the time, everyone on the bodyguard team is doing counter-surveillanc all the time. It is one of the ways you will have to learn how to do multiple jobs at once.

Counter-surveillance is most effective when the bad guy you are watching does not know they are being observed. To do this, it is crucial that you "blend in" with the crowd and covertly do this. Keep in mind that no matter where you are, there can always be some other bad guy watching you. You may think you are on the far outside and looking in, but there could still be a bad guy watching you from behind. For effective counter-surveillance, always try to position yourself so that no one can see you, but you can see everyone else. Also, when conducting this type of work, you always need a reason to be where you are. Meaning, if you are doing counter-surveillance in a coffee shop, you need a reason to be there. It will help you "fit in" and give you a cover story if someone asks you what you're doing. You can't just sit in the corner and stare at your target. If you're in a coffee shop, you should do what people do in coffee shops. Order a coffee or pretend to read a book. Have a reason for while you're there.

## Tip # 37: Advance Work

Advance work is knowing everything about the location you are going to. It helps inform you of strategic information, so you know what to expect when you walk into a place. For example, if you are taking your protectee to a restaurant, you need to know everything about that restaurant. Remember your combat planning from earlier. If you are responsible for protecting your client while you're there, you need to know the most efficient way in and out of the building. Where will you park? Do you drop the client off or walk him in? How close is the nearest hospital? Fire station? How many entries and exits are there in this building? How many people does it hold? Will the restaurant be busy at the time you'll be there? Do you need to call ahead for reservations? Do you get a choice of where to sit? If so, what is the safest and most strategic location to sit? Where are the nearest fire extinguishers, AED, first aid kit? Is the kitchen clean or dirty? Is there anything in the kitchen that your client is allergic to? Are there any impromptu weapons that someone could grab at any time (like kitchen knives)? Do you know the address if you have to call for an ambulance? Where are strategic places that the bad guy could be pulling surveillance on you? What type of clientele does this place usually consist of? There are endless questions that could be answered. The question is always how much do you need to know? The answer is as much as you can. Obviously, how in-depth you go depends on the length of time you have and the threat level. Do you have three weeks to do this advance work, or do you have thirty minutes?

### Tip # 38: Protective Intelligence

Protective intelligence is strategically using gained information to help you keep your client safe. Intelligence is the key to any successful protection detail. Protective intelligence can include anything that can be of strategic or tactical importance to your job. For instance, what type of threat was made to your client? Was it specific or vague? Was the threat overt or veiled? How long ago was the threat made? What manner did the threat arrive in? Was it a phone call, email, text, written letter or was it communicated face to face? What is the relation to the threat and the client? Old friends, co-workers, spouse, strangers? Does the threat have the financial resources or tactical ability to carry out the threat? Does the threat have a history of violence? Where does the threat live? Where do they work? What type of vehicle or vehicles do they drive or have access to? Is the threat working alone, or do they have access to multiple people who may sympathize with them? Any answers to these types of questions can help you as you protect your client. This information should be collected in one Intelligence Document that can be accessed by anyone on the protection team as needed. The gathering of this intelligence should be done legally and can help formulate your plan of how you are going to protect your client.

## Tip # 39: Threat Assessment

Once you have all of your protective intelligence gathered, you now should move into the threat assessment part of your protection plan. A threat assessment will help you put all of your relevant intelligence into one concise package to help you figure out how to protect your client. Once you analyze everything, you can begin making decisions about resources. Once you know if the threat is credible or not, you can decide the best way to protect against it. For example, a high-profile client who is being targeted because of their work and is being credibly threatened by three former criminals will likely require a great deal more resources than one stranger who has made one veiled threat.

## Tip # 40: Thinking Like the Enemy

If you are protecting someone from a threat, the bad news is that most likely, you will be playing defense and will have to "defend" against the threat, who will probably act first. The bad guy usually gets to decide the time and place of the attack; that is their advantage. But we can mitigate this advantage by always being prepared and trained. We have plenty of time to train, plan and put protection strategies in place to increase our defense continuously. The bad guy may get to decide the time and place of the attack, but most likely, we will have home field advantage. Meaning we will know our client's home, office, and places they are going to if we do our advanced work and intelligence gathering correctly. We can have doors locked; alarms turned on, counter-surveillance in place, and all of the tools we've already talked about. We put those things in place because we have to think like the enemy. If you are protecting someone, think creatively about how the bad guy could attack. One of the best ways to protect someone is to think like a bad guy constantly. Constantly think about how you would strike the client and put protection strategies in place for those possibilities.

### Tip # 41: Operational Security

Operational security or "OpSec" is the ability for you to do your job without releasing any information that may be helpful to the bad guy. Just as our goal is to gather intelligence on the threat, the threat's goal is to gather intelligence on us. It can primarily be thought about in two areas: physical (paper, keys, laptops, cell phones, etc.) and virtual (passwords, numbers, schedules, addresses, meeting times, etc.). Operational security includes counter-surveillance and surveillance detection, such as making sure you are not followed or tracked. But it also has things like making sure you do not publish your or the client's information somewhere where a threat could find it and use it against you. Such as posting crucial information on social media. Do not leave intelligence lying around. If you have any notes, printed schedules, tickets, passwords, codes, or phone numbers, do not "forget" them and leave them behind for someone to pick up. Don't leave your cell phone, laptop, keys, vehicle information, wallet, etc. Depending on the threat and the budget, you have to consider tools like burner phones, burner email addresses, ghost numbers, cover names, code phrases, and secure communication with end-to-end encryption.

An example of this is your protectee's itinerary. If the threat is going to assault your protectee physically, they have to know where their target is or will be. Especially if your client is going to be busy with lots of meetings at many places, protecting their itinerary is vital. If the bad guy doesn't know where to find his target, then he cannot attack.

## Tip # 42: Behavior Recognition

Behavior recognition is the skill set of learning about all forms of non-verbal communication between people. As a protector who can potentially face a physical assault, you must be familiar with body language, tone of voice, facial expressions, emotions, clothing, iconography, symbols, and pre-attack indicators. If someone is going to attack you or the person you're protecting, you will need every advantage available when it comes to time and distance. The farther away you see an attack coming, the more time you will have to defend against it. For instance, if you know a common body language movement of someone loading up their weight on their back foot and cocking a shoulder back while making a fist, is a common movement for someone about to throw a punch, then you can react to it faster. Remember, we want to be proactive instead of reactive. You need to know what type of behavior sticks out in a specific social area. If you are at a formal evening event, a bad guy might show up without wearing the appropriate attire. It is something that "sticks out," and you need to pay attention to. You also need to become familiar with how to identify people who may be carrying a weapon. If you can't see someone's hands or waistbands, it is something to pay attention to. Finally, you need to know how people look when they are angry. Someone who is red-faced or grimacing in a way that looks angry may be very close to carrying out an attack.

### Tip # 43: Verbal De-escalation

Verbal de-escalation is the skill of using your words to get out of a bad situation. As a protector, you will often need to help someone calm down or de-escalate their emotions. Calmness and having a plan of what to say to people will be required. Verbal de-escalation skills are crucial. They can help you get out of a bad situation without having to use force. They can help you dissolve a potential confrontation and prevent bad things from happening. The ability to think and speak and use strategic words and phrases can save you a lot of trouble. Obtain suitable training on this, it is a skillset in and of itself, and you use it all the time, on and off the job. Yet, it is one of the things that is trained on the least.

# Part B: Social

### Tip # 44: Social Etiquette

The ability to "fit in" to your environment is critical for bodyguard and executive protection work. It is indispensable if you are working a "low profile" job. A low profile means you are not supposed to be noticed as a bodyguard. A "high profile" job is when you do not care if people know you are a bodyguard or not; in fact, you may want everyone to know you are the bodyguard. Either of these two strategies can be needed depending on the mission, the threat level, and the client's needs. Let's look at a low-profile situation, such as working as the bodyguard on a one-person team for the CEO of a business, and you have to attend a business meeting with him for dinner. The CEO could be meeting with out-of-town guests, and the threat could be anywhere; therefore, you need to stay close to the CEO. But since the people the CEO will be meeting with know nothing of the threat and the CEO doesn't want them to know about it, you need to "fit in" to the group setting. For this type of assignment, you will want to dress like the CEO and play the role of the CEO's "assistant" or something like that that gives you a reason to be there. Not only should you dress the part, but if you are eating dinner at a formal venue, you need to know simple things like table manners, how to order wine, which fork to use first, which glass is the water glass, etc. You need to look and act like you're supposed to be there because, after all, you are there representing the client, and you do not want to cause him embarrassment.

### Tip # 45: Clothing: From Cocktail Hour to the Sleazy Bar

Clothing is a big part of knowing the correct social etiquette. Again, this depends on whether or not you are working a low profile or high-profile detail. And most of the time, you will be working low profile. It is much more common in this industry to operate a one-person low-profile job than running a ten-person high profile team. Again, whatever environment you are working in, you need to have the proper clothing to look the part. Let's say you are working the same low profile protection detail as the above example. Your client is a wealthy business CEO, and you have to attend cocktail hour with him and his business associates.

For a formal business setting cocktail hour, you will need to dress the part. How fancy do you dress? Try to dress to the level of your client as closely as possible. You may not need to look exactly like him, but you will need to dress well enough to make it believable that you are supposed to be there. If your CEO client is wearing a $5,000 suit, you probably don't need a $5,000 suit. But you are going to need something better than an $85 suit off the rack. Make sure you have an outfit of good quality but not flashy. Stick with something safe like black or dark gray—same thing with the tie, not showy but not cheap. The same goes for a different setting. Let's say after cocktail hour, you are now going to a different role on the team, and you are now going to have to conduct undercover surveillance on the threat. So, that evening you will have to be at a sleazy bar, keeping an eye on the threat without them knowing. You will obviously stick out if you wear your nice suit to the bar. You will have to wear regular clothing, blue-collar clothing, or something that "fits in" with the bar's setting. If it's a bar whose primary customer base is bikers, truckers, and gang members, you will again have to dress the part, so others will believe you're supposed to be there.

## Tip # 46: The Little Details: From the Wristwatch to the Tattoo

Continuing with our same example, for a cocktail hour, you will need to pretend to be the CEO's assistant, so you will need to have the conversational skills to make small talk with the other business associates. Cocktail hour is very social, and conversation is very informal, so you will need to talk and interact with others; you can't just stand in the corner and watch everyone. If you do that, you will stand out, everyone will notice you and ask the CEO about you, and you will likely get fired from the job. So, play the part. Ask a lot of questions and exercise your social skills. Also, everyone will be drinking at cocktail hour, but since you are on duty, you shouldn't drink. So, it's best just to ask the bartender for a glass of water, and you can sip that like it's a clear drink, and you will look like you fit in. Fitting in is all about the details. Which means it is more than wearing a suit and tie. Wearing a suit or tie doesn't matter if you do not have the right shoes, wristwatch, or pen in your pocket. If your CEO client is wearing a nice watch and has an expensive pen in his pocket, you will stick out if you are wearing your outdoor camping watch and your "tactical pen." People in these types of settings will notice details like this. Think of the brand and style of your belt, lapel pin, cufflinks, tie, ring(s), and any other accessory. Maybe you have a full sleeve tattoo on one arm, and you will look out of place if that is seen. Just make sure you are wearing long sleeves to cover it up. But again, if you have to change settings on the same day and blend into that sleazy bar later, your long-sleeved business shirt might not work, but a simple t-shirt with tattoos showing will look perfect. Remove your fancy watch and wear your outdoor camping watch or no watch at all. Know the look and environment you need to be in and blend in with your etiquette, clothing, and minute details.

## Tip # 47: Handling the Media

If you find yourself working with a client that is either famous, wealthy, or well-known, there is a good chance you may find yourself interacting with the media. It could be a local or a high-level media presence. Especially if you are out in public with your client, always be aware that you could be being photographed or videoed at any given time. It is different than a counter-surveillance purpose. Fans or the media could be recording your client, and you just happen to be there. As much as you can, you want to stay out of the frame of these recordings if possible. The less you are recorded and photographed, the safer you and your client will be.

On the other hand, you may find yourself dealing with a media person or reporter who wants to barge in and get access to your client. Each situation is unique, but remember, part of your job is to protect your client from embarrassment or interruptions. Getting your client to their next meeting on time may be just as important as keeping them safe. A pushy reporter who wants to do an impromptu "interview" may be a problem. How your client wants you to handle the media, especially unexpected media attention, should ideally be discussed and planned out ahead of time. But if this can't happen, you will have to make the best, common-sense decision at the moment. Always treat the media with professionalism and courtesy without compromising the safety of your client.

# Part C: Educational

### Tip # 48: Terrorism, Counter Terrorism, and Insurgency

If you are going to be protecting someone from violence, you have to understand violence. You have to understand your enemy. You need to learn about previous terrorist attacks and how that kind of violence can impact your mission as a bodyguard. Whether you are protecting someone in the US or overseas, you have to be educated about terrorism, counterterrorism, and insurgency. These concepts are incredibly complex, but that doesn't mean we can't learn about them. One can spend a lifetime studying the theory of terrorism, but you don't have to have a PH.D. in the subject. But you do have to have a working knowledge of the topic. When one thinks about terrorism and counterterrorism, it is easy to only think about war zones or other countries. Remember that terrorism can happen in our own country and our own hometown. It can happen anywhere and at any time.

### Tip # 49: Targeted Violence vs. Random Crime

There are many types of violence. When it comes to protecting a human being from being attacked by another human being, generally, violence can be initially broken down into two sub-categories. The first is targeted violence. It is violence where a specific attacker is targeting a particular target. It is vital when working as a bodyguard or executive protection agent. With targeted violence, you can identify specific things because you may have intel on the threat. For instance, if you know the threat is 6'4" and bald, and this threat has expressly stated he will stab your client with a knife, this can be very helpful on what to look for. Yes, I know these specifics could always change, and just because they say it doesn't mean they will do that exactly, but it can give you a starting point of what to look for. Second, you have a specific attacker that is targeting your client. It also can generally suggest the threat has something personal against the client or the company the client works for. It makes the violence personal. With a random crime, the attack can still be just as violent, but it is unexpected. So, just because you do not have intel that gives you a specific threat doesn't mean something bad can't happen. Most of the time, you will have both of these two types of violence to manage. Just because you have a specific threat doesn't mean you can't be attacked. And just because you don't have a specific threat doesn't mean that a random crime can't happen out of anywhere. Be prepared for both.

## Tip # 50: Stalking and Public Figure Attacks

Another type of crime can be categorized as stalking and public figure attacks. It is a form of targeted violence. It is when you have a specific person trying to harm another. Stalking in and of itself is a vast and complex area to study. But again, just because it can be complex doesn't mean we can't learn about it. Being familiar with stalking behavior and concepts is extremely valuable in the bodyguard profession because a stalker is a widespread reason someone hires a bodyguard. Public figure attacks can include stalking, but not always. If your client is a public figure, they could be a politician, actor, actress, author, speaker, or a wealthy businessman. There are prominent public figures (someone known on the national or international level) or small public figures (like a local business owner or a school board president). No matter where your client lies in this spectrum, know that a public figure can have people who hate them as well as people who are fans. The threat could be a fan that hates them or a fan that really loves the client. If they are for or against the public figure, they can still be a threat. Your mission in protecting a public figure can also be difficult because the very definition of a public figure is that they need to be out in public. They have to be seen. So, they have to be out amongst the people, potentially right next to your threat. It is a very different mission than protecting someone who is not famous or known in public. The mission dictates your tactics, goals, and your protection strategy.

## Tip # 51: Legal Issues and Use of Force Laws of Your Jurisdiction

If you are in charge of someone's safety and security, it is reasonable to expect that you may have to use force in self-defense. One of the most important things to be educated and well-trained on is legal liabilities and use of force laws. Whatever state you are operating in, you must be familiar with the use of force laws in that jurisdiction. Generally, most states have statutes that allow for the legal use of self-defense against someone assaulting you or someone you are protecting. But there may be minor differences in the law from one state to another. It doesn't apply to only the use of force but other issues like a citizen's arrest. If you are working as a private sector entity, you most likely have no other special exceptions or rules than any regular citizen. These legal issues must be clarified with your client when the job begins so that the client's goals do not conflict with your legal capabilities.

## Tip # 52: Budgeting and Writing Proposals

No bodyguard job happens without someone paying for it. In the bodyguarding and executive protection industry, working alone as a one-person team is very common. You are likely to be employed as a contractor and not an employee. It is also expected that before you are hired for a job, you will need to submit a budget proposal for what the job will cost. No one is going to hire you on the spot and give you an unlimited budget. You will have to submit a written proposal on what you charge for your hourly or daily rate and include anything else in the budget that you will need for the job. Think of expenses like car rental, hotel rooms, food, and other travel expenses. And remember, this is just for you. If you are expected to take a job that requires multiple team members, you may be the one who hires the team. So, you will have to write out what you will pay your team and all of their expenses. You have to think through all of these little details when you initially submit your proposals. It doesn't look good if you have to keep going back to the client and ask for an increased budget. A good executive protection agent will be able to think through all expenses needed and articulate them on a written proposal clearly. It is common for you to look at the job and consider the mission requires a four-person team with three armored SUVs. But the client may be expecting you to work as a one-person team and use your personal vehicle. The requirements of the budget will probably have to be negotiated. Be ready to have a good reason for any expense you are asking for.

## Tip # 53: After Action Reports and the Power of the Debrief

An after-action report is a formal written review of a job, mission, or event you've just completed. A simple debrief can be the same thing, only shorter, informal, and can take only five minutes after the event. Either way, a formal AAR or an informal debrief can be powerful to help you learn. It is beneficial if you are working with a team. There are only three questions you ask yourself or your team to conduct an AAR or debrief. 1. What was the mission, and did we complete it. 2. What did we do well. 3. What do we need to improve. It doesn't have to be more complex than that. The power of being honest with yourself and/or your team by answering those three questions will help you highlight your strengths and weaknesses. In this line of work, you cannot make the same mistake twice. You must get better by learning from your mistakes. The AAR/Debrief can be especially helpful with a team because each team member might not exactly know what happened. For example, let's say you have a four-person team, and you protected the client arriving at a large public event, during the event, during an autograph signing, and then back to the airport. This one-night event could be very complex. One team member might not know what another team member did well, or they might not know what another team member did wrong. An AAR or a Debrief can help all team members learn from each other.

# Chapter 4: A Bodyguard's Physical Skills

## Part A: Firearms Skills

### Tip # 54: Handguns

If you are a protector, you need to have skills with specific tools. Firearms are one type of tool. They are one specific tool that can help you with a particular problem, defending yourself or another from the use of unlawful lethal force. If you are going to carry a firearm, there are other tools that you should carry as well. We will discuss those later. A handgun is a good tool because of its size and concealability. Yes, a rifle would give you more capability than a handgun, but a rifle cannot be concealed and worn on your body consistently. A handgun may have its limitations, but it makes up for it in size and concealability. If you are going to carry a handgun, it must only be carried legally. Handgun laws and concealed carry laws vary from state to state and city to city. So, you must be familiar with the firearms laws and self-defense laws of wherever you are working. If you are going to carry a handgun, you must train with it. When starting, make sure you acquire training from an experienced and certified instructor. Like most things in the self-defense industry, there are good instructors and bad instructors. Do your homework beforehand. Make sure you spend your time and money wisely. You must have a skill level with your handgun that is higher than average. It is not enough for you to only get a concealed carry license and then start carrying. You must hold yourself accountable to train with your handgun and become proficient at it. Not only do you need to know all the legal and ethical implications of using a handgun, but you must be proficient in all of the technical skills that go along with it, reloads, malfunction clearing, drawing, holstering, accuracy, speed, target discrimination, cleaning it and fixing it when it is broken. These skills must be at a high level before you ever carry one for work. Because if you do end up having to use one to protect yourself or your client, you cannot miss or make a mistake. You have to be so good in training that you have confidence that you will do the right thing if you use it. Train to a high level and keep training. Shooting is a skill set that will diminish, so you must continually train. A great way to practice and keep your handgun techniques up is to join a shooting sports league and regularly compete in local matches to test your skill set regularly.

### Tip # 55: Shoulder-fired Firearms: Semi-Automatic Rifles and Shotguns

Shoulder-fired firearms like semi-automatic rifles and shotguns can be a great tool in specific environments and missions—the types of protection details where shoulder-fired weapons are out there, although they are scarce. A shoulder-fired weapon extends your range, accuracy, and fighting capability to much longer distances than with only handguns. You are less likely to be expected to use a long gun on a job than a handgun. However, it is still essential that you are capable and proficient with one just in case you show up on a job where you are expected to handle one. So, get training on these types of weapons. Know their capabilities and limitations. It possible you might be on a low-profile detail and carrying a handgun, but a semi-automatic rifle is kept in the trunk of a vehicle so it is close by in case more firepower is needed. People tell me that since they only carry a handgun, they don't need to train with a rifle. However, in my experience, training with a rifle makes one a better marksman and a better tactician, even though most of my jobs are only with handguns. Being capable with the rifle helps you be better with the handgun.

# Part B: Defensive Tactics Skills

## Tip # 56: Jiu-jitsu and Contact Range Martial Arts

As a bodyguard, when you sign a job contract and are legally and ethically expected to protect someone, it is reasonable to expect that you may have to use unarmed skills to defend yourself or your client from an attack. Training in hand-to-hand skills will take time and money. Many martial arts systems offer effective techniques, but like anything else, some are better than others. Divide your hand-to-hand skills into two primary groups: contact range (wrestling, grabbing, throwing, etc.) and long-range (boxing, kickboxing, etc.). Let's look at contact range martial arts first. By far, the best way to invest your time and money is to begin learning Brazilian Jiu-jitsu. Brazilian Jiu-jitsu is a great way to systematically learn concepts like leverage, base, self-defense focused, natural body movements, weight distribution, and controlling another person who does not want to be constrained without injuring them. It is the perfect martial art to learn how to control and subdue someone without harming them. Brazilian Jiu-jitsu is one of the few martial arts that allow you to practice full speed against an opponent who is also going full speed and still without hurting your training partner. Jiu-jitsu helps prepare you for how not to give up when you're losing, and it helps you learn humility because you will often lose and learn from your losses. It helps you discover how to control yourself, make appropriate use of force decisions at the moment and remain calm during physically and mentally intense situations. Something like Jiu-jitsu is so effective because it teaches how to protect yourself when someone grabs you. Once someone holds you and you are physically stuck together, your options of running away, avoiding further contact, or using other tools to defuse the situation have diminished. Especially as a bodyguard when you will often be working in close quarters and if someone grabs you or grabs your client, you need to be able to solve that problem. Other grappling systems like scholastic wrestling, Greco-Roman wrestling, freestyle wrestling, and Sambo are also great for contact range training. Just like shooting, these skills can dimmish, so you must continually train. A great way to do this is to enter local Jiu-jitsu competitions to test your skill set regularly.

### Tip # 57: Boxing and Long-Range Martial Arts

For longer-range martial arts, traditional boxing is a great skill set. Boxing allows you to learn the fundamentals of stance, timing, distance, and proper striking against an opponent doing the same to you. Thus, you study offense and defense at the same time. The fundamentals of fighting in boxing should not be overlooked. Grappling and Jiu-jitsu are extremely important, but you must have other tools in your toolbox if needed. Kickboxing is another good system to learn. Yes, kickboxing incorporates boxing, but it also involves knees, elbows, and feet: all tools that may be needed to defend yourself or a third party. If you have a solid understanding of a good contact range martial art like Jiu-Jitsu and a long-range martial art like kickboxing, you will have the beginnings of the proper defensive tactics skills.

# Part C: Other Tools and Skillsets

### Tip # 58: Emergency Medical Training

When you think about protecting someone, think about the primary things you may have to deal with. Medical issues are significantly more likely to happen than assaults, depending on the threat level. There will be no specific threat for many protection jobs you may get, and you will have to be ready to protect the client from normal day-to-day things. Medical issues can happen anytime and anywhere and can be medical or trauma related. Your client's medical condition will come into play. Meaning your client could drop dead from a heart attack or stroke at any time. How will you react to that? Are they overweight or elderly? Your client could twist their ankle going down a set of stairs. What will you do? Maybe your client has diabetes or has a severe nut allergy. A trauma could happen anytime, like a car accident. What will you do, and where will you go if your client gets injured? CPR, AED, and basic first aid skills are a requirement. But you should be able to offer more. Acquiring training for emergency trauma-related accidents is very valuable. Getting coaching and certifications of an EMT or Paramedic is also highly valued.

## Tip # 59: Flashlight and Low Light Skills

A flashlight is one of the most effective, simple, relevant, and available tools you can have on your person. They are small, lightweight, and take up little space on a belt or in a pocket. But their usefulness is vast. A flashlight can be used in various ways, from identifying unknown persons or potential threats, from using it as a distraction tool that can temporarily blind an attacker to simply lighting up an unfamiliar path for a client walking to their car late at night. You may not need it to find bad guys every day, but there are many times it will prove helpful to light up a dark alley, a dark hotel room, the back seat of a car, or up a flight of stairs in the darkness of a backstage setting. A flashlight is not a weapon and can be carried almost anywhere. However, the flashlight can be used to aid another weapon, like a firearm, if needed. In extreme dark or low light situations like this, you have to be able to see the threat. You have to be able to identify who is a threat and who is not. The ability to quickly light up an area is incredibly helpful.

## Tip # 60:  Non-Lethal Tools: OC Spray and Tasers

Other non-lethal tools also must be considered if you are on a
protection job where a confrontation with a threat is possible. There
are many types of non-lethal tools but let's look at two. OC Spray
(Oleoresin Capsicum) or otherwise known as pepper spray, is a
standard self-defense tool. The right brand and size of a container
of OC spray can be easily worn on the belt and easily and quickly
deployed. The benefit of OC spray is that it is non-lethal, yet it can
have a very effective response against an attacker. Like all non-
lethal tools, there is no guarantee on how any particular threat will
respond to it. However, OC spray has proven to be widely effective
over the years, and its power should not be overlooked. OC spray is
non-lethal. It has been confirmed and documented in the past not
to cause long-term tissue damage and not to have a toxic level.
Some tasers can also be an excellent non-lethal tool; however, there
are more regulations, training, and documentation requirements
for carrying a taser. Additionally, a taser can be more regulated.
Always check the local laws of your particular state and jurisdiction
when looking into these types of tools.

## Tip # 61:  Restraint: Handcuffs and Zip Ties

Whether or not you are legally permitted to restrain someone has
many factors involved in it. It depends on state laws and what you
are legally allowed to do in terms of your hired job. It is not
impossible that you might have to restrain an attacker, but
remember, your primary job as a bodyguard is to protect your
client, not to arrest bad guys. Ideally, you would call the police if
someone needs to be captured. If you are not equipped with arrest
powers by an agency, you have to be very careful with restraining

someone. Restraining someone usually involves some use of force, and you can be liable for depriving someone of their rights. Like any use of force decision, your decision must be reasonable, prudent, and in the best interest of safety. As a private citizen or private sector bodyguard, you may be allowed to restrain someone with a citizen's arrest. But you must know the legal requirements of your state to do so. If you are expected to cuff or restrict someone, you need to carry the appropriate tools (handcuffs, zip ties, etc.) and be trained on properly using them.

## Tip # 62: Impact Weapons

Impact weapons are another set of tools that need to be understood by a bodyguard. Impact tools can be tools like ASP batons, collapsible batons, nightsticks, or a Kubotan. Whether you can carry and use one of these will depend on the details of your contract and the legalities in the jurisdiction you are working in. An impact weapon can be used as a compliance tool or a distractionary tool. It is wise to know the capabilities and limitations of these weapons, whether you are using one or defending yourself from one. Know that any attacker can pick up a stick, pipe, broom, pool cue, a hammer, or any other blunt object to use as a weapon.

## Tip # 63: Knives and Bladed Weapons

Knives or other bladed weapons are other types of weapons that a good bodyguard should be trained on and aware of, both for offense and defense. A simple knife that is legal for anyone to carry can be a deadly weapon facing you or your client. They are sharp and can quickly damage internal organs and arteries, creating bleeding that can lead to death. Again, if and why your carry one will depend on the job and laws. One thing that makes knives so dangerous is that they are very common for people to wear, can be purchased quickly and easily, and are generally unregulated. It is much more difficult for a person to acquire a firearm, acquire the training to be competent with it, and get it in range of your client who is in a protected area. It is much easier for someone to purchase a knife and be deadly with it with no training. Do not underestimate blade and the damage they can do. Another thing that makes knives dangerous is that they can be easily worn and hidden on someone's person. They can be small and easily concealable inside a pocket, belt, or waistband and quickly deployable.

### Tip # 64: Improvised Weapons

Another large category of weapons is improvised weapons. An improvised weapon can be any object or item that can hurt someone. It can be a rock, stick, pen, sharpened piece of plastic, shank, rope, belt, car, boiling hot coffee, or even just someone's hands. Almost anything can be turned into a weapon if someone wants to use it that way; it is vital for a bodyguard to understand. Let's say you are protecting your client during a formal evening dinner with one hundred people in attendance; just because you have ensured that no one in the room has a gun or a pocket knife does not mean that anyone can't attack your client with something else. Think about the environment of a formal dinner. There are likely to be butter knives, forks, or steak knives on every table. There are probably sharp cutting knives in the kitchen. Someone could grab a fire extinguisher and blow it in your face, distracting you. An attacker could throw a heavy glass salt saker at your client head or throw their cell phone or keys at your face. They could even break a water glass and use the shape edge like a knife. Someone could pick up a chair and use that as an impact weapon. Many of these improvised weapons may not cause death but could still cause injury. Always be aware that anything could be used as a weapon against you, even in a controlled and secure environment.

## Tip # 65: Explosives

As a bodyguard, you need to become somewhat familiar with explosives and IED types of attacks. This training must come from credible and certified instructors. You need to become familiar with explosives and learn a general level of safety knowledge on what to do if an explosive is found in or on a car, in a mailbox, at an office, in a home, or in a package delivered through the mail. You don't necessarily need to become an explosives expert, but you need to be familiar enough to know whether or not to call 911 or the bomb squad.

## Tip # 66: Technology

Technology, computers, and IT is rapidly becoming a larger and more significant part of protection. Each year, technology grows and changes, and its capabilities to help you protect your client grow and change as well. You do not have to become an IT specialist. Still, you need to be familiar with email, GPS, cell phones, secure communication apps, radios, cameras, surveillance devices, alarms, motion sensors, and ways to send and receive digitally secure and encrypted messages.

# Chapter 5: A Bodyguard's Transportation

## Part A: Automobiles

### Tip # 67: Responsible Driving

Sometimes the safest thing you can do is make sure your client wears their seatbelt. As a bodyguard, it is very common for you to have to drive your client. If there is no specific threat, remember that any normal driving is statistically probably the most dangerous thing you will do with your client. Car accidents happen quickly and can be deadly. Your job is not just to protect your client from threats and bad guys; it is to keep your client safe at all times. You are the operator of the automobile and are responsible for all passengers. Obey all traffic laws and practice good, safe, defensive driving. Obey all speed limits and be on the lookout for potential traffic hazards. Remember that waiting for a red light is faster than waiting to get a ticket written out. When driving, always try to leave early so that you are not rushed and speeding.

### Tip # 68: Tactical and High-Performance Driving

When protecting a passenger in a vehicle you are driving, it is essential to be trained and proficient in specific driving skills. A vehicle can be unsafe if not handled properly, and threats can use other vehicles as weapons. A good skill set to have is operating a vehicle in high threat circumstances while keeping yourself and your passengers safe. There are driving schools where you can learn high-performance driving skills and operate a vehicle at high rates of speed safely. You can learn turning, driving on the water in low light, using the vehicle as a defensive tool, pit maneuvers, J turns, Y turns, and understanding the capabilities and limitations of a specific vehicle.

### Tip # 69: Motorcade Driving

Motorcade driving is another critical skill. If you are working with a team with multiple vehicles or multiple clients, learning how to drive with others as a team is key. A motorcade is a team of various vehicles that need to travel together for protection. It is another crucial skill to have in your toolbox. For motorcade driving, a plan with assigned roles for each vehicle is needed. Each vehicle needs to know what role they play and where to go. There may be designated cars like the Advance Car (the car that arrives first), the Limo (the car with the client), the Backup (the car that will be used if the Limo breaks down), and a Follow Car (the car carrying the rest of the team). If you are driving in a motorcade, you need to know how far apart and how close together you need to be to the next vehicle. Radio and/or phone communication to each car is essential, and every car must know its role if something bad happens.

### Tip # 70: Arrivals and Departures

Picking the client up or dropping them off from a location should always be given special attention. Arrivals and departures are known as choke points. A choke point is any strategic space where you are at higher risk because your movement is restricted. A choke point is a perfect place for a threat to attack. It is because if the threat knows your client will be exiting the car by the front door and walking into the office, they know where your client will be. Your client will have to be at that exact location, and the threat knows this, so all the threat has to do is wait for the arrival and then strike.

Arrivals and departures are also dangerous because they are transitional spaces. A transitional space is any location where someone moves from point A to point B, and the transition can easily divert their awareness. For instance, if someone is exiting the car and entering a building for the first time, they tend to focus on things like where do I go? What door do I go in? Am I parked in the right spot? Am I too early or too late? Is this the correct building? These things can distract someone, making them an easy target.

## Tip # 71: Vehicle Attacks

Attacks on, in, or around vehicles are very common. A vehicle can be a choke point, a transitional space, and a vehicle's space can often be less secure, allowing an attacker to drive in and out quickly. For instance, if you are dropping the client off on the side of a street, it can be easy for an attacker to drive by, attack, and drive away quickly. All of these elements should be considered when making your plans. Where is the safest place to drop off your client? Where is the safest place to park the car? Where is a potential choke point? Is this a transitional space? Does this parking area have public access?

## Tip # 72: Public Transportation

Negotiating public transit with your client can be very challenging as well. Reservations and arrangements have to be made ahead of time. And your client's schedule may change after you've made the reservation. It can be challenging with public transportation because you have to adhere to their policies, timelines, and fees. Add in the difficultly of utilizing this public transit in a city or country you have never been in. In a foreign country, you are almost always going to use some form of public transportation. It is where the positives of good advanced work come in. For instance, if you were traveling with a client to a foreign country you have never been to, good advanced work can help you and keep you and your client safer. With good advanced work, you can know what hotel you will be staying at, including what floor and room. You can then use that hotel manager to help you hire a trusted driving company. You can then use that driver to help you find the quickest ways in and out of certain parts of town.

# Part B: Attacks and Tactics

### Tip # 73: Managing Choke Points

A good protector learns from history. One thing that can significantly improve our chances of surviving an attack in the future is the study of past attacks targeted at protected people. Again, this is usually focused on targeted violence on public figures. If you begin studying this subject matter, you will find a large number of attacks against protected figures that take place in and around vehicles. Either where the target is getting out of a vehicle or getting into a vehicle. It is for the reasons we mentioned earlier that make the vehicle a choke point. Some of this is out of your control. If you have to drop the client off, you have to drop them off. But there are some things that you can control. For instance, you can change the time of the drop-off, and you can change the car's exact location. Maybe instead of pulling up directly in front of the door, you can pull up ten yards in front of the back door. Perhaps you can leave plenty of room between you and the car in front of you, leaving you enough space to quickly pull away if needed. Or maybe all you can do is watch better and have more team members stationed at the known choke point.

## Tip # 74: Ambush Response

If you are driving your protectee from one location to another, be aware that you could be attacked en route. You will need to pay special attention to specific choke points like bridges, alleys, construction, detours, or any area that funnels you into a narrow location and slows you down. Especially, be aware of times when you are forced to stop, like railroad crossings, car accidents, or spontaneous construction. A common tactic in certain countries is for a vehicle ahead of you to purposely get into an accident or just a fender bender with you, forcing you to stop. Always maintain a good distance between you and the car in front and behind you. As you are driving, always be thinking about ways that you could creatively escape if ambushed. Can you get around the car in front of you? Can you jump the curb? Can you drive on the sidewalk if needed? If you are ambushed while in a vehicle, one of the best tactics is to keep moving and drive out of the ambush. It makes you a moving target and will likely get you out of the danger zone. The purchase and installation of a dashcam that records everything can also be a helpful tool if there is a legal issue resulting from your actions or counter actions from an attack.

# Chapter 6: A Bodyguard's Environments and Missions

## Part A: Operational Goals

### Tip # 75: *Man to Man vs. Zone Defense*

If you are protecting one human being from another, there may be times when you will be working in close quarters in and around lots of people. If you are working with a team with a higher profile client, you may need to work together with your teammates on a specific strategy of physical placement. Think of it like football, where for each play, each player had a distinct role for the play to be successful. For example, let's say you have to protect your client at a formal evening party in an event hall that seats 200 people at round tables. It is a large event, and the client will be walking around mingling with various people throughout the event. You have a four-person team, and your mission is to have at least one person within thirty feet of the client at all times. You have two primary strategies you can use. One is a "zone defense" strategy. You divide up the venue into four equal quadrants, and each one of you takes a quadrant. When the client is in your quadrant, you move in the proper way to keep an eye on them. When they move out of your quadrant, you hang back and let the other team member take over. It takes communication and coordination. Option Two is to have at least one team member next to the client the entire time. It may not be feasible depending on the nature of the threat and the environment.

## Tip # 76: Formations

If you are in an environment where a threat requires a protective formation around the client at all times, you have a few options. If you are by yourself, you have to remain in the most strategic position possible and constantly move as the client moves. You should always be close enough to respond to the client if you need to protect them, but you should be far enough away that you do not prevent them from doing their job. If you have two people on the team, having one person in front and one person behind the client is preferred. If you have three or more people, you can position you team so that you form a perimeter around the client. It can be a three-person triangle, a four-person diamond, or another shape with five or more people. You should have a working knowledge of how all of these positions work. Just like a football team, each person in a four-person diamond has a specific assigned role. And you will need to be flexible and adaptable to change positions and roles at a moment's notice.

## Tip # 77: Being the Gray Man

The "Gray Man" is a term that describes someone who does not stand out. This skill set is incredibly useful in protective operations for a variety of roles. For instance, if you are conducting undercover surveillance on a threat, you need to look and act like someone in the crowd. If the bodyguards are wearing suits and ties, you should not wear a suit or tie. The point of being the Gray Man is not to look like you are there to protect someone. But you can jump in to help in an emergency if an attack occurs. It does not only mean clothing but it can apply to hairstyle, appearance, body language, mood, or activity level. Remember, the threat usually has the advantage in the time and place of the attack. As protectors, we generally cannot predict when and where the threat will take place. So, our advantage is that the bad guy doesn't know the number of people on our team... and we can hide people in plain sight.

### Tip # 78: High Profile vs. Low Profile

There are generally two strategic decisions that need to be made with any protective operation. First, are you going to use a high profile or low-profile strategy? Low profile is when you are trying to be discreet, be the gray man, and not advertise yourself as a bodyguard. It can be used to help hide the size of your team. High profile is when you intentionally try to display strength and size, and you want to stand out for a tactical reason. There are strengths and weaknesses of each strategy. The power of low profile is that threat does not know how large the protection team is and if they are armed or not. The strength of a high profile is that it can deter the attack because you may present too strong a force for the attacker. A weakness of a low profile is that you may not be able to identify yourself to law enforcement if an emergency happens. A drawback of a high profile is that you may be attacked first, before the client, because the bad guy knows who to take out first.

# Part B: High-Risk Missions

### Tip # 79: Operating in Austere Environments

In specific jobs, you may be required to travel and work in a country or an environment that is unfriendly, dangerous, high-crime risk, and uncomfortable to live and work in. These areas could be developing countries with scarce resources or political unrest; the fact these areas are in need or dangerous may be the exact reason your client needs to go there. Maybe they have a business interest in that region. Another austere environment that is common is a hurricane, flood, or disaster site. Maybe your client has a charity or foundation that helps support people in need. Unfortunately, many places with the greatest need are also dangerous. Lack of stable politics, local law enforcement, and the presence of gangs or criminals increases the likelihood your client may be attacked. Be prepared to travel to one of these areas at a moment's notice; if you are going to work in one of these areas for any amount of time, you have to have certain necessities planned out. How will you and your client get good water to drink if you can't drink water out of the tap? What food will you eat that won't make you sick? Where will you stay if there are no safe hotels? How will you drive and get around if you don't know who to trust? Things that can help prepare you for these last-minute jobs are staying informed on worldwide news, disasters, or significant political changes. Have updated vaccinations (Hepatitis, Malaria, Yellow Fever, Meningitis, etc.) so you are ready to travel at a moment's notice. Have an updated passport with plenty of blank pages for last-minute Visas. An international driver's license is very easy to obtain. These are all things that can help set you up for success if one of these jobs comes up.

## Tip # 80: Kidnapping and Ransom

When traveling abroad, especially while protecting someone who is either easily recognizable or is obviously of high net worth, you should always be aware of kidnapping and ransom. In some regions of the world, things like kidnapping and holding someone for ransom is more common. If a person is connected to business, is known to have money, looks like they have money, or just looks like they come from a country with money, they could be a target for kidnapping. Kidnapping and ransom aren't always for one hundred million dollars like the movies. There is a common tactic with criminals called "Express Kidnapping," where they will kidnap someone and hold them for a couple of hours to get a couple of hundred bucks in cash. Learn about and watch out for this kind of thing. Some companies have Kidnap and Ransom Insurance if their employee is held and needs emergency money. You can also attend classes and training dealing with kidnap, ransom, and terrorist emergencies that can help prepare you for what to do if you run into one of these situations.

## Tip # 81: Escape and Evasion Concepts

If you are traveling to other countries or unstable locations or have the potential for violence, you must always have a backup plan to get out of that country or area. For instance, a nation is unstable, and you fly in to begin your job. Once you start, civil unrest erupts, you need to leave the country, but the airport is taken over. As a result, you may have to rent a car and drive out. Or maybe you drove into the country from one road, but that road is now blocked due to riots or becomes a conflict zone. Therefore, you will need to have a secondary route of where you need to exit the country. If you are going into one of these countries, you should become familiar with all surrounding countries, so you know what the best route of escape is.

Another good thing to think about is what if your client is seriously injured or has a severe medical episode, and there are no good hospitals in the entire country. There is medical evacuation insurance that can be purchased ahead of time. These insurance packages can include emergency extraction from one country to another if specific medical care is needed.

# Part C: Operational Settings

## Tip # 82: Formal Settings

As a bodyguard, it is very common to accompany your client to formal dinners, charity events, fundraisers, or speaking engagements. These formal events can have many attendees where you or your client is in the spotlight, figuratively or literally. These environments can be challenging and logistically complex due to media presence, other high-profile clients, other bodyguard or executive protection teams in the same room, and a complicated program of things that need to happen on stage and on time. What if your client is engaged in a meaningful conversation with a colleague, and you know they are supposed to be on stage in one minute? How will you handle it? Do you go up and remind the client of their speaking obligation? Will you go to the emcee and tell them to stall? Or will you do something else? You will have to know how to protect your client without getting in their way or holding up the event.

## Tip # 83: Residential and Personal Settings

A bodyguard will often likely be hired to work in residences and other personal settings. Protecting someone in their own home presents its own challenges. It is their personal space, and you have to be very careful how you work in it. To you, it may be just another job, but for them, it is their home. Be very cautious and respectful when someone allows you into their home. Everyone has different standards and different boundaries. Like any other protection detail, the more you can clarify with your client ahead of time, the better. While working in someone's residence, you may have to be ready to receive other family members, high-profile guests, or simple tasks like taking the family dog out for a bathroom break. There may also be times when the client leaves with another teammate, and you are required to stay back and guard the residence all alone. It can feel like an uneventful job, but their home is their most sacred and trusted space, so it must be protected.

# Chapter 7: A Bodyguard's Relationship with the Protectee

## Part A: The Protectee

### Tip # 84: Celebrity Security and the CEO

Any type of job can have its positives and its negatives. Being a bodyguard for a high-profile individual like a celebrity or a CEO can come with things like more resources, more money, and maybe a better working relationship with law enforcement. But this type of protectee can be challenging since you may have fans coming up to you and the protectee all the time. You may have to deal with the media. Learn to notice the directions of cameras and cell phones and try to stay out of the frame. You can protect your client better if you remain anonymous. You don't need to be in the pictures on the paper. You may have to deal with other workers or employees in your client's life that feel they have the right to interrupt your protection plan because they 'have to' talk to the CEO right now. Sometimes, your celebrity client wants to leave the building but is continually stopped by fans, and the celebrity doesn't want to appear rude to the fans. You can come in politely and professionally and "remind" the star they have an urgent meeting to get to so they can leave. Then you can talk to the fan, apologize your client had to go. It is one way you can help the client "save face" and give them an "out" to stay on schedule.

### Tip # 85: The Single Parent

Doing bodyguard work is not always with lights, cameras, and celebrities. It is very common to be hired for protective work for a protectee who may be a single mom stalked by her estranged husband. These cases can be challenging because the client might not have a lot of money, which means fewer resources and fewer people on your team. This type of client may also not have the luxury of having a flexible work schedule or have the money or time to take off of work. This client may have to deal with the new stresses of having their lives in danger while still managing their life, work, kids, school, etc. This type of client may not be accustomed to working with people through all aspects of their daily life. All people handle stress in different ways, and you have to be prepared to help your client manage the stress and emotional trauma that may come with these types of situations.

## Tip # 86: The Servant and Leader Role

Regardless of what type of protectee you may be working with, it is essential to remember that you, as the bodyguard or the executive protection agent, have to fulfill both a servant and leader role. You have to be a servant because you have to be willing to follow the client's lead. They are the one who is paying your check, and you need to fulfill their expectations of what they hired you for. You have to have a humble attitude and not allow your ego to prevent you from doing seemingly servant duties like opening a door, carrying luggage, picking up trash, running errands, scheduling meetings, or any little thing that is asked of you to help you protect your client. You must be able to switch roles and be a leader as well. For example, if your client hired you to be the security expert, you must figure out how to "lead up" and utilize your expertise. What if a situation occurs where your client (who is your boss, technically) wants to go somewhere that is unsafe? They are in charge, but when do you step in when you know they are doing something that could be dangerous to them? You will have to be prepared for these types of decisions because they will come up.

### Tip # 87: Developing Rapport

Developing rapport with your protectee is vital. It is a skill set that you can learn. First, you have to gain your client's trust. If they cannot trust you, they will not listen to you regarding security matters. Second, you must develop good social skills and be able to communicate that you are a professional and worthy of someone's trust. It usually has to be done in a very short amount of time upon meeting your client.

In most cases, you will not get a formal two-hour sit-down meeting where you get to interview the client on what all they want. Most likely, you will be introduced to your client with a handshake; you may be able to ask one or two questions. People will often develop first impressions within 5-10 seconds, which gives you very little time. Developing rapport is the ability to make sure the client knows that you are a professional, you respect what they do, and you will not get in their way. You need to be able to communicate that you can help them, and you can "add value" to their work life, not get in their way.

# Part B: The Protective Circle

### Tip # 88: Children as Protectees

When working as a protection agent, you may be given the opportunity to work with various types of people to protect. If another team member is guarding your client, you may have to watch the kids since the kids may be vulnerable to an attack. Being hired to protect children can be very difficult yet very common. You may have to take them to school, pick them up from school, help them with homework, take them to soccer practice, and do all kinds of activities. It is not always what someone initially thinks about when they see themselves as a bodyguard but sometimes children are the ones in need of protection the most. Children can be vulnerable and, depending on their age, may not be able to provide things for themselves. When protecting children, you have an amazing opportunity to help them learn and develop their own skills. Do not see this type of assignment as a punishment as many do. See it as an opportunity to truly help a child and their family.

## Tip # 89: *The Protectee's Family and Friends*

With most executive protection roles, you will be expected to provide a level of protection for multiple people at once. It is not always only one person you are protecting. You have to figure out who all is in your circle of protection. Remember, if there is a threat out there wanting to hurt your client, but they can't attack the client because of their security, the threat may try another strategy. They may try to harm or attack the client's family members, friends, co-workers or even damage their property. How these types of job specifics get done will always be different in every detail and every contract. But you have to be ready for a situation that is flexible and changing. What if you are assigned to protect a client for an evening's formal dinner. And when you arrive to meet with the client, you see the client has brought his wife and four kids. The client tells you to stay with and protect the kids while he goes and does his own thing. What will you do in this type of situation where you don't have enough resources, and the job is changing rapidly? Will you honor his request since he is the pay writing your check? Or will you clarify with him that the threat is against him and not his family? You have to think on your feet and think through these possibilities before they show up.

### Tip # 90: Non-human Clients

Most protection work is about protecting human beings from other human beings. However, there are certain cases where a protection agent is hired to guard non-human items. For example, you can be employed to protect things of value. Racehorses can be worth millions of dollars, and protection agents are hired to guard them all of the time. Protection agents can be employed to protect all kinds of things from jewelry, fur coats, and computer hard drives. These types of jobs can be very abnormal, but the pay can be extremely high. These types of jobs are not very common, but they are out there, so be ready if such an opportunity arises.

# Part C: Boundaries

### Tip # 91: Boundaries: Do Nothing Illegal

Executive protection agents are often in situations where they have to make crucial decisions. It is where character comes in. To protect yourself and your career, you have to be aware of the bad things out there that can get you in trouble. Trust and character are the most important things you have. You have to do your job while remaining honorable to your character. If you are with a client who has money and asks you to do something illegal, unethical, or anything against your moral code, always say 'no.' Nothing illegal is worth sacrificing your career over. Do not think that you have to do what they say just because the client is the boss or they are writing the check. If you lose your job or get put in jail, then you can't protect anyone. So, do yourself a favor and make up your mind you will not be tempted to do anything illegal.

# Tip # 92: Boundaries: A Protectee's Advances

Another topic to be aware of when working as a protection agent is the possibility of sexual or emotional advances by the client. It can happen in this industry because, much of the time, an executive protection agent is working with a client for very long hours. They can be together at home, at work, on personal time, etc. If someone needs protection, they need protection all the time. Boundaries have to be established so you do not put yourself in a situation where you can be accused of anything improper. As you develop rapport, trust, and a relationship with the client, you may get to know one another very well. It has happened in the past where clients and bodyguards have become too emotionally or physically close. And when this happens, usually, the job and the character of the people involved are found to be lacking. Be aware of this possibility and do everything you can to protect against it.

# Chapter 8: A Bodyguard's Industry Credibility

## Part A: Licenses and Certifications

### Tip # 93: Bodyguard and Executive Protection Training

To be a professional takes dedication. There are many other careers and life experiences that can help you in your career as a bodyguard. Occupations such as law enforcement, firefighter, military, security, psychology, IT, or legal specialties can help you. However, experience in these areas does not automatically make you qualified to be a bodyguard. They may help, but no one resume makes you automatically qualified. Therefore, even if you do not have experience in one of the above fields, you can still be successful in a bodyguard career. So, regardless of your background, if you want to be successful in the bodyguard industry it is best to obtain relevant and specific training. There are executive protection schools and bodyguard training academies that you can attend. Many of them are well worth their time and money. Not only does this allow you to learn from professionals who are already working in the industry, but these schools can get you the appropriate certifications and licenses to get started.

### Tip # 94: Medical Licenses

Having emergency medical training is extremely valuable in the protection industry. If your primary role is protecting someone, suffering a medical emergency (heart attack, stroke, seizure, etc.) may be more probable than a physical assault. Or if there is an assault and your client is injured, the only thing faster than driving them to the emergency room is to be your own emergency room.

You can easily obtain certifications as an EMR, EMT, or Paramedic in your area. Emergency medical skills are not only valuable, but the certificates that come with them are even better. It shows prospective employers you are serious about training, serving others, and investing in your own skill sets.

## Tip # 95: Concealed Carry Licenses

For many executive protection jobs, you will need to be armed with a concealed handgun. Each state and many cities will have different laws regarding the concealed carry of a handgun. It is essential to know where you can and cannot carry a concealed firearm in the area you live and work. It is also important to know which states have reciprocity with your state. Just because you have a concealed handgun permit in your state does not necessarily mean you can carry it in the state next to you. You may, many states and reciprocity laws that honor each other's permits, but they may not. And even if another state accepts your permit, you still have to abide by that state's firearms laws. So, even if both states honor the same license, the states may still have different specific firearms laws. It is on you as the handgun owner and the permit holder to know the regulations of each state and jurisdiction you are working in. If you are going to carry a concealed handgun, make sure you have the proper licenses and certifications to do so.

## Tip # 96: Private Detective Licenses and Security Regulation

Remember that each state has different laws and regulations on what you can and cannot do in the private security industry. Some states have no rules whatsoever. Some states have many restrictions on the private security industry where you cannot even advertise a "security business" of any kind unless you have a certain level of license from the state. Some states require that you have a private detective's license to provide executive protection services or any security services that allow you to carry a concealed handgun. Being a true professional means that you have the skills to seek out and discover what the rules and regulations are in your area. You must have the proper credentials and licenses. Do the research, find out what you need to do, get the right certifications. There are no shortcuts.

# Part B: Breaking Into the Industry

### *Tip # 97: Gaining Experience*

Once you have the proper training, licenses, and certifications, the bodyguarding industry can be challenging to break into. Just because you are trained and licensed doesn't mean you're automatically going to get a high-paying job where you get to wear sunglasses and an earpiece protecting celebrities. It is a unique industry that still operates on word of mouth, networking, and handshakes. It is because trust and honor are so important. If you are going to protect someone, you have to be worthy of confidence, trust, and integrity. And you have to demonstrate that trust and honor over some time and earn a good reputation. Once word gets out in the industry that you can be relied on, you might get asked to work some low-level jobs to prove yourself.

Then you can get your foot in the door and begin working your way up. I broke into this industry with zero experience. After I got the training and my proper certifications, I did jobs for free to gain experience and build my resume. At first, I could only find partime executive protection work, so I worked a second job to support myself. I drove overnight to different states to work jobs without anyone paying for my hotel or travel because I needed the experience. I took low-level jobs as anyone breaking into any industry needs to do. I took dangerous and high-risk jobs when no one else would take them. Then I slowly began putting together a resume and demonstrating that I was a professional, dependable agent who took my job seriously. I would always arrive early and leave late. Those things paid off, and I was able to take better and better jobs. This type of work is not for everyone, but it is excellent work for those who like it. You can break-in. It can be done, but it takes hard work, commitment to professionalism, dedication to training, and doing each part of the job with excellence over a long period.

## Tip # 98: Building the Resume: Honesty

Your honor and integrity are your most precious items. If you do your job with a good work ethic and are honest with all of your dealings, people will trust you and remember you. Your honor can be very easy to lose, and it is tough to gain back. In most cases, once you lose it, you will never get it back. Honor is something that is given to you by someone else. You cannot give it to yourself. You can only earn it by doing your job well, ethically, and with excellence. Having honor is about doing what you said you would do. It is about fulfilling your commitments. Honor is about not lying or giving in to peer pressure; it is about not compromising your values and beliefs. Being a protector or a security agent is all about honor; you either have it or don't. Not only do you have to be honest with others, but you have to be honest with yourself. Self-honesty is difficult, but you must have it. If you cannot be honest with yourself, you will not be able, to be honest with others.

# Part C: Treating Yourself Like a Business

### Tip # 99: Working as Contractor

Most bodyguarding and executive protection jobs you will get at first will hire you as an independent contractor. When working as a contractor, you are not an employee and have to pay your self-employment taxes at the end of the year. So, a contractor job may sound like it is high-paying at first, but you must factor in that you have to pay taxes out of that high wage at the end of the year. When you are working as an independent contractor, especially in a job that could be dangerous or create liability for you, it is in your best interest to set up a business entity where you can work under. Depending on your state, an S-corporation or an LLC may be an excellent way to go. This corporate entity provides an extra layer of protection from your personal life if something bad happens. If you are working under your corporation and someone sues you, and they win, they can only take assets of the legal entity of your corporation. They cannot take anything you own personally, your house, your car, etc. Obviously, each legal case is different but in general, having a corporation is the best way to go. Any serious contractor has a legal corporation they work under. You must treat yourself like a business.

### Tip # 100: Living Will and Life Insurance

Other things that professionals have are living wills and life insurance for your loved ones. If you are working in a job that can potentially kill you, you need to have these things written out ahead of time. Taking the time and getting a proper will, will help your family if something terrible happens to you and your die on the job. It is a reality of the profession we choose, and it is what we sign up for. Take it seriously because it is. A testament will help your family be able to make after-life decisions when you are gone, instead of them worrying about what "you would have wanted." Do them a favor and take the time to do this. Life insurance is the same concept. Once you are gone, you can continue to provide for your family and help them with expenses. Funerals, legal matters, and insurance issues can be costly, so do your loved ones a favor and get some life insurance. It is a way to help your family and honor them once you are gone.

## Tip # 101: Networking, Referrals, and Getting Jobs

A lot of the executive protection industry works on networking and referrals. Once you work with other protection professionals, you learn things about them. How early do they show up for work? How well-trained are they? How seriously do they take their job? How courteous are they to others? Do they have good equipment and tools? How hard do they work? You will notice those things about other agents, and you will remember who you would like to work with and who you would not like to work with in the future. And guess what, they are noticing those same things about you. Word gets around this industry fast. Mostly, when people think about networking, they think about getting work from others. I disagree. I believe networking is about giving other people work. If you come across a job that you do not want or are not qualified for, pass it along to someone you trust. They will remember that and will likely return the same favor to you. That is how you network; you show other people that you are valuable. That is how you begin to build a resume, and that is how you strengthen your reputation.

# About the Expert

Cody Blocker C.P.S. is a Certified Protection Specialist and an honor graduate of the esteemed Executive Security International. Cody worked as the Security Director of a large organization for over ten years and currently works in the private security industry. He has worked as an Executive Protection Agent in various roles in multiple states in the US and overseas, including conflict zones. Cody's unique skill set has allowed him to gain experience and specialize in the areas of surveillance, counter-surveillance, threat assessment, and advanced work. He is a licensed Private Detective and a licensed Emergency Medical Technician (EMT). Cody is certified by his state's Highway Patrol to teach Concealed Handgun Certification Courses to responsible citizens. He has trained and consulted with over 100 organizations across the country in various security capacities. Cody has over twenty years of training in Japanese and Brazilian martial arts and is a boxing, mixed martial arts, and Brazilian Jiu-Jitsu competitor. Cody is also a competitive pistol shooter and has amassed thousands of hours of continuing education in combative, tactic, driving, shooting, surveillance, and intelligence training from national and international experts. Along with other protection professionals with whom he has worked closely, he teaches self-defense, pistol combat, surveillance, threat assessment, and security operations to teams and individuals. He can be reached at his website www.avoidthefight.com.

HowExpert publishes quick 'how to' guides on all topics from A to Z by everyday experts. Visit HowExpert.com to learn more.

# Recommended Resources

- HowExpert.com – Quick 'How To' Guides on All Topics from A to Z by Everyday Experts.
- HowExpert.com/free – Free HowExpert Email Newsletter.
- HowExpert.com/books – HowExpert Books
- HowExpert.com/courses – HowExpert Courses
- HowExpert.com/clothing – HowExpert Clothing
- HowExpert.com/membership – HowExpert Membership Site
- HowExpert.com/affiliates – HowExpert Affiliate Program
- HowExpert.com/jobs – HowExpert Jobs
- HowExpert.com/writers – Write About Your #1 Passion/Knowledge/Expertise & Become a HowExpert Author.
- HowExpert.com/resources – Additional HowExpert Recommended Resources
- YouTube.com/HowExpert – Subscribe to HowExpert YouTube.
- Instagram.com/HowExpert – Follow HowExpert on Instagram.
- Facebook.com/HowExpert – Follow HowExpert on Facebook.
- TikTok.com/@HowExpert – Follow HowExpert on TikTok.

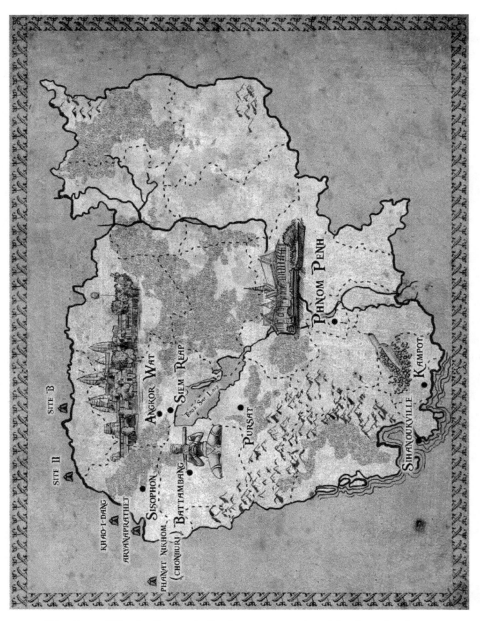

Kingdom of Cambodia map indicating areas mentioned by the artists in
this book. ©2021. All rights reserved. This image may not be used or
duplicated without express permission in writing from the author.

# Introduction

My father was born in the province of Kampot, to the southwest of Phnom Penh, in a place called Tani Tuk Meas. While I know very little about his childhood, I like to imagine that daily life was much like what we see in idyllic paintings: coconut palm trees swaying in the warm summer winds, green rice fields, people making offerings at the local Buddhist temple. I like to imagine my father running along the road on his way to elementary school, wearing the typical uniform of a white shirt and blue shorts or trousers. Sadly, much of my connection with my father comes through my imagination.

On April 17, 1975, communist guerillas known as the Khmer Rouge marched into Phnom Penh and other provincial cities, declaring victory. At first, people cheered, thinking that the bombing and war they had endured for more than a decade had finally come to an end. Instead, that day marked the beginning of nearly four years of terror. The Khmer Rouge implemented a radical Maoist and Marxist-Leninist policy with the goal of transforming Cambodia into a classless society, abolishing money and private property, traditional education, religion, and cultural practices. People were forced into the countryside to undertake arduous agricultural work from morning to evening, with little food to sustain them. Schools, pagodas, mosques, stores, and government buildings were turned into stables, granaries, torture centers, and prisons.

During the Khmer Rouge regime, more than 2 million people died of starvation, disease, overwork, torture, and execution in what became known as the "killing fields." Among those were my father's parents, grandparents, siblings, cousins, friends. Cambodia was not spoken of in our house, and as far as I knew, it was a bad place--or at least, a place I believed had stolen my father's happiness.

It wasn't until I traveled to Cambodia for the first time that I actually began to see the beauty and brilliance in Khmer culture. I remember one day very distinctly. I had taken a taxi with some friends from the capital city of Phnom Penh to Siem Reap, where the Angkor temples are located. I of course wanted to visit the famous Angkor Wat first, but it was early afternoon when we arrived, and our taxi driver insisted it would be best to wait either until evening to see the sunset or until the next morning to see the sunrise over Angkor Wat, so instead we went to visit the Bayon, part of Angkor Thom.

Built in the 12th century by King Jayavarman VII, the Bayon encompasses hundreds of huge faces carved into stone, facing north, south, east, and west. I had gone expecting to see magnificent monuments, but not faces in the stone, faces that seemed serene, at peace. The tranquility reflected in the gentle smiles and partially closed eyes of each face stood in stark contrast to nearly all of my beliefs and perceptions about Cambodia as a grim place of war, destruction, and trauma. I looked up at them and literally fell to my knees, overwhelmed with emotion.

For the rest of the afternoon I walked among the many faces, and felt that they were watching me, comforting me. While silent, they spoke to me.

This was a pivotal moment, because I realized just how much I had been focusing on Cambodia and my Cambodian identity in a negative way. Without discounting the trauma and suffering endured during the Khmer Rouge regime (and we will never, ever forget), I realized that period is but a very short fragment within the timeline of Cambodian history. The Khmer Empire once encompassed most of what is now Thailand and Vietnam. The Khmer built complex cities and spectacular temples without modern tools or equipment, reflecting Buddhist and Hindu cosmology on earth. They expressed their love of music, dance, martial arts, cooking, adornment, and other creative endeavors on the temple walls themselves, through intricate carvings that tell tales of both everyday life and ancient mythos.

## The Power of Art to Connect, to Heal

Under the Khmer Rouge regime, approximately 90 percent of Cambodia's artisans were killed. The regime wanted to erase all vestiges of outside influence or elite, "oppressor" culture, and targeted artists--painters, singers, martial artists, and dancers--for execution.

Yet just as the Khmer Rouge sought to eliminate traditional arts, post-war Cambodians seek to rebuild them. In so doing, they strive to repair and heal their shattered spirits.

**Figure 1.** Faces in the Stone, Bayon Temple, Angkor Thom. Photo: Christine Su

**Figure 2**. Gentle Smiles, Bayon Temple, Angkor Thom. Photo: Allison Choate

## Cambodians in the United States

Following the fall of the Khmer Rouge regime in Cambodia in 1979, thousands of refugees fled the country. Approximately 145,000 refugees relocated to the U.S. between 1979 and 2002, with the majority arriving between 1980 and 1985. Traumatized and thousands of miles from their homeland, Cambodian refugees faced significant challenges in resettlement and adjustment.

First, in an attempt to distribute the thousands of refugees so as not to "burden" any one city or state, U.S. relief organizations and government agencies relocated Cambodians to different regions, resulting in cultural and linguistic isolation. Second, refugees came with memories of trauma inconceivable to many Americans, yet agencies directed them to areas with few resources or professionals with the knowledge and experience to assist them. Third, most came with no money or possessions, and lacking skills necessary to obtain employment. Unable to secure jobs, many refugees lived in poverty or relied upon government assistance. Others worked long hours in factories or other jobs that did not require advanced education or fluency in English.

The adult refugees brought with them their children and other relatives who were born or very young during the Khmer Rouge regime or were born in the refugee camps. This group became known as the "1.5 generation."[1] They found themselves caught in-between their Khmer heritage and their contemporary lives in the U.S. Their parents relied upon them to help navigate life in the U.S. on one hand, yet implored them to maintain Khmer cultural values and traditions on the other.

Some scholars distinguish the 1.5 generation even further, using the terms "1.25 generation" to refer to those who were born in Cambodia (or transitional refugee camps) and came to the U.S. as adolescents (13–17 years old), and "1.75 generation," those who were born in Cambodia or the camps but came to the U.S. at a very early age (0-5 years old), noting that there is a spectrum of adaptation and acculturation.

Those of Cambodian heritage born in the U.S., known as the 2.0 generation, also found themselves in-between: neither wholly Cambodian nor wholly American. Furthermore, the direct trauma experienced by the refugees, if not addressed, can pass down within families and communities, creating "a lasting effect that worsens with each generation[. . .]and a culture of silence that creates internal and external trauma for children and youth."[2]

Indeed, a 2011 survey of 500 1.5- and 2.0-generation Cambodians in and around Long Beach, California (with the largest Cambodian population outside of Cambodia) revealed that nearly half of the respondents reported symptoms of depression, including loneliness, fear, insomnia, cutting and other self-harming acts.[3]

And yet, as Cambodian American writer Sokunthary Svay notes, the members of these new generations occupy a unique liminal space that offers opportunities to provide distinct perspectives, especially as expressed through the arts.

In their creative work, she continues, they find "a way to heal old wounds and to reinvent oneself: from damaged to healed, survivor to successor, old world to current world, 1 to 1.5," to which I would add "to 2.0."[4]

Art has the power to connect, to convey emotions, thoughts, and memories, and to facilitate healing.

## Voices of a New Generation: The Book

When I returned to the U.S. after my first trip to Cambodia, I promised myself that I would help rewrite the limited narrative that has defined Khmer American culture. I want to honor and acknowledge our complex history, but convey that Cambodian heritage is a source of dignity, not shame. To this end, I decided to write a book about Khmer American artists. I want to highlight the creative talents and imaginations of the Cambodian American community, to provide space for artists to share their experiences and journeys.

The artists who narrate their stories in this book are members of either the 1.5 or 2.0 generations. They are friends and colleagues who opened their hearts and allowed me to observe the world through their eyes and hear them speak to the world through their art. They are the voices of a new generation.

I am humbled and grateful to present this book.

Author's note: In this book, I use the terms "Cambodian" and "Khmer" interchangeably. There is much debate about the difference between the terms and whether and when one is more appropriate than the other, but as the artists use both in describing themselves and their work, I choose to follow suit.

# Chapter 1

## Ancient Khmer Martial Arts
## ក្បាច់គុណបុរាណខ្មែរ

Walking along the cool sandstone corridors of Angkor Wat, one of many extraordinary temples in northern Cambodia, one can almost feel the vibrancy and energy of life as it existed during the ancient Khmer Empire (9th to 15th centuries).

Built in the 12th century and dedicated to Vishnu, Angkor Wat's five main towers symbolize the five peaks of Mount Meru that form the center of the universe and the home of the gods in Hindu mythology.[5] Seven concentric seas, represented at Angkor by the enormous moat surrounding the massive monument, encircle and protect Mount Meru. The temple's interior construction is a complex intersection of galleries, passageways, and terraces. Elaborate bas-reliefs carved into its walls depicting creation narratives, scenes from the *Reamker*, and epic battles with kings and *nak jambaang* (warriors) engaged in different types of *kun* (combat) complement the magnificence of its architecture.[6] Angkor is a sacred place.

The term *kbach kun boran Khmer* refers to the array of martial arts developed and practiced throughout the Khmer Empire for centuries. *Kbach kun boran* played an integral role in Khmer armies' victories over their enemies, and its practice required physical, mental, and spiritual preparation.

Those who mastered the different styles of *kun* were much respected and admired, and these *kru* (teachers) were sought after to pass on their knowledge. Novices spent years if not decades studying and training.

**Figure 3**. *Nak jambaang* (warriors) marching into battle, Bayon Temple.
Photo: Christine Su

**Figure 4.** Khmer warrior fighting against the Cham, Bayon Temple.
Photo: Allison Choate

## Defining Kbach Kun Boran Khmer

In this work, I use *kbach kun boran Khmer* (which literally translates to "ancient Khmer martial arts") as the umbrella term to describe a variety of martial arts styles. The different types of *kbach kun boran Khmer* fall under three broad categories, sometimes called "door systems": hand-to-hand combat without weapons; combat using weapons; and grappling.[7] Within these larger categories are more specific *kbach kun*, including:

- *pradal serey*: "free fighting"/freestyle kickboxing
- *bokator* (sometimes called *l'bokator*): a combat and defense system with techniques and moves inspired by animals
- *dambong veng*: combat involving the use of a long staff
- *bok chambab*: wrestling

Perhaps the best-known, especially among martial arts enthusiasts, is *pradal serey* (freestyle kickboxing), which has ancient origins, perhaps as early as the Funan period prior to Angkor, and continues to be very popular today.[8] Cambodians love to attend live competitions or watch them on television. Traditional instrument ensembles accompany *pradal serey* matches with music called *vung phleng pradal* or *vung phleng klang khek*, performed by *sralai* (oboe), *skor* or *sampho* (drums), and *chhing* (cymbals), in two parts.

The first part, a slow, melodic composition performed prior to the match, is an invocation that pays respect to the spirits of the ancestors and former teachers and asks them to instill confidence in the fighters.

The second part is a faster-paced piece with a pulsating drumbeat, played throughout the actual boxing to rouse the crowds, stopping only when a fighter is knocked out or the allotted time runs out.[9] A match consists of five rounds, each lasting for three minutes, with a two-minute break in between.

Recently, with the production and popularity of films such as *Jailbreak* (2017), more attention has focused on *bokator*.[10] *Bokator* was designed for use in battle, and soldiers trained to use their elbows, knees, hands, feet, and even heads to strike opponents, as well as various weapons. *Bokator* techniques mimic the styles of certain wild animals and as such, include different moves named horse, alligator, *naga* (sea serpent), eagle, crane, and so forth.[11] The documentary film *Surviving Bokator* (2018) chronicles the contemporary movement to revive *bokator* in Cambodia and tells a powerful story about reclaiming cultural identity and building bridges between generations. Cambodian officials have applied to have *bokator* included in the UNESCO Intangible Cultural Heritage list.[12]

## Foundations of *Kbach Kun Boran Khmer*

While each of the *kun* styles is unique, certain principles, postures, and patterns serve as their foundation. The core of *kbach kun boran* consists of 12 *mae kun* (techniques) that guide the use of body parts (hands, elbows, feet, knees, head) and additional implements (sticks, staffs, swords, and spears), and 12 *twear kun*, which prescribe specific body postures and complex footwork patterns.[13] The term *twear* means "door," which is fitting as doors can either allow or block access to a space, and the *tvear kun* serve this function for warriors confronting their opponents.

As with other Cambodian arts, the Khmer Rouge sought to extinguish *kbach kun boran* during their regime (1975-1979). The Khmer Rouge perceived martial arts masters as threats to their totalitarian control, and systematically rooted out both *kru* and their students for execution. Still, a handful of knowledge-bearers survived. In this first chapter, one such individual, Vannak Pen (aka *Lok Kru Kirihingsà*) shares his story of how influential--indeed, central--*kbach kun boran Khmer* has been in his life, and how crucial it is for him to pass on knowledge of this traditional art to his sons, Tanaka and Viro. In the next chapter, Tanaka in turn shares how his father and *kbach kun boran Khmer* have guided him.

## Artist Encounters

I first met Vannak Pen while I was working as the Director of the Center for Southeast Asian Studies at Ohio University. I facilitated an annual Khmer Studies conference, and I wanted to make the conference experience something more than reading of academic papers. I wanted those who attended to learn about Cambodian history and culture from Cambodians themselves as well as engage in scholarly dialogue. To this end, I went searching for the Cambodian community in southeastern Ohio.

While we had several international students from Cambodia studying at the university, I found that the population of resident Cambodian/ Cambodian Americans in Athens, Ohio was one: me.

About 90 minutes north, however, in the Columbus area, I found a thriving Cambodian community.

I began to make inquiries about cultural events hosted in Columbus and started to meet with community members. At one event I met Vannak Pen, and even during that first meeting, I noticed his calm and peaceful demeanor. He and I spoke at length about a group of young Cambodians to whom he was teaching *kbach kun boran Khmer*. Many, he noted, were at risk of getting involved with gangs or other negative elements because there was little to detract them.[14] Vannak decided to form a class in which he would teach *kbach kun boran Khmer* to provide the family, community, and purpose that the youth needed. He invited me to observe his class, both in practice sessions and later in performances at the Khmer Buddhist temple. His students captivated me not only with their physical skill, but their focus and concentration as well.

*Lok Kru Kirihingsa* and his students graciously made the drive down to Athens for the Khmer Studies conference not only the first year I was at Ohio, but for several years thereafter. Their participation provided insight into the ancient art and added a new dimension to the conference. More recently, Vannak and Tanaka relocated to California from Ohio, as I had several years prior, and I was delighted to reconnect with them and find out how *kbach kun boran Khmer* has continued to play a positive role in their lives.                                      -*C.S.*

## My Story: Vannak Pen

I was born in Srok Thma Koul, Khum Chrouy Sdau, Phum Nikom Krao in Battambang province in Cambodia in 1967.

**Figure 5**. *Lok Kru* Kirihingsa (Vannak Pen).
Photo courtesy of Vannak Pen

Between my birth and my eventual arrival in the Khao-I-Dang refugee camp on the Thai border after the fall of the Khmer Rouge, my family and I moved many different times.

A distinct memory from my childhood is that my cousins and I found all kinds of ways to entertain ourselves. During this time (early 1975), there were no iPads, iPhones, or any kind of technology--just stones and bamboo sticks to play with. One day, I was playing with my cousins in the jungle and we came across what we thought were all kinds of cool "toys." They were actually grenades, cartridges, and ammunition that had been left behind by soldiers. For some reason, my older cousin, Chorn, decided we should burn all of them and see what happened. And so we did.

As a young boy I had never seen these "toys" before, so I wasn't sure exactly what was going to happen, or why everyone ran after they set the toys on fire, so I continued standing there.

I remember my cousin yelling at me, *"Ah prokach, jos ah'ang nov kalaing neng tver ey?!? Rut!"* ("Hey, why are you still standing there? Run!") Even when we didn't see soldiers or combat right in front of us, we were surrounded by vestiges of war.

## Life under the Khmer Rouge

When I was about 8 years old, the Khmer Rouge gained control of the whole country. We were still in Battambang, but moved to a place called Makhoeun, and then to Poy Angkor village. The Khmer Rouge told everyone in this village, including my family, that if we didn't leave that the area would be bombed by the U.S or that the Vietnamese would invade and kill us—either way, it was urgent that we leave. So all of the families in Poy Angkor moved to Kotosaut.

Under Khmer Rouge control, everybody had been forced to undertake agricultural work: picking rice, watching the cows to make sure they ate the grass, and collecting feces for fertilization. When I was about 10 years old, I was forced to work on a project to build a dam. It was around 1977 or 1978 that I remember being the darkest times for all of us. This was when the number of killings had started to increase. Around 1978, my father was accused of being an enemy of the Khmer Rouge because he happened to mention aloud to a pregnant woman that during earlier times, people (especially pregnant women) never had to work this hard. Upon learning of this, the Khmer Rouge confronted him and planned to kill him; luckily, his life was spared because he was an acquaintance of the *mae-khum* [commune chief] during this time.

## Learning *Kbach Kun Boran*

After the Khmer Rouge were overthrown by the Vietnamese, my family relocated to Khao-I-Dang refugee camp on the Thai-Cambodia border. It was in Khao-I-Dang that I learned martial arts from a teacher named *Kru* Chea Chomran. He taught me the ancient art of *kbach kun boran Khmer*. I learned so much from him, and when I was 13 years old, I participated in my first tournament fight. The prize for winning the fight was a chicken, which I wanted to win to bring back for my family. I fought with someone the same age as me, the same height and size as me, and probably much more experience than me, and I won.

When I brought the chicken home, I didn't tell my family how I got it because my father was against me learning martial arts. He preferred traditional classroom education. My father pushed me to learn and wanted me to be educated in English because he believed that one day the family would come to America and would need someone able to speak English and translate for others. (He was right--once we came to the U.S., I had to serve as the main translator for my parents, who relied on me for help, especially with medical or legal stuff.) Little did my father know, however, that when he thought I was at school, I was learning *kbach kun boran* from Kru Chea Chomran!

While we were happy to have escaped the Khmer Rouge, life in Khao-I-Dang was also difficult. There was constant gunfire between the Khmer Rouge and the Vietnamese close to the camp, which frightened us, and conditions in the camp were unsanitary and crowded.

One memory I will never forget is when a friend of mine snuck out of the camp into Thailand to find produce to bring back to re-sell (this is one way people survived there). Unfortunately, the Thai police caught him. I saw him in handcuffs, and I walked over to him, hoping to help, but instead, the police arrested us both, and decided to deport us back to Cambodia without our families! They dropped us off at the border crossing. Of course, we wanted to be reunited with our families, so we undertook the long walk back to the camp. Along the way we saw many dead bodies--whether they were Thai, Khmer, Vietnamese, we didn't know--but there were so many. On the journey back we ran into some Thai bandits who wanted to rob us. But since we had just been deported, we didn't have anything to hand over. I looked at my friend and said in Khmer: "I think their guns are fake. Let's fight them and run for it."

I hit one of the men, who happened to be the biggest of the group, and when I did so, the others (who were smaller) ran away, and my friend and I eagerly headed back to the camp. When we got back to Khao-I-Dang, we saw the same Thai policemen who had deported us, but instead of arresting us again, they were impressed that we actually made it back, and in fact gave us some food as a reward. We stayed in Khao-I-Dang until 1983, when we were sponsored to come to the U.S.

I remember an incident on the airplane on the way to the United States that was the first of many that signified that my life was going to be very different from what I had known.

The flight attendant asked what I wanted to eat, and I saw something on the tray that I thought was ice cream or some sort of sweet dessert made with condensed milk. I asked for that and took a big bite out of it, and almost vomited! It was a stick of butter!

**Life in the U.S.**

When we arrived in the U.S. I enrolled in school in Rochester, New York, where I immediately felt out of place. Even though the environment was very diverse, I faced discrimination and was bullied by others: Whites, Blacks, Hispanics, and sometimes even other Asians. At that time I didn't speak much English, so I relied on learning people's body language.

When I felt frustrated, I remember my English teacher telling me, "Put your head down and put in the work. Try to communicate in English at home and avoid speaking your native language." He advised me to watch American television or listen to the radio, and I remember watching shows like *ThunderCats* and I imitated the characters: "ThunderCats! ThunderCats! Ho!"

It was very difficult for me, being in a strange (and cold!) place, and it was very lonely. Still, my *kun* training had taught me to be strong and persevere. Somehow, I completed high school, and soon thereafter enrolled in community college.

I started my educational journey studying criminal justice, but soon learned how dependent that major was on being fluent in English, so I switched to computer science. I discovered another new language--that of computers--which I was able to pick up quickly. I graduated with my associates degree and landed my first job as a low-end PC repair technician making $10 per hour.

Soon thereafter, I met my wife (who is also Khmer) in Columbus, Ohio and we married and settled there. Once we had a baby on the way, I realized that my $10 per hour position was not going to be enough to support my family, so I went after other jobs. I became an application support specialist, and then a network engineer. I also realized that if I wanted to go further in my career, I needed to continue my education, so in 2004, I decided to go back to school.

While still working full-time, now with two children, I attended Franklin University part-time. My work schedule was very demanding, and it took 40 minutes to drive from my workplace to my school. I would have to rush to class right after my shift. Between working, studying, commuting, and taking care of a growing family, it was very stressful.

During this time, I once again relied on what I had learned in my *kbach kun boran* training. I wish I could have studied with another Khmer *kru*, but there were no *kbach kun boran* teachers in Columbus. But I was able to study other martial arts forms: Kung Fu, Karate, Tae Kwon Do, and Ju Jit Su, with multiple teachers. I loved all of them because they reinforced my self-discipline and fostered my self-confidence. I completed my bachelor's degree in computer science and transitioned into my career in software development and engineering.

It was at that point that I realized that while as I mentioned I loved all martial arts, I had been neglecting that of my own heritage. I was ready to become more invested in my own cultural art. I also felt a strong pull to pass my knowledge on to my children and others in their generation. I decided to turn back to *kbach kun boran Khmer*, and if there were still no teachers to be found, I would become the teacher.

## Teaching *Kbach Kun Boran Khmer*

I was the first person in Columbus to revive the ancient art of *kbach kun boran Khmer* and initiate its teaching. I was determined to revive it, so I arranged to perform a demonstration at the local temple to show the community what I planned to do. With their blessings, I began to teach *kbach kun boran* in the Columbus community, and met many wonderful students.

I founded the Kun Khmer Warriors Westgate club in Ohio with the goal of not only teaching combat techniques but instilling the values inherent in *kbach kun boran* into the minds of Khmer youth as well. Many of these youth had faced bullying and discrimination in school, like I had, and were leaning toward getting involved in gangs. I knew that would lead them down the wrong path, and they could get badly hurt, killed, or end up in prison. I knew that *kbach kun boran* had really helped me, and I knew it could help them, too. Self-confidence fostered through this art form reduces students' fear throughout their lives.

## Applying Ancient Teachings in the Modern Era

I have great respect for the teachings inherent in martial arts, through which I not only overcame the adversity in my life, but to begin to heal from the trauma I had faced as well. They helped me develop a feeling of self-control in environments not within my control and provided spaces in which I could express myself and truly feel free.

The benefits of *kbach kun boran Khmer* are both physical and mental. I decide what to teach based on what level of experience a given student has. For beginners, in addition to the basic movements, we focus on learning the history of *kbach* and outlining its rules. For intermediates, we teach more advanced conditioning exercises that require strength, flexibility, and endurance. Practicing the *mae sam* and *twear* helps to develop physical strength by emphasizing muscle contraction and expansion; stimulating the body in this way can make one faster and stronger.

The mental benefits are more difficult to measure, but drawing on my personal experience, martial arts were essential in maintaining my sanity! When I went back to school, sometimes on very little sleep, while raising two kids, playing and coaching soccer, and working full-time, teaching *kbach kun boran* principles helped me to stay focused and calm. I believe my older son, Tanaka, relied on these principles while he was in college, and my son Viro (in college now) does. I have loved seeing their growth, building character, improving mental focus, and developing toughness through sweat.

**Figure 6**. *Lok Kru* Kirihingsa practices a *kbach kun boran* move with his son, Tanaka.
Photo: Vannoroth Ngoc

**Figure 7.** Carving of (*wai kaeng*) elbow move,
Bayon temple. Image: ThundernLightning,
"Elbow Strike in Khmer Martial Art" (Wikipedia)

**Figure 8.**
*Lok Kru* Kirihingsa demonstrates *wai kaeng* during
training. Photo: Vannoroth Ngoc

\*\*\*\*\*\*\*\*\*\*\*\*\*\*\*\*\*\*\*\*\*\*\*\*\*\*\*\*\*\*\*\*\*\*\*\*\*\*\*\*\*\*\*\*\*\*\*\*\*\*\*\*\*\*\*\*\*\*\*\*\*\*\*\*\*\*\*\*

**Author's note:** *Lok Kru Kirihingsa* has outlined the *mae kun* and *tvear kun* in an illustrated manuscript that I hope he will one day publish. It outlines the philosophy behind *kbach kun boran Khmer*, the combinations of *mae kun* and *tvear kun* that comprise the distinct genres, and drawings of specific moves with explanations as to when and why a given move is used. Currently, he refers to this writing when teaching his students and it is not available to the public, but he has given permission to include an excerpt in this book (Fig. 9).

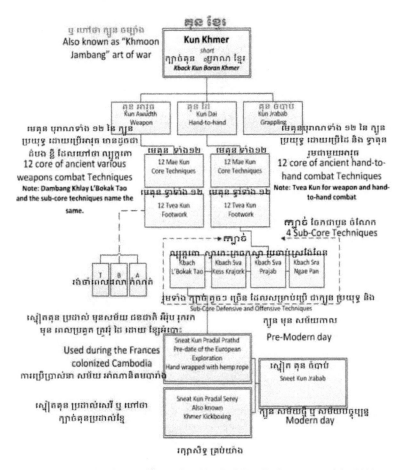

**Figure 9**. *Kun Khmer* styles, outlined by *Lok Kru Kirihingsa*, copyright 2000. Used with permission.

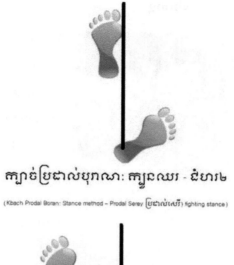

ក្បាច់ប្រដាល់បុរាណៈ ក្បួនឈរ - ជំហរ២

(Kbach Prodal Boran: Stance method – Prodal Serey ប្រដាល់សេរី) fighting stance)

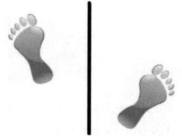

ក្បាច់ប្រដាល់បុរាណៈ ក្បួនឈរ - ជំហរ៣

(Kbach Prodal Boran: Stance method – Prodal Serey ប្រដាល់សេរី) fighting stance)

**Figures 10a** and **10b**: *Tvear* foot patterns used in *pradal serey*.
Graphics courtesy of Kun Khmer/Vannak Pen, copyright 2000.
Used with permission.

Above are examples of *tvear* foot patterns. The *tvear* in Fig. 10a is a fundamental "fighting stance" used in *pradal serey*. The weight distribution is 90% on the rear foot and 10% on the lead foot. According to *Lok Kru Kirihingsa*, this *tvear* is excellent in preparing for an offensive attack as it allows for rapid forward and backward movement. The *tvear* in Fig. 10b is one best suited for kicking (with either lead or rear leg) and/or defense against kicks. The hips and body should be completely square, with weight distribution at about 70% on the rear foot and 30% on the lead foot.[15]

## My Story: Tanaka Nhong

**Figure 11**: Tanaka Nhong.
Photo courtesy of Vannak Pen

I was born in Columbus, Ohio in 1996, and have one younger brother, Viro. I had a happy childhood. I loved being outdoors. At first, I didn't think I was unlike others because I didn't understand that kids saw each other like that, as insiders and outsiders. It was when others singled me out that I learned I was somehow different.

One moment I remember was when I was in the third grade, during lunch. We had all just finished playing and I couldn't wait to get my food because I had heard they were serving sherbet ice cream which was my favorite! We were all excited, but a group of kids ran up to the front of the line with their teacher and shoved me to the back.

"Hey, no ditching!" I said, indicating that they should not cut in front of me. The other kids looked back and said, "You go to the back because you're black!" I was very surprised and responded, "I'm not black! I'm brown!" It hadn't occurred to me before that because of my skin color I was expected to be subordinate to them.

Despite the discrimination and intolerance of others, however, I have always known that I am Khmer, and I take pride in my Khmer heritage. Some Khmer parents did not speak of Cambodia or the war with their children, but in my family, from a young age, I heard many stories.

It is interesting how my parents, whose backgrounds are very different, had similar experiences. My father grew up in a rural area in Battambang, where schooling was scarce and food sometimes even scarcer, whereas my mother was born in Pursat into an educated, financially stable family. But even though you might say they are from different ends of the spectrum, their experiences after the Khmer Rouge took over were certainly similar.

In April 1975, my grandfather (my mother's father), who had been a pilot under the Lon Nol regime, was taken away to be killed in what became known as the Po Chrey Massacre. He managed to escape his first capture and reunite with his family, but soon thereafter was found again and killed, shot in the head in front of them. As my father mentioned, he too had to confront violence and death during this time. I do think that this trauma is passed down intergenerationally; that is, as their son, I am affected by their stories and experiences, even though I wasn't a physical witness to what they endured.

### Learning *Kbach Kun Boran*

I was very involved with *Kun Khmer* Warriors in Ohio, first because my father insisted; later, because it became an integral part of my identity.

By the age of about 13, I began to take the lead in choreographing performances and demonstrations and recruiting others into the club. Being involved in *kbach kun boran* was a point of pride for me. It was also somewhat nerve-wracking, first because I knew how much *kbach kun boran* meant to my father, and second, because when performing I felt that I was representing Khmer culture and my community. I wanted to make sure that I represented the absolute best way.

Before an event begins, we perform what is called *pithi tvai bongkum kru* (ពិធីថ្វាយបង្គំគ្រូ) or *tvai kru,* an essential ritual in which we pay respect to our ancestors who protected the Khmer warriors of the past and ask them to continue to do so in the present. *Tvai kru* is a spiritual moment for the fighter to connect with the ancestors in preparation for representing them in battle. It's really heartfelt. It's not necessarily mandatory but it does help connect the individual fighter to his or her sense of purpose.

There are so many distinct moves and combinations of moves in *kbach kun boran Khmer.* It takes years and years to learn them, so it's difficult to explain concisely.

I can say that in *kbach kun boran* there are 12 main defense or counter techniques. *Mae som thom* is one of the first techniques you learn, and it involves redirecting your opponent's attack by stepping outward and shifting your body outside of your opponent's circle. It is fundamental: this is why it's called *mae som thom* (*som* means practice and *thom* means large or big).

**Figure 12**. Members of a *kbach kun boran Khmer* group perform the *pithi tvai bongkum kru* before a demonstration at Ohio University in 2011.
Photo: Christine Su

With *mae som thom* as the foundation, there are then other "add-ons" to it that describe using specific body parts or moving in certain directions. *Mae som thom knong*, for example, also has as its goal redirecting your opponent's attack. But in this technique, instead of redirecting outward, you move *knong* (inward) to counter the opponent's punches. It's complicated! That is why to become a true master, you really have to be dedicated to study and practice.

*Kbach kun boran* has always uplifted me. It is my escape from stress or anxiety. When I want to feel rejuvenated, I turn back to it. It's important to understand that *kbach kun boran* is not only a physical sport—it is an art form. When I choreograph moves for a performance, I try to make sure that a move fits with the skill and ability of the person who will demonstrate it. I have to feel what works and what doesn't.

Creating and choreographing are very much like putting together the pieces of a puzzle. It gets frustrating when moves don't feel or look right, but when they do, it excites me inside and excites the crowd watching the performance as well.

I continued practicing *kbach kun boran* into my college years. I attended Ohio State University and pursued a very competitive academic program, and definitely relied upon my *kun* training when I was feeling overwhelmed. *Kbach kun boran* sustains me spiritually. It provides me with a level of reassurance that I can't really explain. It has helped me to feel a sense of control with myself. Perhaps it's like my father mentioned--that *kbach kun boran* helps to give you a sense of control in an environment not within your control.

I started working as a Nursing Assistant at a senior living facility at the age of 18 and have continued my work in healthcare ever since. I completed my bachelor's degree from Ohio State, and I plan to continue my education and work in the health field. In the future, I hope to handle data analytics for hospitals.

Our family moved to Riverside, California in 2019. We haven't started a *kbach kun boran Khmer* group here, due in large part to the [COVID-19] pandemic, but I hope to revive it.

*Kbach kun boran* is about training and disciplining the mind, body, and spirit, and through my dad's teaching it has certainly done that for me. When my current job as a consultant required me to make a big, nerve-wracking presentation, my executive director advised me to put myself into the mindset of when I was practicing *kbach kun boran*.

That clicked right away for me. We can walk away from the gym, but the mind is always working and we have to regularly check in on our mental health. *Kbach kun boran* definitely served as a catalyst for me to understand what that meant. When you live a life motivated by doing the things you love, you find empowerment within yourself and through your actions, and you empower others.

**Figure 13.** Members of *Kun Khmer* Westgate practice *kbach kun boran* kicking moves.
Photo:
Vannoroth Ngoc

**Figure 14:** Similar move carved in bas-relief, Angkor Wat.
Original photo by Peter Park. Image available via:
https://en.wikipedia.org/wiki/Pradal_serey#/media /File:Knee5.jpg

While I will always love and respect *kbach kun boran*, I have also started to explore other Khmer arts. I have learned some folk dances and am studying how to play the *roneat ek* [a type of Khmer xylophone]. It's definitely a learning curve!

When I was young, I used to dislike training--it was something I "had to" do rather than something I wanted to do. But as I matured, I came to see its value, which led me to want to know more about other areas of our culture and heritage. I have remained curious and love exploring what it means to be Cambodian.

When I think about being Khmer, I think of our ancient history, when the Khmer ruled a huge empire and were the heart and soul of Southeast Asia.

When I think about being American, I think about being a part of the same story as many others who came to the U.S. from different parts of the world to find their "American Dream." I feel proud being both.

**Figure 15**: Tanaka Nhong and his father, Vannak Pen, at Ohio State University graduation, 2017. Photo: Narin Nhong

# Chapter 2

## Classical Dance
## របាំបុរាណ

> Khmer classical dance is a technically complex and aesthetically beautiful, refined and stylized form with a codified vocabulary and body line/silhouette. Story-based dances are hallmarks of each. In Khmer classical dance, these dramas typically take place in a mytho-poetic realm populated by gods and kings, demons and fantastical beings.[16]

Carved into the walls of the many temples of the Angkor complex, in northern Cambodia, one finds intricate sculptures of *apsara*, celestial nymphs revered as mediators between heaven and earth in Cambodian cosmology, and *devata*, divine beings who both guard and greet visitors to the sacred spaces.[17] According to Hindu legend, *devas* (gods) led by Hanuman, the monkey king, and *asuras* (demons) led by Ravana, the demon king, engaged in a giant tug of war, pulling on the tail and the head of a great *naga* (sea serpent) in the universal battle between good and evil. The back-and-forth movement from pulling on the *naga* churned the Sea of Milk, an ocean of immortality which contained the elixir of life. From this churning arose the beautiful *apsara*, who flew to the heavens to dance for the gods.

Occasionally the *apsara* would descend from the heavens, their graceful movements calling upon the gods to bestow blessings on earthly kings. Khmer kings in turn, seeking to communicate and find favor with the gods, conducted extravagant rituals in which humans replicated the dances of these ethereal beings.

**Figure 16a.** Center scene from bas-relief of the Churning of the Sea of Milk, Angkor Wat. On the left are the *asuras* (demons) and on the right are the *devas* (gods) pulling on the *naga*, with the Hindu god Vishnu in the center.

**Figure 16b. (inset)** The dancing *apsara* created from the churning appear and fly toward the heavens above. Photos: Christine Su

## Dance and National/Cultural Identity

Today, Khmer dancers emulate the curved hands and lithe postures of the *apsara* and *devata* in numerous dances. The 19th century King Ang Duong codified the various gestures, movements, and costumes of classical dance based on interpretations of the Angkor carvings, which teachers then used to choreograph various dance compositions. In the 20th century, for example, Queen Sisowath Kossamak, the mother of Norodom Sihanouk, choreographed the now-celebrated *Robam Apsara* (Apsara Dance), intending to make her granddaughter, Princess Bopha Devi, the first professional *apsara* dancer. Indeed, the Princess began training at age 5, and became the prima ballerina of the Royal Ballet of Cambodia at age 16.[18] As classical dance began to be performed outside of the palace and became accessible to and recognized by a wider audience, Cambodians viewed the dancers not only as royal artists, but as national symbols of Cambodia as well.[19] Suppya Helene Yut, a former dancer with the Royal Ballet and an advisor to Princess Bopha Devi wrote,

> While [*Robam Apsara*] was a new creation, the choreography gave viewers a sense of continuity of this 1960s contemporary dance with the legacy of a millennium. Since then, the Apsara dance has bec[o]me a symbol of Khmer cultural identity, performed in the homeland as well as in the Cambodian diasporas around the globe.[20]

Princess Bopha Devi continued to perform *Robam Apsara* and other works throughout the world until the coup d'état of 1970, which deposed Prince Sihanouk, after which she fled

Cambodia.[21] Because of the Khmer Rouge terror and its unstable aftermath she was unable to return until the 1990s, but when she did return, she served as Minister of Culture from 1999 to 2004 and was instrumental in reviving Khmer dance in the post-UNTAC era.[22]

**Figure 17**. *Devata sculptures,* Angkor Wat. Photo: Christine Su.

Dancers and musicians who survived or trained under those who survived the Khmer Rouge feel called to relay their knowledge to a new generation, such that these arts are not forgotten.[23] One of the premier organizations engaged in this work is the Khmer Arts Academy in Long Beach, California founded in 2002 by Sophiline Cheam Shapiro, a member of the first class of dancers to graduate from the Royal University of Fine Arts in Cambodia after it reopened in 1980 (from 1975-1979 the Khmer Rouge had closed all schools).

At Khmer Arts Academy, students train in dance (both classical and folk) and learn traditional instruments from instructors taught and mentored by *Neak Kru* Sophiline.

In 2006, *Neak Kru* Sophiline and her husband, John Shapiro returned to Cambodia to open the counterpart of Khmer Arts in Cambodia. They now manage the Sophiline Arts Ensemble located in Takmao, Kandal province, outside of Phnom Penh.[24] Both organizations are dedicated to sustaining and fostering Cambodian dance across borders through training, research, outreach, creation, and performance.

In Cambodian refugee communities in the U.S., dance has come to signify identity and cultural pride. Classical dancers perform dressed in ornate costumes: beautiful silk *sampot charabap* woven with silver or gold thread, tied, or folded around dancers' waists and secured with gold belts, beaded or sequined *sbai* (sashes) worn over their shoulders, elegant crowns balanced on their heads, and numerous bracelets, arm cuffs, anklets, and other adornments including fragrant flowers added to complete the human expression of the *apsara* and *devata*. Various gestures in the dance represent elements of nature (e.g., flower, bud, leaf, fruit) and body postures communicate meaning (e.g., love, sadness, shyness); in combination, they can tell stories.[25] Furthermore, distinctive costumes signify specific characters: princes/princesses, gods/goddesses, giants, demons, monkeys, and other roles.[26]

At important celebrations, dance is always present, and classical dance is something Cambodians look to both as a symbol of the former greatness of the Empire and of the exquisite artistic talent and beauty of the Khmer people.

I grew up in a community without many Asians in general, and to my knowledge, no Cambodians. My mother (who is from Scotland) and father wanted my sisters and me to be as American as possible. Whose parents don't want their children to be accepted and successful in their neighborhoods and schools? As a mixed-race child, I felt markedly different and alone, and so I, too, wanted to do whatever I could to fit in. So until I was much older, I knew almost nothing about my Khmer heritage. My father didn't offer information, and I didn't dare ask, because I knew it was painful for him. Unfortunately, in not wanting to dredge up painful things, I also failed to benefit from knowledge of wonderful, creative things, like Cambodian music, dance, and art.

When I was a graduate student at the University of Hawai`i (UH), I learned about an event taking place at the East-West Center, a think-tank and research center on the UH campus. Several dancers from Cambodia had come to take part in a special program to share their stories in the aftermath of the Khmer Rouge. This intrigued me, and I attended. I recall watching the members of the group take the stage, and as I watched the classical dance they performed, emotion overcame me.

By that point in my life, I had studied some Cambodian history and knew about the deliberate attempts by the Khmer Rouge to destroy art and artists. In watching the dance that evening, my first experience of a live Cambodian dance performance, however, I realized that while the Khmer Rouge may have suppressed this extraordinary art form during its regime, they did not succeed in extinguishing it.

Rather, these dancers were living proof of the determination to re-create and share Cambodian arts and culture. To this day, that performance stands out in my mind as one of the most beautiful things I have ever seen.

Because there were several scholars of Cambodia in Hawai`i at the time, especially at the East-West Center, I was able to participate in programs and festivities I had theretofore never experienced.

And I got to dance.

At one point, I was able to learn the *robam kuo trolauk* (the coconut dance), a folk dance often enjoyed at Khmer New Year celebrations.

**Figure 18.** A younger me dancing the *robam kuo trolauk* at the East-West Center, circa 1996. Photo courtesy of the author (photographer unknown)

Classical dancers start training at a very young age, and I was already in my 20s when I first learned *robam kuo trolauk*, so I did not even dream of performing classical dance myself. However, I adored watching the *apsara* dancers and how their movements wove together stories.

As I got to know some of the scholars and dancers, I felt like I belonged for the first time, not through assimilating or conforming, but rather, by discovering. I was gaining greater understanding of what "Khmer" means.

This chapter shares the stories of two Khmer women: Reaksmey (Mea) Lath and Heidi Hou, and how dance has shaped their belief systems and guided their actions, and continues to play a defining role in their lives.

## Artist Encounters

I first met Mea Lath when she volunteered for the Cambodia Town Film Festival in Long Beach in 2013, and our paths continued to cross. She often came to the Bay Area to perform with *Neak Kru* Charya Burt, an acclaimed master dancer and choreographer based in northern California (and the sister of *Neak Kru* Sophiline Cheam Shapiro), so I saw her perform in person from time to time. I knew she taught at the Khmer Arts Academy in Long Beach, and when I considered writing this book I knew that I wanted to interview her.

I met Heidi Hou in 2015, while assisting with an in-country Khmer language program which attracted many Cambodian heritage students. In between language classes, she told many anecdotes about her family history. I knew hers, too, was a story I needed to share.                                          -C.S.

**Figure 19**. Reaksmey (Mea) Lath makes offerings to the ancestors, especially the *kru robam boran Khmer* who have passed on, but whose spirits live on through the dance. Photo: Rosie Hin

*Author's note: On June 14, 2021, Lok Yiey Em Theay, the last surviving dancer from the original Royal Cambodian Ballet, passed away in Cambodia at the age of 89. This chapter is dedicated to Neak Kru Em Theay, with love, appreciation, and respect for her lifelong devotion to preserving and teaching Khmer dance.*

## My Story: Reaksmey (Mea) Lath

My name is Reaksmey, but I usually go by Mea. The last syllable of my full name is pronounced like the English word "me," but many people pronounce it like "may." The latter is a more common Khmer name, which means "ray of light." But my

**Figure 20**. Reaksmey (Mea) Lath. Photo courtesy of Mea Lath.

name, Reaksmey, is the Khmer version of Lakshmi, the Hindu goddess of prosperity and wisdom.

It's hard for me to put into words how much Khmer dance has meant and means to me. It is beautiful and graceful, yes, but each dance is so much more than hand and foot movements and body postures. Khmer dance tells a story, and when I perform Khmer dance, I become a character in that story. Sometimes, it's almost like I am transported back to times when court dancers performed for ancient kings, and I am part of preserving that history so it is not forgotten. Because so many dance masters were lost during the Khmer Rouge, it was an honor for me to learn from those who continue to practice.

Now, as an instructor, I feel an almost-overwhelming responsibility to pass these stories, these traditions on to members of younger generations.

## Early Life

I was born in Site B, one of the refugee camps on the border with Thailand. Then in 1992, my parents and I were sponsored by an aunt and uncle to come to the U.S. I was exposed to many cultural events here in Long Beach, like Khmer New Year, and when I was growing up, I would watch the dancers performing at these events.

I was mesmerized by their elegance, dressed in beautiful costumes and adorned with golden headdresses and jewelry. Of course, there were other types of dances (like folk dances) performed as well, but it was the classical dancers, the *apsara*, that captivated me. I loved the origin story, with Kampu and Mera, and the *apsara* appearing from the churning of the sea of milk…it was a whole other world.

I myself didn't start dance classes until I was 12. I was a very shy child, and it was difficult for me to tell others that I wanted to dance, too. But I met a girl around my age who was taking dance classes at the Arts of Apsara, a performing arts program at the United Cambodian Community (UCC) run by *Neak Kru* Sophiline Cheam Shapiro. She and I (and her mother and my mother) became friends, and I finally mustered up the courage to ask to take the classes there, too.

Two weeks after I started at Arts of Apsara, *Neak Kru* Sophiline and her husband, Pu John Shapiro, left Arts of

Apsara to start the Khmer Arts Academy (KAA) here in Long Beach. I followed my teacher, and for the first few years, we didn't have a physical space, so we practiced wherever we could--in *Neak Kru*'s living room, even in her backyard! Eventually we found our current space here on Obispo Avenue, and we have been here ever since.

I pretty much grew up in this space. Much of both my time and my identity have revolved around Khmer dance. I will say that in the beginning, I wasn't one of the best dancers, but I was really dedicated to dancing and just loved being at KAA.

**Figure 21**. Reaksmey (Mea) Lath in
*apsara* costume. Photo by Love Studio

## Leaving Long Beach

When I was 18, I left Long Beach to attend San Diego State University. I always had thought I would go to Cal State Long Beach, like many of my friends, but leaving Long Beach turned out to be one of the best decisions I've ever made. For one, I learned so much about how others (outside of Long Beach) viewed Cambodians, and having distanced myself physically from it, I was able to examine my community from a different perspective.

I hadn't realized how challenging our situation was until I got out of it. While there are many wonderful things about east-side Long Beach, life there was difficult. The refugees were traumatized by what they had gone through, and then found that they had to rebuild their lives in an unfamiliar place with unfamiliar practices and procedures. A lot of the hurt and distress manifested itself in negative ways, like distrust, community disputes, and even violence.

Those youth growing up there often found themselves lost, confronted with discrimination and intimidation from peers, and torn between becoming American and remaining Cambodian. But when you live in that environment every day, while it may have been uncomfortable, it was "normal"--it was what I knew.

San Diego is where I gained my independence. I attended San Diego State University, where I studied journalism and public relations, and I was able to take a step back from my life and try new things. I got involved in extracurricular activities and joined a sorority. I hung out with people outside my community and had to do more things for myself, since my mom and siblings were far away. I was homesick, but I really think I needed that time away.

I will admit that there were times in San Diego when I didn't feel proud to be Khmer. There weren't many Cambodians there, and what people thought they knew about Cambodians wasn't flattering. People would make jokes, like "Oh, I saw your relatives in 'Gangland' on tv last night--the Tiny Rascals gang, right?" I began to realize how little people know about Cambodia and Cambodians. It's not all Khmer Rouge and gangs. I started incorporating things about Cambodia and Khmer culture into my studies. If I wrote a research paper, it had something to do with Cambodia. If I wrote a news story, I wanted it to relate to Cambodia somehow. I wanted to show that we as a people have something rich and beautiful and vibrant. We have a history that goes back thousands of years. Those four years [1975-1979, when the Khmer Rouge were in power], shouldn't be all that define us, nor should the gangs be all that define us. There is so much more.

## Coming Full Circle

During my junior year, while I was still in San Diego, I was asked to join the Khmer Arts Academy as an instructor. I was thrilled, but to be an instructor, I would *have* to be there in person. This was before the days of ZOOM, but even using other online tools, it just wouldn't be the same trying to teach dance remotely.

` So, from my junior year until I graduated, I went back and forth from San Diego to Long Beach *every weekend*. I was also an apprentice of *Neak Kru* Charya Burt at the time, and she is in northern California, so I was flying up there once a month for six months, as well as back and forth between San Diego and Long Beach. It was exhausting, but it was so meaningful, because while I had been part of a dance group in San Diego, I wasn't connected to it the way I was connected to KAA. For my first two years in college, I felt like there was a piece of me missing.

When I started teaching, I felt whole again--even though I felt like I didn't know what I was doing. That is, there is no instructor's manual, no guidebook, no training telling you how to teach dance. You teach what you know.

Here in the U.S., we don't have structured formal arts education for Khmer dance the way they do in Cambodia. We don't have the Royal University of Fine Arts where you train to become a Khmer dancer.

For people here, Khmer dance is not a vocation; it is more like a hobby, something we do for cultural preservation. But when I started teaching dance, I feel like I found my purpose. I feel like it was dance and learning in this environment that guided me to become who I am today, and I wanted others to realize and experience that. Shifting from being a student to being a teacher, then, I felt so empowered.

Dance is not just about movements and music; it's about learning the incredible and complex history that gave birth to the dance.

**Figure 22**. *Neak Kru* Mea assisting young dancers
in preparation for performance. Photo: Kristina Sam-Chem

Khmer Arts Academy is a safe place for exploring one's identity as both Khmer and American. My time at KAA centers on teaching the young students about values and ways of approaching things, like leadership and coping mechanisms and strategies for dealing with difficult situations. I think it's working. For example, in general the high school dropout rate for Cambodian Americans is quite high. But I am so proud to say that at least 95% of our dancers finish high school. I believe they take the lessons they learn in dance into their "regular" lives in the outside world.

Many in my generation, the 1.5, were kind of lost because they weren't grounded in their culture. They knew their parents were Cambodian, but they didn't know what that truly meant beyond trauma and displacement. They didn't really know who they were or where they came from, literally or figuratively. You need to know where you come from before you can get where you want to go.

## Vision for the Future

We have about 20 students at KAA, which is fewer than in the past, when all our classes were free. During that time we had 60-65 students, and this whole studio was filled. Now, however, to stay afloat we do have to charge a small amount for classes, which I think is fine. Sometimes when things are free we undervalue them.

I think that the students who are here now are more invested in the art of dance and more dedicated to it. They aren't forced to be here; they choose to be here. Some can only come two hours per week (one day of class), but some are here *every single day*, and not just for dance; some are learning traditional instruments, for example, so they are here even longer. I am here every day except for Sunday.

In 2006, *Neak Kru* Sophiline and Pu John moved back to Cambodia to establish Khmer Arts there. It is exciting being part of an intercontinental organization! I did have the opportunity to go to Cambodia and train there several years ago. That was some intense training! Plus, that was my first trip to Cambodia, and it was very emotional for me to be in the place where the art that means so much to me was created centuries ago.

My dream is to help heal the community by establishing a strong foundation upon which the next generation can build. The dream is big and I know that it will take a lot of hard work and time to achieve. My goal with the KAA space is to rebuild and restructure  it so that students learn not only the arts themselves, but also, how to run an arts nonprofit. I want them to learn leadership and administration and marketing skills, so they can build up their resumes. I want there to be a curriculum that students who wish to can follow and learn not only the performance of dance, but also other roles in arts management. They can complete the curriculum and become an instructor, for example, or take on a bigger role in KAA.

I also feel that KAA can play a part not only in preserving the arts of the past, but in crafting the arts of the future as well. I love traditional dance, but also feel it's important that the youth feel like they are a part of the creative process and not only reproducing past works. Pu John and *Neak Kru* Sophiline encouraged us to try innovative and inclusive works. I am really excited about one such program we started called "Roots and Shoots."

In "Roots and Shoots," the youth create their own works and tell their own stories. The mechanics are based in tradition--that is, as in classical dance they use hand movements to convey meaning--but they use these to tell their own stories. They may create a classical dance to a popular U.S. song, for example, or tell a story about a recent experience in the U.S. They may use non-traditional instruments to accompany a classical dance.

On one hand, when you put classical dance into more modern contexts, the works may resonate better with members of the younger generations. On the other hand,

I feel that engaging youth in this way helps them to relate to older generations--they (re)connect through dance.

To that point, I was thrilled to be involved with Disney's work as a cultural consultant for *Raya and the Last Dragon* (2021). I and other members of KAA met with Disney representatives during the planning process and creators there asked for our input from the Cambodian/Cambodian American perspective, especially regarding Khmer mythology and dance. I would love to continue to do this type of work-- that is, ensuring Cambodian perspectives are included in artistic projects about Asians or Southeast Asians.

I would love to start a dance class for older Cambodian women, in which we could focus on dance for health and wellness and developing self-confidence. There were many times when KAA would perform and some of the older folks would watch us and cry. I think they feel like without the arts a part of their identity is missing (well, it was taken away, or they were forced to hide it) and when they see the dance, they think back to pre-war times. It also helps them to open up.

There is one dance called the Sentimental Dance, for example, which features a prince and a princess who fall in love but end up getting separated. We performed this for the Dream Beyond Foundation [for seniors, established by Nancy Lee] and an elder came up to me afterward and said, "That is like my story! I fell in love, but my love and I  also had to be separated from each other during the war..." She felt moved to share her story with me because of the dance.

I am so grateful to my instructors and mentors--*Neak Kru* Sophiline Cheam Shapiro, *Neak Kru* Charya Burt, and Bong Prumsodun Ok—for teaching me about the greater narratives that inform our Khmer identity. I like to tell the youth to see themselves not as compelled to come to dance because their parents or relatives want them to, but rather, as willing students seeking to be part of something greater, something bigger than themselves, that not a lot of people get to experience.

Every opportunity to dance, to connect with the spirits of our ancestors and honor the gods, is a gift.

**Figure 23**. Dance is a gift. Photo: Sophia Chhoeng

## My Story: Heidi Hou

As a child, I recall my days being filled with the sounds of loud Khmer karaoke in the house, blasting tunes of Ros Serey Sothea and Sinn Sisamouth as my grandparents took turns with the microphone. I also recall that every time

**Figure 24.** Heidi Hou
Photo courtesy of Aron Chek,
Cambodian Student Society, CSULB

there was a [Los Angeles] Laker game, the living room of my grandparents' house would be filled with relatives shouting "DEFENSE!" and rooting for Kobe Bryant and Shaquille O'Neal, taking up every nook and cranny of space to hover over the television. And I recall that both work and play time always came to a halt at ten minutes to 6:00pm, to give our household of nine time to prepare for dinner, which we shared sitting on the floor on a *kantheil* (woven straw mat).

My childhood entailed language barriers and broken English, and home-cooked Cambodian *samlaw* with occasional McDonald's happy meals and In-n-Out burgers. My two working-class parents had to keep up with the "9 to 5"--and often hours well outside of that--in order to support our family, which caused them to be away much of the day.

As a result, my brother and I spent much of the time with our grandparents. But we were surrounded by love, and it was through my grandparents that I first came to know about Cambodian history and culture.

## A Twist of Fate/Destiny

In the 1970s, my grandmother, Pheakkdei Khiev, was a schoolteacher living in Phnom Penh. At the time of the Khmer Rouge takeover, she was 22 years old, married to a lieutenant in the Cambodian military, and the proud mother of a 3-year-old girl, Pichenda (my mother). When the red nightmare swept through, my grandmother's husband, her three younger brothers, and her father (a doctor) were all taken prisoner. She never saw or heard from them again, and she can only speculate about their fates. Only by concealing her occupation and education (she had attended university in Phnom Penh) was she able to protect herself and her daughter from being killed. She was forced to toil in the rice fields, and even her daughter, who was still a toddler, was put to work chasing birds by making noise, to keep them from eating the rice plants. A pot lid and a stick were my mother's only toys.

Before the communist invasion, my grandfather was a farmer living with his mother, brother, and sister. Many stories tell of the emptying of the cities and movement of urbanites to the countryside, but even modest farmers were not immune to the Khmer Rouge's onslaught.

My grandfather's brother was murdered outright, and while his own life was spared, he retained little else. He was forced to endure 14-to-16-hour workdays, and during the rice harvest, the workday extended even longer.

Even as someone who already knew how to work in the rice fields, he was exhausted and often sick from overwork and little food. The Khmer Rouge felt no pity for illness or injury, and many adults and children died in the fields.

Life was hard for all, but for my grandmother, a difficult life soon became unbearable. One of the Khmer Rouge leaders in her commune had become attracted to her and demanded that she marry him. Refusal to accept such an offer almost always resulted in fatal consequences. My grandmother, however, did not want to marry him, which meant she had to escape as soon as possible.

With a diamond ring she had hidden from her captors, she was able to bribe female cadres who served the meager food to the workers each day. The women disclosed to my grandmother the most favorable time and place from which to escape. With a young, malnourished daughter and very weak herself, she fled from the camp. She didn't know what awaited her, but she could not fathom the idea of marrying a member of the Khmer Rouge and having him become her daughter's father. Somehow, they made it to another village.

My grandmother knew that she had to hide her identity to protect herself and her daughter, so she used a different name and invented a different background, one not associated with the city or with education. She and her daughter were able to stay in the village, but in time, another Khmer Rouge cadre became attracted to her and wanted to marry her. She found herself in the same plight as in the previous village.

But another man witnessed her fear and offered to marry her himself to save her from a horrible fate. This man was my grandfather, Vanna Kong. They were married in their dirty, torn work clothes.

**Figures 25a and 25b.** Left: My maternal grandfather, Vanna Kong, and Right: My maternal grandmother, Khiev Pheakkdei, circa 1965. Photos courtesy of the Hou family

In November 1978, fate took another strange twist: Vietnam invaded Cambodia. This invasion eventually resulted in the overthrow of the Khmer Rouge regime in January 1979, nearly four years after they had initially established power. My grandfather, grandmother, and mother were able to escape the country and ended up in a refugee camp on the Thai border.

While happy to be free from the Khmer Rouge, life in the camps was far from safe or pleasant. They moved from camp to camp, living in three different camps in just one year.

While in a camp in Chonburi, my grandmother gave birth to my aunt, Pichreatrey--a living symbol of their family's resilience. The family of four eventually left the camps and migrated to Indonesia, where they stayed for two months before being sponsored to come to the U.S. Despite the uncertainty of what life there held for them, hope for creating better lives for their children helped them to persevere.

## Life in Long Beach

Like many Cambodian refugees, they landed in Long Beach, a beacon of hope for a new start. Like many refugees, they needed government assistance when they first arrived, but they were determined to become independent. To help them adapt to life in America, both of my grandparents attended night school English classes. To earn extra money, my grandfather collected newspapers from trash and recycling bins and delivered them to recycling stations. Two strangers had become husband and wife and ultimately true companions, supporting each other throughout their struggles--and their happy moments.

In 1984 and 1986, they welcomed two more children, a girl (Pichvichea) and a boy (Marvin), my aunt and uncle. Life continued to move forward, and my beautiful mother (Pichenda) was soon introduced to my father, Anthony Hou. They married in 1992 in Long Beach.

**Figures 26 and 27.**
My mother (Pichenda)
and father (Anthony
Hou) on their wedding
day in 1992.

Photos courtesy of
the Hou family

## The 2.0 Generation

I loved growing up near my grandparents, aunts, and uncles as well as my parents. Yet as a child who was both Cambodian and American, I felt like I was not fully either.

I consider myself lucky that both of my parents spoke English, yet since we spoke only English at home, I didn't know their native tongue. And despite the care and attention of my grandparents, I felt distanced from them, because the language barrier often affected genuine communication. I knew a few phrases in Khmer, and while my attempts to speak with my grandparents made them smile, I knew I wanted that feeling of temporary joy to last much longer than 10 seconds.

Growing up second-generation is a balancing act. I had two cultural identities that should've felt in unison with one another, but instead felt like they were pitted against each other. At one point, I decided that I wanted to challenge myself to learn a new Khmer word each day. I discouraged my father from speaking English to me, asking him to speak Khmer instead, and to correct me if I was wrong. I was not ashamed to sound funny, because for the first time ever, I really wanted to learn. I spent nights at the homes of both sets of grandparents, and soon, their broken English and my broken Khmer seemed to fit together. I loved discovering this part of me, to feel the joy of being able to communicate clearly with the people who raised me day after day. Learning the language, and in turn learning more about my heritage, brought about a new confidence in how I viewed myself inside their homes, which was vital because outside was a whole different world.

When I went to school, kids always used to ask, "What type of Asian are you?" At first, I was proud to tell other kids that I am Cambodian, but then I learned that they associated "Cambodian" with "gangbangers" and refugees who were dirty, "ghetto," uneducated, dark-skinned, and poor.

Hearing these stereotypes day after day, I started to believe I *was* what they said I was. I began to be ashamed to tell people I was Cambodian, so I when asked "What are you?" I would nonchalantly tell them I was Chinese, or Japanese, or any other better-known Asian so that people would just nod their heads. Doing so saved me from the burden of constantly having to explain my ethnic origin. Being Cambodian was to be an "other," and as I child, I longed to fit in with my peers, not to stick out. But at home, with family, I was accepted and loved.

When I was about seven years old, my maternal grandmother, Claudine, who had been living in France, came to live with us for a few months in California. She spoke only French and Khmer, but the moment she heard Elvis Presley's "Blue Hawai`i" coming from my radio, a smile of recognition spread across her face. We bonded through a shared love of music. I played that song every night for us. She, in turn, taught me Buddhist chants (mostly in Pali or Sanskrit) to repeat to protect me as I slept. I remember this as a wonderful time, because she and I connected in a way that didn't require that we fully understand each other's spoken languages. After she returned to France, I wanted to know even more about my heritage, and so I started learning classical dance with teachers at the Cambodian Association of America.

## Dance and Identity

Dance transformed me. Through the movements and gestures, we as dancers told stories about what the Khmer believed, what they valued. I might say that I became more Khmer through dance. While when I first started learning dance I had never been to Cambodia, dance transported me there. I imagined myself as the *apsara* on the walls of Angkor Wat that I had seen in pictures, dressed in elegant silks with elaborate gold headdresses. I trained for more than 10 years.

As I became more skilled as a dancer, I also became a teacher. I had the opportunity to work with youth through a non-profit called the Cambodian Fine Arts Heritage Relief Foundation (CFAHRF), which helped to raise funds for medical missions and humanitarian support to various orphanages in Cambodia. I love teaching. I want Cambodian youth to be proud of their heritage, and know that they can gain confidence in themselves when they are immersed in dance. Dance is not just physical--it is emotional, mental, and spiritual as well.

I started teaching dance to students in the Cambodian Student Society at Cal State Long Beach while I was still in high school. I knew that I wanted to attend Cal State Long Beach, and to continue to grow as a member of the Cambodian community. I loved the camaraderie of that group--here were Khmer students, plural--I was not the only one!

It was at CSULB that I was able to enroll in formal Khmer language classes for the first time, and it turned out that the Khmer language instructor was my great aunt, Outay.

**Figure 28.** Heidi Hou in classical dance costume.
Photo courtesy of the Hou family

As she taught language, *Neak Kru* Outay also told us about her personal history in Cambodia, which made me think about what my parents might have gone through.

Strangely enough, as much I loved my Cambodian heritage, I realized that I still knew relatively little about my parents' experience. At home we ate Khmer food and sang Khmer karaoke, so I felt surrounded by Cambodian-ness, but mom and dad rarely spoke about Cambodia.

My parents were introduced to each other in Long Beach, and since my brother and I were born and raised here, we didn't know what their childhoods in Cambodia were like, or even the details of their early years in the U.S.

My mother was too young to remember much, and my dad preferred to only talk about positive things, like the work ethic he gained as a child in Cambodia. He would wake up before the crack of dawn to sell fresh bread and lottery tickets and deliver newspapers on the back of his older brother's bicycle all around town before the other kids were even awake. He talked about the joy of tending to all his animals on the farm and maintaining the garden with his grandfather every day. He hustled from a young age to enjoy the little things his earnings could buy, and he loved being surrounded by siblings and family. Yet whenever the war came up in conversation, the air always got a little heavier. There was pain and sadness in my father's eyes anytime I asked about our family history. While I was longing to understand all he endured, I knew when to stop asking. I knew I would never be able to fully understand his journey. In those still and silent moments, I was just happy to know he survived.

## The Garden

Our family lives in north Long Beach. From the front, our house looks like many other houses in the area, which is to say that it is a beautiful house, but it doesn't stand out as ostentatious or out of the ordinary. What *is* extra-ordinary about our house is the backyard.

Walking through the backyard is almost like being transported to another world. There are pathways that meander through the space, happening intermittently upon unique structures that my dad built, with places to sit and take in the beauty of the surrounding environment. Along the pathways and the perimeter are dozens of different types of plants and flowers my dad tends to carefully every day, perhaps similar to those he nurtured with his grandfather years ago. I believe that in tending them, in pruning the dead leaves, allowing the new buds and shoots to come through, he finds comfort and solace.

This is his creative space, the space that allows him to express himself in the way dance does for me.

**Figure 29.** My father's garden.
Photo: Heidi Hou

In his garden, he finds peace.

**Figure 30.** My father, Anthony Hou, in his garden.
Photo: Heidi Hou

# Chapter 3

## Fine Arts
## វិចិត្រសិល្បៈ

In the early 2000s, strolling down Street 178 in Phnom Penh heading toward the riverfront, you would pass by the Royal University of Fine Arts (RUFA) and the National Museum on the right side. On the left side you would find shops full of paintings, etched silver, wooden and stone sculptures, and other arts-related items, many created by RUFA's students. Indeed, the street became known as "art street" among both visitors and locals, a treasure trove filled with beautiful keepsakes and artisan crafts.

There were certain iconic themes to be found among these crafts, particularly the paintings and wood carvings.

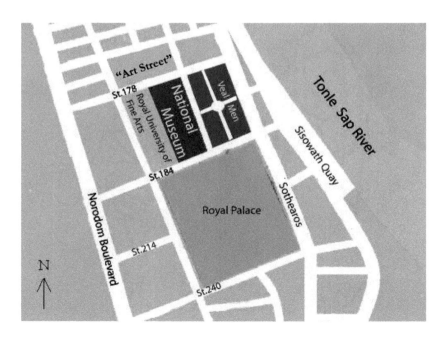

**Figure 31**: Area showing RUFA, National Museum, "Art Street," and the Riverfront, Phnom Penh. Map source: https://www.cambodiamuseum.info/en_information_visitors.html

If you wanted to purchase a painting of the front view of Angkor Wat, or a wooden or stone mini-representation of the four-faced sculptures of the Bayon or King Jayavarman VII, for example, there were dozens to choose from, all painted or carved in a similar manner, albeit by different artists. Many a tourist returned from Cambodia with a shellacked wood carving of an *apsara* or *devata*--the celestial goddesses whose likenesses line the walls of Angkor--purchased from one of the Art Street shops. And while these reproductions reflect the reverence and respect for that Cambodians hold for their country's ancient history, when the Khmer Empire ruled much of mainland Southeast Asia, there is an undeniable uniformity in these pieces.

This homogeneity of what became known as "Cambodian art" is actually, at least in part, a colonial imposition. Indeed, "beginning with their supposed 'rediscovery' [by the French] in the 1860s, the temples of Angkor became the centerpiece for the colonial inscription of a quintessential Khmer culture."[27] With strong French encouragement, Angkor and its environs became the symbols of Cambodia, upon which "Cambodian art" and artists should focus.[28]

## The School of Cambodian Arts

In the late 1800s, French naturalist and scholar Henri Mouhot traveled throughout Southeast Asia, sketching flora and fauna, drawing maps, and taking notes on his findings.

When he visited Cambodia and came across the ancient capital of Angkor, he wrote:

'In the province still bearing the name of Ongcor [sic]...there are...ruins of such grandeur, remains of structures which must have been raised at such an immense cost of labour, that, at the first view, one is filled with profound admiration, and cannot but ask what has become of this powerful race, so civilised, so enlightened, the authors of these gigantic works? One of these temples[. . .] is grander than anything left to us by Greece or Rome...' [29]

The French, who retained administrative control over Cambodia until independence in 1953, lamented what they believed to be "neglected" monuments and sought to revive not only interest in, but attention on Angkor as the pinnacle of Khmer history and culture.[30] The artist and educator George Groslier (1887-1945), for example, felt that Angkor represented an idyllic authentic Cambodia and therefore should be the focus of Cambodian study in the arts. In 1918, the School of Cambodian Arts (aka École des Beaux Arts) was established under Groslier's direction.

The School's curriculum required copying certain forms or archetypes defined as "Cambodian art." Classes established compulsory frames of reference which trapped Cambodia in the Angkorian past, even as the lives of Cambodians themselves changed in the early 20th century. Teachers at the School hung drawings or placed models at the front of the classroom that students were to copy to learn the "right" way of creating Cambodian art.

As Ingrid Muan writes, "the point of the lesson was to eventually absorb these canons of representation so thoroughly as to be able to render them without the drawn example."[31]

What became convention was that which Groslier and his colleagues defined and outlined, and moreover, that they believed foreigners would purchase as "authentic" souvenirs of Cambodia.

"In the curious geography of consumption that would ensue," writes Muan, "Cambodians would produce 'traditional' hand-made things for a distant clientele while relying on French manufactured goods for their everyday modern lives."[32]

## The Royal University of Fine Arts

Art, however, is dynamic. What defined Cambodian art transformed over time, particularly outside of the School environment and within it after Groslier's death in 1945.

By the 1950s and 1960s, other influences emerged in the works of contemporary artists, even those who trained at École des Beaux Arts. While there is insufficient space to explore the works of these independence-era artists in detail, art historians note that the styles and techniques of these works reflected more freedom and originality than the Groslier-era propagation of multiple reproductions.

In 1965, the School of Cambodian Arts was transformed into and renamed the Royal University of Fine Arts under the direction of a new rector, Vann Molyvann, the famed independence-era architect who designed many unconventional and innovative buildings in Phnom Penh, including the Olympic Stadium and the Chatomuk Conference Hall. Molyvann's administration encouraged students to show their individual styles and personalities.

Prior to the outbreak of war and unrest of the 1970s, "the promise of those shaping the new institution was that innovative forms of 'Khmer Art' would be realised [sic]."[33] But the Khmer Rouge soon crushed Cambodian artists' innovative or individualistic notions.

**Figure 32**. Chatomuk Conference Center, by Vann Molyvann.
Photo: Christine Su

## Returning to "Khmerness" after the Khmer Rouge

Following the overthrow of the Khmer Rouge, exhausted and traumatized Cambodians understandably searched for ways to re-identify and re-center themselves. In this pursuit of rebuilding Cambodian culture, they returned to not only pre-war ways of thinking, but to the purported pinnacle of Khmer power and prosperity--the idyllic Angkorian empire--as their preferred narrative. The fantasy of an ancient kingdom in which benevolent rulers looked after a vital populace served as a stabilizing factor in what was still a very unstable world. Indeed, when RUFA reopened in 1980, in reestablishing the curriculum, the administration basically revisited and reinstated the Groslier canon.

> The images encountered in contemporary Cambodia [. . .] referenc[e] subject matter gleaned from colonial stereotypes of Cambodian identity (Angkor, traditional dancers, tropical landscapes). The vast majority of forms encountered in Cambodia today are haunted as well by the formal logic of Groslier's training. It is as if the model and its copy—as well as the procedure taught for its multiplication—have become a form of identity, a "Cambodian" way of making art. [34]

wrote Ingrid Muan in 2001. Her poignant remark supports my description and interpretation of the paintings and sculptures that filled the art shops on Street 178 in the early 2000s.

In 2021, many of these shops have been replaced by hotels (including an enormous Hyatt right across from the National Museum), restaurants, and spas, and some have simply closed down. The inventory in those that remain seems less abundant. Admittedly the COVID-19 pandemic of 2020 devastated the tourist industry and decreased demand for artwork and souvenirs in general; however, the definition of "Cambodian art" is again broadening to include a range of topics and interpretations. Just a few of the many galleries currently supporting and exhibiting contemporary work include:

- Phnom Penh: *Assasax, DinArt, JavaArts, Kbach, Khmer Sense, Romeet, Sra'Art*
- Siem Reap: *Batia Sarem, Mirage, One Eleven, Open Studio Cambodia, Theam's House*
- Battambang: *Lotus, Loeum Lorn/Tep Kao Sol, Make Maek, Romcheik5, Sangker*

This is by no means a finite list. One could plan a weeks-long trip spent visiting the many galleries and speaking with the artists.

Furthermore, with the emergence and visibility of contemporary arts in Cambodia, there have been exciting developments in thought-provoking dialogue between Cambodian and Cambodian American artists.

In this chapter, we meet two Cambodian American artists, Sayon Syprasoeuth, born in Cambodia of Lao-Nyaw descent, and Alan Khum, a San Francisco native, as they share their interpretations of Cambodian identity.

## Artist Encounters

I actually met Sayon Syprasoeuth for the first time in Cambodia in 2019. I attended an international conference on genocide in Phnom Penh and ran into him there. I immediately recognized him because I have worked with the Lao community and seen his work in that context. I introduced myself and learned that he had an exhibit at Meta House, a well-known independent arts and media center which had recently relocated to "Art Street." I attended his show and knew I wanted to get to know him and his work more closely.

I met Alan Khum in the Tenderloin in San Francisco. Ratha Chuon Kim (also featured in this book) managed the Cambodia exhibits for the annual Mid-Autumn Harvest Festival held there. Alan displayed some of his work at these festivals, and also created paintings on-site. I was mesmerized by his work, ranging from fantastical portrayals of Hanuman in action to soothing sketches of sleeping cats. I knew I wanted to share his incredible gifts and transformative work in this book as well. -C.S.

## My Story: Sayon Syprasoeuth

I was born in 1967 in Sisophon, Cambodia, close to the Thai border. The area is now called Krong Poi Pet. I think Sisophon used to be part of Thailand until the early 20th century. Because of its location, there are a lot of ethnic Thai and Lao-Nyaw as well as Khmer living in the Sisophon area.

**Figure 33.** Sayon Syprasoeuth, wearing a T-shirt created as protest art, stenciled with the image of Xiao Zhen Xie.
Photo courtesy of Sayon Syprasoeuth

My family is Lao-Nyaw, a minority group that has lived along the Cambodia-Thailand border for centuries. I learned from speaking with other families that the ancestors of the Lao-Nyaw living in this area were originally traders who came with their goods. Eventually they decided to stay.

The families in the village where we lived were mostly Lao-Nyaw, and I remember families speaking Khmer, Lao, and Thai in different situations as I was growing up. I never learned to speak Khmer myself as my family left Cambodia when I was quite young to take refuge closer to Thailand.

Also, because of what was happening in Cambodia at the time, they didn't want me to learn Khmer language--hearing it brought back bad memories of the trauma they experienced.

From what I remember I had a happy early childhood. I remember going into the woods to hunt for food with my dad for example, playing with my siblings, and just being a child. During this time in the early 1970s, I remember there were soldiers (whom I found out later were the Khmer Rouge) milling about the area, but we were concerned with our everyday lives as farmers and didn't focus our attention on them much. We knew there was something brewing early on, but we just made sure we didn't get in their way or cause any problems. Back then farmers and peasants were not the targets of the Khmer Rouge; rather, it was wealthy, elite people they wanted to overthrow, but as it turned out people from diverse socioeconomic backgrounds were caught in the chaos, arrested, put in labor camps, and eventually executed. When we were able, we set out to escape into Thailand.

Sisophon is not very far from Thailand in terms of distance, but the journey there on foot was arduous and agonizing. I remember that my mother was very pregnant with my youngest brother at the time, and having to walk in that state, through thick jungle covered with landmines, along dirt roads that transformed into mud ponds during the raining season was very difficult for her. But somehow, we made it.

At first, we stayed in a Thai village. Unfortunately, we could not remain there indefinitely because we were considered illegal aliens. So we moved to a refugee camp named Aranyaprathet. It was there, out of chaos and confusion, that I began to create my own world and submerge myself in creating, making things like shadow puppets and clay sculptures from whatever I could find, and embracing nature through play and exploration.

I think perhaps that living in a border town, amongst various groups and speaking various languages, started my interest in hybrid identities, and being able to do that today is to "code switch" easily. Today I identify as a Cambodian artist, a Lao-Nyaw artist, an American artist, and an international artist. Or, I like to say that I am just being an artist. As my old art professor used to say, just be an artist and address the issues that you want to bring attention to right now.

## Making Art in the Camp

We were in Aranyaprathet Refugee Camp for a few years, and during that time, there was little to keep us occupied. Food was dropped off every month, I think. I remember going to "downtown" and was lucky enough to find a truck where people were giving food away. The camp school was a makeshift lean-to, since everything in the camp was temporary and overcrowded.

I was a curious child, so I began to try to entertain myself by exploring my surroundings. I was a child, so I used my imagination and created my own worlds in which to play. On some nights we would throw up a square cardboard box and you could see there were bats flying towards it. Sometimes there would be packs of them. Since the sky is so dark, you can only see them when the lights below reflect off their wings. You really have to look closely to see how fast they fly and maneuver while in the air. I often wondered if they were hungry and desperate like we were, only they lived in the sky, and had their own problems. That was my thinking at the time.

I also made small sculptures of animals and people from the dirt. It was so easy and accessible since there was lots of thick rich dirt all around me. When it rained there was thick mud to use (things got messy and I remember that people got their flip-flops stuck in the mud while walking). I was able to create shadow puppets from materials I found. I was able to set up a makeshift theatre with a plastic screen and a candle, and I put on shadow puppet shows. I found a plastic bag, cut it open and stretched it to make a screen. Then I found plastic bottles to cut into body parts: a round head, two arms, a body and two legs. I made a hole through each piece to connect arm to body and legs to body, and then I poked a stick through the body for me to hold the puppet, and then it was done.

The other kids in the camp were really entertained by what I created, and I thought in my head, Wow--what an amazing thing I can do to command such power. Other adults from the distance looked on with delight as well. We were all mesmerized by the light and shadows and our own imagination. It was all movement and not much dialogue, but that experience was the first time I saw clearly how art could affect people, and how it could create another world for them. I felt that I could help to transport people away from the chaos and confusion of the refugee camp through these shows, through art, and I felt good about that, like I had something to contribute to make life there more bearable.

**Moving to the U.S.**

When I was about ten years old, my family was sponsored to come to the U.S. by the Lutheran Church. Everyone living in the refugee camps knew they needed to be sponsored to leave for life in another country, and believed it was just a matter of time and luck as to when an individual or organization would select their family to sponsor.

**Figure 34**. Sayon circa age 9, Aranyaprathet Refugee Camp. Photo courtesy of Sayon Syaprasoeuth

Sponsorships by religious organizations were not unusual, and families were desperate to get out of the camps, so many accepted these offers. I don't think we thought much about religion or the possibility that anyone would try to change ours. (I was raised Buddhist).

I found out much later that those who did not get selected lingered in the camps for years, and once the refugee program dissolved were repatriated to Cambodia and left to survive on their own.

We landed in Elkader, Iowa. We arrived in March 1980, and I remember that there were streetlights all along the roads, and I saw snow dancing in the dark sky as it was dropping down to the street, with the streetlights illuminating it. I had never seen snow, and I thought it was beautiful, the air so clean and fresh.

We were a family of nine, and the only Asian family in Elkader. This was both good and bad: good in that most people were very friendly and welcoming, because they knew who we were and knew some of our story; bad because there was no Lao or Khmer community to associate with. We didn't speak English, and we were not used to the cold weather or the food, so it was a very isolating experience. After much searching, we finally found we had a cousin in a neighboring town (about 45 minutes away), and I remember we were so happy to meet them and to no longer feel alone. We also found out that we had an uncle who was living in Torrance, California, and had heard that there were a lot of Lao and Cambodians in Long Beach, not far from Torrance, and decided to relocate there in 1984.

I have to say that it was amazing to grow up in Long Beach. The immigrant community there was growing, and there was so much color and energy happening at that time. I felt lots of excitement and there was a sense of freedom. Living here was easy for the first few years. I really don't know what happened or when things started changing. I don't know if it was individual attitudes, a sense of entitlement, or just an enduring survival mentality.

But as more immigrants came in from Central and South America, Long Beach started to get more crowded, and tension began building. There were tensions between Southeast Asians and other ethnic groups, and there were assaults, fighting, and eventually drive-by shootings.

I was trying to fit into American life while maintaining my Asian identity but doing so was difficult. It was hard to try to negotiate two cultures: one, as a youth trying to fit in America and two, a translator and breadwinner for my family, amidst a precarious environment.

My artwork came to reflect this duality. Many of my works juxtapose opposites: immigrant/refugee, Asian/American, masculine/feminine, beautiful/grotesque. I found that making art helped me to escape from the dysfunctional world around me, but early on I didn't know that I would pursue art as a career.

After high school I attended Long Beach City College (LBCC) but wasn't very serious about my studies. I was the only one in my family who really wanted to pursue college. Because I didn't have any role models, I had to figure things out for myself through trial and error, and self-doubt and other challenges led to many mistakes.

Like many children of immigrants and refugees, I had learned that making money was very important, and that my studies should aim towards something that would allow for that. I understood this perspective, because we started out with virtually nothing, but I wasn't finding anything that filled my soul or gave me personal satisfaction.

## Becoming an Artist

After 8 years on and off again at LBCC, I eventually decided on an art major. I finished at LBCC and then transferred to California State University at Long Beach, where I received my Bachelor of Fine Arts. I graduated early since I spent so many years at LBCC and had built up extra credits. Later I went on to Claremont Graduate University for my Master of Fine Arts degree, which I completed in two years. I got very little financial aid, so during all of my schooling I worked full-time. Many people wonder how I did it. I was fortunate in that after high school I also attended a trade school to learn graphic design, which was at its infancy at the time (1990s), and with that training I landed a production job doing advertising layouts. I started there in 1996 and accumulated many years of service and related vacation time, much of which I used to attend my classes.

I have always been an artist in the sense that I have always been creating. When I started making art more seriously, however, I was trying to unpack who I am and where I came from.

When you are a refugee, you don't know the extent to which trauma affects you because you are living moment by moment. When you take the time to reflect and process what happened, only then you can begin to heal.

It's interesting: people sometimes ask me what my art means, but I don't like to give too much of an explanation. I like art to be interpreted by individuals, to see what emotions it triggers in them.

I do like to engage in dialogue with people on what my experience was and how my personal narratives inform my work. What people think they know about an artist when they look at their work is only the surface; it's hard for others to know the amount of self-reflection the artist went through in creating a piece, or the kind of narrative the work is trying to present.

At first, I really felt connected with oil painting, because of the smell and the fluidity of the materials, and of course this has been a creative medium detailed in our history books for hundreds of years. Painting seemed be a good way to tell stories. I later realized there are many ways to present narrative storytelling besides painting, and I started using other materials and mediums. I like to work with mixed media. I really like 3-dimensional art and sculpture and have dabbled in photography, which to me is very accessible. I also like relying on my design skills to manipulate images and using them to tell another kind of story.

One of my more mysterious pieces is *Catching Fireflies* (2008), which draws upon our family's belief systems. When I was a child, my mother would tell me stories about how important it was that I do good deeds and practice good, moral behavior, otherwise when I died my soul could be banished to the realms of suffering.

*Catching Fireflies* is a hanging sculpture created from my own hair, glue, and glitter to form a kind of net. The net is created by a person's good deeds, and will help to catch and save that person from falling into hell.

**Figure 35**. *Catching Fireflies*. 12 ft by 5 ft.
Photo courtesy of sayonart.com

## Connection to Community

As an artist, I feel so blessed to be part of the Long Beach community. There is so much talent and inspiration here. I lived in Orange County for about ten years but came back to Long Beach in 2014, and I have been able to be involved with the community in a number of ways, such as community gatherings, civic activities and of course creating art with other likeminded artists, businesses, and supporters.

First, I have been a part of the staff at United Cambodian Community (UCC) since November 2015. I was brought on as a Program Coordinator to create an after-school art program for local high school students.

I currently serve as Youth Program Manager. As part of this role, I became involved with a project called "Living Arts Long Beach," a six-month program of free after-school arts classes for students ages 14 to 25. The program aims to expose people to different types of art, so we have students participate in a range of activities and complete a variety of projects with a professional artist. Some of our projects we have shared are silk-screening, Khmer traditional dance, and collage. We've visited an architecture studio; we've offered a moviemaking class. We have also had field trips to various arts-related venues, including the Long Beach Museum, the Long Beach Opera, and the Long Beach Symphony.

"Living Arts Long Beach" is about much more than making art. This program provides a safe space for youth to express their feelings and emotions, which in turn helps build their self-esteem, communication skills, ability to work as part of a team, and many other areas of personal growth. At the end of the program, the students display their work at a local gallery or arts organization. They receive a certificate of completion and invite family and friends to come and view their work at an art reception. This is a very proud moment, for them, for their families, and for me.

Second, I have been fortunate to participate in the Global Hybrid project since 2008. Global Hybrid is an arts exchange program that started between Long Beach and Cambodia. The idea, started by my friend and neighbor Denise Scott, was to mount a show in Cambodia and then have local Cambodian artists create their own art in response and dialogue with us.

Then we would bring the show, including some of their art, back to Long Beach.

It's important to have that exchange of ideas, of dialogue, because many of the artists who were artists during the sixties and seventies were killed for embracing creativity and western ideology. It's been fulfilling to begin that dialogue again. The program has since expanded to include Korea, which is exciting. We want to show that self-expression is important for community and spiritual prosperity.

Third, I was able to create a mural as part of the Cambodia Town Mural Project. When I started working at UCC, the director told me that I was going to take on this project. I had no experience creating murals, so I was very nervous, but I liked the challenge. I wanted to find out from the community what they wanted to gain from this mural, so I held a series of meetings to hear their ideas and get a sense of what they wanted these murals to represent. I asked participants in the meetings to draw what they wanted to see in the murals. After five such meetings we ended up with images guided by these discussions and drawings.

The result was *The Spirit Within,* a 30-by 60-foot mural on the corner of Anaheim Street and Dawson Avenue in the heart of Cambodia Town in Long Beach, completed in 2017. The mural presents four large Apsara dancers, which evoke a sense of cultural pride and the beauty of the Khmer people, to greet visitors to the space. The mural also includes images of elephants, sea turtles, and Irrawaddy dolphins, which are endangered in Cambodia, as well as cultural references like Angkor Wat, the Bayon, and the *daem tenout* (palm tree).

**Figure 36.** *The Spirit Within* (completed 2017), on the corner of Anaheim Street and Dawson Avenue in Cambodia Town, Long Beach, CA.
Photo courtesy of www.visitcambodiatownlongbeach.com

## Vision for the Future

The unprecedented events of the past two years (2020-2021) have affected me, as they have all of us, in so many ways.

In terms of my art, the recent past has brought me back to my artistic roots. For example, nowadays I am hearing gunshots, witnessing injustice against African Americans and unequal treatment of different groups, observing violence and the destruction of property (e.g., in downtown Long Beach in the wake of the George Floyd incident) that is very reminiscent of the war climate in Cambodia and turmoil and angst of the refugee camp experience. And now there are uprisings in violence against Asian Americans. There seem to be these random assaults, caught on video, that have been very shocking to watch. My hope is that people will come together to try to better understand of the root of these problems: systemic racism, fear, misinformation, or a combination of all of these.

We as a community need to look at ourselves, how we see race, colorism, hierarchy within the worlds we occupy and the greater world beyond. As an activist I created protest art, a stencil of Xiao Zhen Xie, a 75-year-old woman attacked in San Francisco in 2021, fighting off the perpetrator, a male in his late 30s.[35] I have emblazoned it onto t-shirts and wear it to show my support for the Asian American community.

Furthermore, our shelter-in-place directives due to COVID-19, while isolating, have given me time to reflect on my life, my role as an artist and responsibility in the world.

**Figure 37.** Close-up of the Xiao Zhen Xie stencil.
Image courtesy of www.sayonart.com

There is both beauty and darkness in all times and all things. Creating art allows me to express my voice and make visible the injustices in our world. I create out of lived experience as I did as a child back in the refugee camp, but I now have the intelligence to see how my work can be used to effect change. I am eager to share the body of work that results from this reflection in the near future.

## My Story: Alan Khum

I was born in San Francisco, California in 1987 and have spent my whole life here.

When most people think of Cambodians in CA, their minds jump immediately to Long Beach, but in the past, especially before the earthquake of 1989, there was a much larger Khmer population in the Bay Area than there is now.[36]

**Figure 38.** Alan Khum, live painting at the Mid-Autumn Harvest Festival, Tenderloin, San Francisco, Sept. 2015. Photo: Christine Su

My parents came to California as refugees from Cambodia. I grew up in Bayview, which has a bad reputation but was and is a great creative resource for artists. There was so much energy and vibrancy in San Francisco in the 1990s, and so much diversity--ethnic, social, economic, political--all of which inspire artists to create. I used to take public transportation to and from high school, and I liked to look at the graffiti and murals in different parts of the city, and they are part of what drew me to become an artist.

In the Tenderloin, for example, right on the corner of Olive and Polk streets, there is a huge mural by Johanna Poethig that incorporates elements of different Southeast

**Figure 39a. (full mural)**
"Strong Roots, Healthy Tree" Mural by Johanna Poethig installed in
San Francisco's Tenderloin District. (1989)

**Figure 39b. (inset 1)**
Women dressed in
clothing representative of
their home countries and
cultures, with traditional
architecture in the
background.

**Figure 39c. (inset 2)**
A section of the
Churning of the Sea of
Milk legend depicted
in the mural.

Photos: Don Fallon

Asian cultures: Cambodian, Lao, Vietnamese. You can see Southeast Asian style architecture reflected there (structures resembling a Buddhist temple and stupa), and a big piece of the mural depicts scenes from an ancient legend about how Cambodia came into existence. I loved how my Cambodian heritage was reflected in my environment. My love of art in public spaces became an integral part of my future work.

## Cambodian Values, American Expectations

My parents went through a very difficult time in Cambodia during the Khmer Rouge period and then in the refugee camp. The memories are very painful for them, so they didn't tell me a lot about that time. I heard bits and pieces as I was growing up, but it was very difficult for them to talk about. They believed it was something better left in the past, although I know they will never be able to forget. They did, however, bring with them traditional Cambodian values--humility, respect for elders, importance of family, hard work--which were consistently stressed in our home. I haven't been to Cambodia as an adult, so my work reflects the experiences and interpretations of my parents, though I have done a lot of reading and research on my own.

One show I put together was "Obscure Origins," a solo exhibition at SOMArts Cultural Center.[37] In this show, you find many images based on Cambodian folk stories. So, you will see *naga* (sea serpents) and *yeak* (ogres) and *garuda* (half-man, half-bird) and other folkloric characters in my work.

But other pieces reflect my American upbringing, so you will also see the Golden Gate Bridge and cat meme popular culture. And sometimes the pieces include images from both Cambodian and U.S. culture, which speaks to the complexity of being both Cambodian and American.

On one hand, I don't truly know or understand the culture of my/my family's origins, and there is a void there, a piece of my identity that is missing or incomplete. On the other hand, I don't feel like I fit neatly into American culture either. It is difficult to put this liminal feeling into words; rather, I choose to express this through my art. Certainly, other children of refugees in the 1.5 and 2.0 generations have experienced similar uncertainty; in our hybridity, we are caught between the traditional Cambodian values I mentioned and an American lifestyle that values individualism, instant gratification, and emphasis on youth.

### Becoming an Artist

When I was very young, I loved watching cartoons on Saturdays and even in the early mornings during the week while eating breakfast before going to school. I remember trying to draw and imitate cartoons like *dragonball z* and *Pokémon*. My sister was an artist and had an internship at an art gallery (Meridian Gallery) in 1997, when I was 10 years old. She would let me go with her to the gallery and I would get to see projects and artwork everyone else was working on, which I took in as inspiration.

When I was in high school, I was interested more in graphic design, video games, computers, and graffiti, in addition to cartoons and animation. I was fortunate to be able to learn Adobe Photoshop in High school and took a digital media class in which I played around with collaging and manipulating digital works.

This was a game changer: I felt like I had so much freedom and had endless ideas about what I could create. I thought about pursuing animation and 3D art as a career because of movies by Pixar and DreamWorks, but I wasn't sure if I liked digital art as much as or more than traditional art, and I was invested in graffiti. When I was a junior in high school, I interned at the same gallery as my sister had, Meridian Gallery.

I studied art formally in college. I began at City College of San Francisco and started taking multimedia classes such as web design and flash animation, which was pretty big around this time (circa 2005), as well as traditional art classes. I did some freelance work in web and graphic design on the side, to help pay for school.

At one point, however, I met an instructor, artist Fred Kling, who changed the way I look at art. I think working with him helped to steer me back toward more traditional art. He was kind and generous and pushed me to be a better artist regardless of my situation. At the time, I couldn't afford many art supplies, so he gave me his personal wooden box of paints and easels and I was able to experiment with watercolor and oil paints. Through Fred, I met other artists and started going to art shows. Fred suggested that I should submit my work to shows and not be afraid to just go into small local boutiques and show some of my work. I did just that and started getting my artwork shown in those boutiques, in local galleries, and at pop-up events. Prior to that point I had been focusing on digital art, but after meeting Fred I found a balance between traditional and digital. Incidentally, Fred had visited Cambodia in the 1960s and would tell me about his time there, so we had that connection as well.

I earned an associates degree in arts and humanities, and then continued on to San Francisco State University, where I earned my bachelor of arts degree in painting and drawing. At SFSU, I really began to explore different mediums.

**Figure 40**. Alan Khum, "Laocoön and His Cats."
Image courtesy of Alan Khum Arts

I already loved both watercolor and oil painting, but also ventured into trying new (for me) things like wood cutting, 3D art, sculpture, and installation art.

By the time I graduated from SFSU, I had been heavily involved in the arts community in the Bay Area: I was exhibiting my own work in galleries and curating the work of others and collaborating on projects with other artists. I love doing all these things. I started to participate in Cambodia- and Southeast Asia-related events more, too. I loved being part of Khmer New Year and the Mid-Autumn Harvest festival, held right in the Tenderloin and hosted by the Southeast Asia Arts and Culture Coalition.

## What I Create

In addition to images from Cambodian mythology, I also like to paint what I imagine everyday life in Cambodia to be like. So you will see stilt houses and Buddhist temples in my work, for example. And of course, you will see cats. I love cats – I call myself ប៉ា ឆ្មា (Pa Chhma) which means "Cat Daddy."

I went through a particularly rough patch in life at one point, during which I felt very alone, and I relied on my cat as not only a pet, but also as a friend. Having my cat, Misty, was a very healing presence that helped me emotionally and mentally, so every cat painting I do reminds me of her and how she kept my spirit up during those hard times.

Cats are ubiquitous in my work. Cats are great because they are survivors, fierce defenders in the face of danger, so including them in my work is symbolic, especially when the work is about Cambodia, the war, and the refugee experience. Cats are empathic, and I think art should function in an empathic way; that is, the work should resonate with the audience in some way. If you're a cat person, you will understand what I mean.

**Figure 41**. Alan Khum, "Chma Kyom" (My Cat).
Image courtesy of Alan Khum Arts

Cats also have a quiet strength, a silence; but silence is not weakness. Their penchant for watching a situation carefully and for an extended period of time before taking action has proven a clever strategy. Finally, cats are very humorous, and when you are dealing with heavy topics, you need humor sometimes to break the tension. A cat can be very serious and almost angry, but in a split second can do something so funny you have to laugh out loud.

## Art in Public Places

I have been very fortunate in that I have always been a working artist. A lot of what I engage in centers around social justice issues, like immigration politics or racial inequity. I like my art to make an impact. In addition to exhibitions, I have also done commissioned art for clients, and for the city of San Francisco.

One of my most memorable projects was *Art Wraps for the Heart of Tenderloin* (2017), which involved creating vinyl wraps to be installed on traffic control signal/utility boxes and trash cans for a duration of several years. I was one of seven artists chosen to contribute to the project. I created my designs using vivid colors (and of course, cats) to bring some brightness into the space. The project was well-received by the neighborhood, and I liked that I was giving back to the community which inspired me so much.

## Vision for the Future

The unprecedented events of the past two years have affected me--as they have affected all of us-- in so many ways. In terms of my art, it is interesting because the recent past has in a way helped me to understand my parents' experiences more. For example, we are contending with so much violence and abuse of power, injustice, and unequal treatment, and while I was not physically present in Cambodia with my parents, I know these things are very reminiscent of the war climate there and in the refugee camps.

**Figures 42 (top), 43a (above) and 43b (right)**
*Art Wraps for the Heart of Tenderloin*
art projects.

Photo (top): Tenderloin Museum Facebook
page, provided by Alan Khum
Photos (above and right) courtesy of Alan
Khum

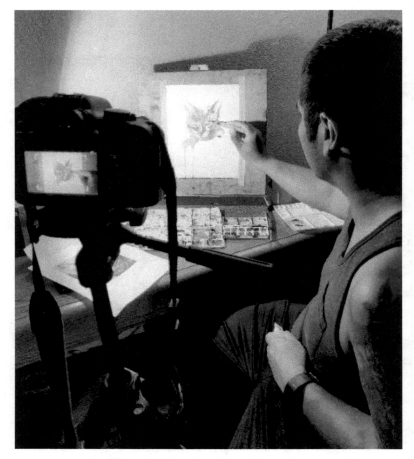

**Figure 44**. Alan Khum in creation mode.
Photo: Alan Khum Arts

Moving forward, I hope to continue to create art that blends the different aspects of my identity and family history, and the more I learn, the more authentic my work becomes.

# Chapter 4

## Contemporary Music
## គន្ត្រីសម័យថ្មី

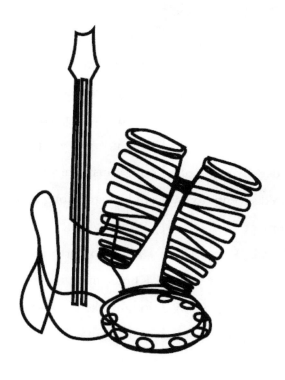

On March 28, 2021, twenty-two-year-old Cambodian rap artist VannDa released a music video of his newest single, entitled "Time to Rise." By April 1, the video had more than 2,000,000 views on YouTube. By April 6, it had more than 6,000,000 views. By April 10, it had 10,000,000 views. By April 30th, it had 35,000,000 views, and by May 25th, more than 52,000,000 views.[38]

That rap is popular in Cambodia is not surprising; rap had become part of urban Cambodian Americans' music repertoire in the 1990s, and it soon crossed the seas and has since proliferated in Cambodia. What was perhaps unanticipated was that "Time to Rise" was not just a rap song and video recorded by a popular young musician, but a rap song that featured seventy-five-year-old Master Kong Nay on an archaic instrument.

Master Kong Nay is a virtuoso performer on one of the oldest and most revered Khmer instruments: the *chapei dong veng* (hereafter, *chapei*), a long-necked, two-stringed lute that dates back centuries in Cambodia. The *chapei*, played at weddings, funerals, and other community events, is accompanied by singing with lyrics that relate traditional folktales or draw from Buddhist teachings, make social commentary or share important news or information. Indeed, as the COVID-19 pandemic spread throughout the globe beginning in 2020, Master Kong Nay produced a public service announcement using the *chapei*, singing lyrics urging

Cambodians to wash their hands and social distance to avoid catching the virus.[39]

Born in Kampot in 1946, Kong Nay went blind at the age of four after contracting smallpox, but he did not let his lack of sight stop him from appreciating and studying music. His family members were masters of traditional instruments themselves, and Kong Nay developed a particular affinity for the *chapei* and began studying it formally when he was 13. By the time he was 15, he was playing *chapei* professionally, and became skilled and popular enough to make a living doing so. He was also a gifted lyricist, able to improvise quickly and tailor songs to be timely and relevant.

In 1975, when the Khmer Rouge took over, Kong Nay and his family were forced to undertake hard labor in the rice fields, something not easily accomplished by a blind person. Additionally, in most cases the Khmer Rouge killed known musicians outright. In Kong Nay's case, however, they asked him to play songs extoling the greatness of the Khmer Rouge. Perhaps because of his ability to spontaneously modify *ayai* or *chapei* songs to serve their cause, the Khmer Rouge did not execute him. Kong Nay survived the regime, but many of his family members, including two of his brothers, did not.

Master Kong Nay is one of the few remaining *chapei* masters in the world, and in 2016, the *chapei dong veng* was inscribed in UNESCO's list of Intangible Cultural Heritage in Need of Urgent Safeguarding.

But returning to the popularity of "Time to Rise," one unfamiliar with *chapei* might question why someone would include it and Master Kong Nay together in a rap composition, and why VannDa's 21$^{st}$ century audience would be so enthralled with the final product.

Upon closer examination, however, one finds remarkable similarities between *chapei* music and rap, both in terms of the social commentary in their respective lyrics and the cadence of the music and singing. Thus the appeal to a younger audience is not as shocking as it first may seem.

## Beginnings of Cambodian (/American) Rap

When Cambodian refugees came to the U.S. in the 1980s, many relocated to metropolitan areas like Chicago and Los Angeles, and ended up in neighborhoods within those areas that were under-resourced and underserved. Long Beach, California, which now has the largest Cambodian population outside of Cambodia, is less than 25 miles from Los Angeles.

Rap was beginning to flourish in Los Angeles and young Cambodians in the metro area followed rappers like NWA and Tupac Shakur, whose songs addressed unsavory encounters with police, drug abuse, gun violence, poverty, racism. These themes resonated with Cambodian youth, struggling to navigate U.S. culture in general and survive unwelcoming and dangerous environments in particular. Cambodian Americans themselves soon adopted rap as a medium to tell their own stories.

While the rap genre was new to Cambodia when it became popular in the 2000s, however, some of its basic sounds and rhythms have been part of Khmer music for centuries. The beloved Cambodian tradition of *ayai*, for example, involves two singers who engage each other to see who is the better impromptu performer. In some *ayai*, the format is call-and-response, in which one singer asks a question and the other must ad-lib a response right then and there. The audience expects the lyrics produced by both singers to rhyme and entertain, and they especially like humorous responses.

Similarly, freestyle rap in the U.S. often involves a "battle" between performers who come up with their lyrics on the spot, with the winner determined by the audience. So these two musical styles, generated thousands of miles and thousands of years apart, may be more alike than different.

In the lyrics to "Time to Rise" (excerpt below), VannDa speaks of the respect contemporary musicians and artists must have for their predecessors and the knowledge they can pass on, rather than pretending past experience is no longer relevant.

VannDa:

*We have art in our souls like the sculptures on our temple walls*
*Art is the soul of Cambodia*

*View those artists as you would view the sculptures of our temples*
*Respect them as teachers to defeat your enemies*

*Open a page in history and show those who prefer ignorance,*
*you hear me?*

**Figure 45. (above)**
. VannDa with Master Kong Nay.
Photo courtesy of Baramey Production

**Figure 46**. (left) Khmer
artist VannDa
Photo courtesy of
Baramey Production

In response, Master Kong Nay sings (and in the tradition of *ayai*, his words rhyme):

> *Brothers, sisters, uncles and aunties,*
> *I am Kong Nay and would like to testify*
> *Chapei dong veng, lakhon bassac, ayai chapei*

VannDa interjects, noting the youth's desire for autonomy:

> *Modern music of the youth*
> *A generation over the age of 20*
> *They wanna fly like the birds*

But Master Kong Nay reassures him (and us) that:

> *They are flexible with the sounds of modernity and evolve it with our tradition.*

In other words, ancient and modern music can not only exist simultaneously, but can be mixed and merged to create original compositions and styles as well.

## Artist Encounters

I first met praCh, the first artist featured in this chapter, years ago when I was living in Hawai`i. At the time I was heavily involved in cultural programming for the Cambodian Community of Hawai`i, and we hoped to engage our youth more fully, so for our Khmer New Year celebration that year, we invited praCh to perform. We met when he came for that performance and have been friends ever since, and I knew without question that I wanted his story to be told in this book.

The second part of this chapter introduces Laura Tevary Mam. I met Laura Mam at one of the opening events for the first Cambodian Town Film Festival in 2013 and have followed her career since that time.

As a young woman, Mam relocated to Cambodia to pursue a music career in 2014. Somehow, this 2.0-generation American who at the time spoke little Khmer had the prescience to know that Cambodia was fertile ground for planting the seeds of an "original music" movement in which creativity would be reawakened, and that would ultimately support the resurgence of a true collaboration between ancient and modern (or between *chapei* and Stratocaster) such as that between Kong Nay and VannDa.

She shares her journey with us as well.                    -*C.S.*

Continuation of lyrics from "Time to Rise,"
provided courtesy of Baramey Production:

Master Kong Nay:

> *It's time to rise as high as the stars*
> *May both men and women be blessed*
>
> *To the male and female artists who seek to fulfill their dreams*
> *Go forth and open the new chapter of the treasured arts inherited from*
> *me, Kong Nay*

VannDa:

> *I said time to rise, time is priceless, rise beyond the sky*
> *Like Master Kong Nay who rose beyond the stars*
>
> *I do this with my utmost ability, not carelessly but with precision*
> *I said time to rise, bright as the sun a million miles away*

## My Story: praCh Ly

I was born in Cambodia in 1979, although I am not certain on what day or in what month. 1979 was the year that the Vietnamese over- threw the Khmer Rouge, but there was

**Figure 47**. praCh Ly.
Photo courtesy of prachly.com

mass confusion and shock following the overthrow, and Cambodians didn't suddenly become free and go back to normal lives, so marking dates on a calendar (or even having a calendar) was not high on the list of concerns. But I know that it was sometime in 1979. I also know I was born in an area of Battambang called Ka Prach, after which I was named.

Soon after that, we relocated to a refugee camp and then to the United States. Growing up as a refugee kid in the U.S. was not exactly fun. There was a lot of bullying, name-calling, and violence against Cambodians. The streets were dangerous for all of us, and some Cambodian youth, not accepted by the mainstream or even other minority groups, formed gangs to cope. It was easy to get caught up in that life.

When I was nine years old, I got a job in a video store, making $5 a week, plus the manager let me take two movies per night home for free. I used to stay in the store from the time I got out of school until closing, enraptured by the films.

Outside of the store, sitting on the sidewalk, there was a man selling bootleg copies of albums on cassette tapes. I stopped to talk with him a few times, and at one point I decided buy a couple of tapes, one of which turned out to be a copy of NWA's *Straight Outta Compton* (1987). When I listened to that album, my mind was blown. The issues and events they were rapping about were things that resonated with me: racial tensions, violence in the streets, police brutality. Our first apartment in Long Beach was in the 69th Street apartments. Walk one block to 70th street, and you're in Compton.

I started collecting and listening to rap whenever I could. I was in middle school at the time, and I remember I received an assignment to write an essay about a song that was important to me. I wrote about Too Short's "The Ghetto," an amazing song whose lyrics about life, ("Trying to survive/trying to stay alive") seemed to tell my story as well. Growing up listening to rap and hip-hop and living in similar circumstances, it was natural that I would ultimately choose rap to express myself.

This was a difficult time for the U.S., especially in the LA area. In the early 1990s, an African American man named Rodney King was beaten by four White police officers during his arrest following a high-speed car chase. He was badly hurt and hospitalized, and later brought a legal case against the four officers for excessive force.

At the trial, three officers were acquitted, and the jury couldn't reach a verdict for the fourth. Within hours after news of the acquittals emerged, riots broke out throughout LA. For six days, people vandalized and looted businesses, set cars and buildings on fire, and attacked each other in the streets. It was terrifying. I remember the sounds of gunshots and seeing the fire and smoke. The morning after one of the night riots, I walked to the video store where I had worked, only to find that it had burned down.

When I first started to rap, I was reacting to this environment. I also started to act out myself. My parents saw that I was heading down a dangerous path, and were worried about my safety, so they sent me to live with my older brother in Florida. That was the best thing they could've done for me. I had never really talked with my brother about Cambodia or the refugee camps before, but when I was there, he started opening up about what he had been through and describing what he felt: fear, hunger, exhaustion, uncertainty, hopelessness. I realized that I had stories to tell that were more important than glorifying gang life and drugs, and that led to an evolution in my music. When I came back to Long Beach, I had a notebook full of rhymes.

## Becoming the #1 Rapper--in Cambodia

I cut my first CD, which I ended up calling *DALAMA: The End'n is Just the Beginnin'* (1999) in my parents' garage. I didn't have a mixing board or sound system, so I had to make do with a karaoke machine (fortunately nearly all Cambodian American homes had one during that time).

I started to tell stories, stories my family had told me and stories about my own experiences through poetry, through song, through rap. This first album was kind of like an autobiography for me, and a history lesson for those who rejected us or were biased against us. I found sound bites from old Khmer Rouge propaganda speeches and put them in some of the songs. I rapped in both English and Khmer. I let my feelings about the genocide be known.

I had no money for any marketing, so I did the cover art and printing of the CDs myself. I decided to rent a booth and sell copies at the Khmer New Year celebration in Long Beach. There wasn't much interest at first, as there were all kinds of foods and other items for sale, and no one really knew who I was. But at one point, the power went out in the main area that they had set up for singers and band members, so the music stopped temporarily. I saw an opportunity, so I kind of snuck onto the stage and started rapping. I performed the song "welCome" from my first album a capella and when I finished, there was silence.

Then, slowly, people started clapping and coming up to me asking who I was, and where they could find my music. The next thing I knew, there was a line of people waiting in front of my booth to buy my CD. It sold out!

One of the people who picked up the CD was DJ Sop, a deejay in Cambodia who happened to be in Long Beach at the time. He took the album back to Cambodia, started playing it there, and it took off like wildfire.

I had never been back to Cambodia, and definitely wasn't promoting it there, so wasn't aware of its popularity. It wasn't until a reporter called me and asked how I felt about having the "#1 Album in Cambodia" that I found out that my music was more far-reaching than I had thought. At first, I thought my friends were pranking me, pretending to be the reporter, so I hung up on him. Fortunately, he called back.

He said the album as it had been sold in Cambodia was called *Khmer Rap,* and there was no artist identified on it. Someone had replaced my cover artwork with a picture of a child holding a rifle and made and sold dozens upon dozens of bootleg copies. In fact, when I went to Cambodia some years later, someone tried to sell me my own album! I did end up buying a few copies.

The beats and the lyrics (in both English and Khmer) on the album were really resonating with youth. It's hard to believe, but most youth in Cambodia who grew up in the 1990s and 2000s hadn't learned about the Khmer Rouge in their history classes.[40] So they were learning through my music.

## The DALAMA Trilogy, Continued

In 2003, I recorded the second album of the *DALAMA* trilogy, *DALAMA: The Lost Chapter.*[41] My first album was pretty raw, in terms of the language I used (I swore a lot). It definitely allowed me to express my feelings and frustrations. The language on the second album is more intentional; that is, I was selective about my words, and didn't use a lot of profanity. After the success of the first album, I thought that the second might attract a wider audience, not only other rappers or hip-hop musicians, but community members and youth (like my nieces and nephews), and I wanted to create for them as well. Turns out I had a lot to say-- there are 21 tracks on the album![42]

I also incorporated more traditional Khmer sounds, like *khloy* [flute] and *pin peat* [traditional Khmer music ensemble]. One of the pieces, *refleXion*, is popular with the older community members because it is *ayai*, something they love.

**Figure 48.** Cover art for *DALAMA: The End'n is Just the Beginnin'*.
Image courtesy of praCh Ly

It was important to me to bring these things into the work, because not only are they part of our ancient history, but musicians were among those the Khmer Rouge tried to destroy. Putting those who remain on the album shows that they are not gone. We were able to collaborate with Ho Chhim Chan, an incredible *pin peat* master who survived the Khmer Rouge, for example.

Soon after I recorded the second album, I had another incredible experience that brought together past and present for me. Cambodian Living Arts (CLA), an arts non-profit founded by genocide survivor Arn Chorn-Pond, invited me to travel with a group of their sponsors to Cambodia to meet CLA masters and students. Of course I said yes. I was one of about 30 who made the trip. After I arrived, two very interesting things happened.

First, I arrived in Phnom Penh and was outside of the airport when a Rolls Royce pulled up. The car door opened, and inside was my dad! This was a complete surprise. He had been in Battambang, making arrangements to build a huge Buddha statue next to Wat Ek, and Ming Ravynn Karet-Coxen of the Nginn Karet Foundation (www.nkfc.org) arranged for him to come from Battambang to meet me. It was surreal.

We spent some time together, riding in *cyclo* around the city, not speaking much, but just enjoying each other's company. I remember riding around the Independence Monument and just taking in the sights. It is a memory I treasure.

Second, at one point during the trip we were all gathered in a restaurant listening to Cambodian traditional music being played live. I heard the distinctive sound of the *chapei dong veng;* when I looked over at the stage, there was Master Kong Nay. I was so captivated by his playing and singing that I left my food on the table and went over to sit by the stage to take it all in. This was Master Kong Nay!

Listening to him play with words and rhyme—like the freestyling we do in rap—was amazing. I introduced myself to him and knew that I wanted to come back someday to work with him. Later, I approached some people and started tossing around an idea for a fusion project: to return to Cambodia to record Cambodian American rappers and Master Kong Nay singing *ayai* and playing the *chapei*, making music together. Some producers thought it was a great idea, and the next year, I returned with two colleagues of mine, Silong Chhung and Thy Pich, both of whom are also Khmer American rappers.

We met Master Kong Nay and his wife in Phnom Penh in his home near the White Building (which has since been torn down). What an amazing experience, to hear his stories about life in Cambodia before the war, about life under the Khmer Rouge, about reviving interest in traditional music among Cambodia's youth.

During that same trip I was also fortunate to be introduced to the *sadieu*, an ancient one-stringed instrument that very, very few people still know how to play. The *sadieu* is made from a long piece of wood with a string stretched from end to end, similar to a bow, and about one-third of the way from the top there is the shell of a large gourd. The musician places the shell over his heart, and the echo of his heartbeat forms the basis for the song. It is amazing.

Before the end of the trip, we went to a recording studio and recorded quite a few songs with Kong Nay, which I took back to the U.S. intending to include them on my third album.

**Figure 49 (above).** praCh meeting with Master Kong Nay and his wife
in Phnom Penh. Photo: Silong Chhun

**Figure 50 (left).**
The rare *sadieu*, played
by Sinath.
Photo: Silong Chhun

We had the good fortune to be able to record the sounds of the *sadieu* as well, played by a young man named Sinath. It was extraordinary, an experience I will never forget.

Right before I left Cambodia, too, Master Kong Nay wrote and recorded a song about me. Coming up with the melody and the rhymes on the spot, he sang about my birth in the refugee camp, of my journey to the U.S., of the gangs and violence of the Long Beach streets. He even sang about how I recorded my first album in my parents' garage. Master Kong Nay is a living legend, and for him to take the time to tell my story was a once-in-a-lifetime thing.[43]

My third album, *DALAMA: Memoirs of the Invisible War*, hasn't been publicly released. I want to include the recordings from that second trip to Cambodia on the album. It has been brewing for years; there is just so much material (actually, between the second and third albums I wrote more than 50 songs) and it requires a lot of remastering and other work before it is ready for public release.

I have also been venturing into other areas. In 2004, for example, I wrote some original music for a play showing in New York City called *Eyes of the Heart*, about a Khmer woman who suffers from psychosomatic blindness as a result of her experiences under the Khmer Rouge. I have been really active in planning the Cambodian New Year celebrations at El Dorado Park. I have been giving lectures and presentations at different universities across the U.S. I wrote some additional music for *Enemies of the People* (2009), an award-winning documentary directed by Rob Lemkin, which follows Cambodian journalist Thet Sambath, a Khmer Rouge survivor, as he sets out to interview former Khmer Rouge top leaders. I helped to produce *Paulina* (Caylee So's award-winning short film) in 2012. I contributed music for *Samnang* (2013), which takes place in Long Beach. It has been extremely busy and productive.

## Cambodia Town Film Festival

One of my proudest moments was when we launched our Cambodia Town Film Festival (CTFF). CTFF started as a dream around 2009, and I was amazed to see it come together.

We held many discussions about what CTFF should be: when it should be held, how it should be managed, what types of events to include. Caylee So and I are co-founders and co-directors, and we have put together some amazing programs, launching the first CTFF in 2013. CTFF is a *multi-day* festival, not just one or two film screenings, showcasing the cinematic talent of Cambodians in diaspora. We host interviews with directors, panel discussions, dance, and other live performances throughout CTFF weekend.

We created CTFF to provide space for filmmakers to showcase their work and network, to connect Cambodian and Cambodian American artists, and especially since we screened in Long Beach, to promote community and local businesses.

The first film to open our first festival was *A River Changes Course* (ARCC), directed by Khmer American Kalyanee Mam.

ARCC (2013) captures the stories of three young Cambodians: one living in the forests of Ratanakiri, another supporting his family as a fisherman on the Tonle Sap River, and yet another who leaves her rural village searching for a steady income in the garment factories of Phnom Penh. They all struggle to maintain traditional ways of life while the modern world closes in around them. This film and others in the festival addressed a critical issue in Cambodia: how to reconcile tradition and change, preservation and modernization.

For some of the Cambodian filmmakers, coming to CTFF was their first time ever leaving Cambodia and/or coming to the U.S., so it was really important that we let them know how much we appreciate their work and want to foster connections. For some of the Cambodian American filmmakers, too, watching films by Cambodians at CTFF was the closest they had come to visiting or returning to the homeland. Many were born in refugee camps or in the U.S. and have no first-hand memories of Cambodia. They learned about it through these films, and through their connections with their Cambodian artist counterparts. CTFF has even spurred some Cambodian Americans to make the trip.

Throughout all CTFFs to date, the films speak to the human condition, not only Cambodian or Cambodian American situations, and reach and inspire multiple audiences. A committee comprised of academics, practitioners, and community members decides which of the many films submitted should be screened.

## Building a Bridge Between Generations

One of the things we have done each year is to incorporate a film from Cambodia's "Golden Age," the 1960s and early 70s, when hundreds of films were being produced and screened. During the first CTFF, for example, we included *Orn Ey Srey Orn* (1972), directed by famed director Ly Bun Yim, known for putting never-before-seen special effects into his films, and really capturing the audience's attention. People in Phnom Penh flocked to see his films.

*Orn Ey Srey Orn* is a classic story about a love triangle, and about different social classes and how they can affect relationships. The soundtrack is music by Sinn Sisamouth. AND, we put in English language subtitles, which was no easy feat. It had never been done before, and Khmer language has so many nuances that are difficult to translate. But I am so glad we did that. There are many Khmer Americans who are not fluent in Khmer, or at least not fluent at the level needed to understand all of the dialogue, and we wanted them to be able to appreciate the film. And of course, there are non-Khmer in our audience as well.

We have continued to include at least one "classic" film in CTFF each year, including another by Ly Bun Yim, *12 Sisters* (1968), which has ogres, a flying Pegasus, and all sorts of special effects. It is amazing to be able to see what previous generations produced and what audiences experienced with these films, long before computer-generated imagery (CGI) or visual effects (VFX).

## Coming Full Circle

At CTFF 2019, the last CTFF we were able to hold in-person before COVID-19, I was so honored and humbled that we screened *In the Life of Music* (2018) as our featured film. While as I mentioned earlier I have contributed to other films, this film, which I helped to produce, brought together my love of music, my love of Cambodia, and my love of film. Because it centered on "Champa Battambang," a true classic 1960s Cambodia song, and how it was so meaningful to members of three different generations, it brought a lot of things full circle.

I think the film offers something for individuals in each of these generations. They can see their own stories reflected in various parts of the film, but it also speaks to the relationships between members of different generations. We do a lot of talking about how distant we have become from our parents, and how much intergenerational misunderstanding there is. But in the film, while acknowledging those challenges, we also get a glimpse into how music can connect us, no matter how different the characters and their lives.

I wanted to continue that theme throughout the weekend. I decided that as part of the program I would perform some of my music. Let me rephrase that: my friends [Sam Tea and Silong Chhun] convinced me to do a live performance. I hadn't planned on it, but they asked, and I said that if they would get up there and perform with me, I would do it.

The year 2020 would mark the 20-year anniversary of the release of my first album, *DALAMA: The End'n is Just the*

*Beginnin'*, so CTFF (held in September 2019) would be an appropriate time to announce that. Can you believe that? 20 years. As I said I hadn't planned it, but I realized that it was a good time to revisit the songs and see how they resonate with today's audiences, and to reflect on my own work considering how I have changed, how the world has changed.

In a promotional piece for CTFF 2019, I wrote:

> Many things have changed over the past 20 years, not only for me but for the diasporic Cambodian community, and yet one thing we all retain is our identity as Khmer. We struggle with it. We fight with it. We defend it. We embrace it. And now, twenty years later, I will be performing a show to commemorate it.[44]

It was out of the ordinary, being up on that stage. The house was full. I was a little nervous, and I don't really get nervous. But this was important to me. By CTFF number 7, we had grown so much. I had grown so much.

I actually got kind of emotional during the performance because these songs are my story--no, *our* story--and I have gotten to know the community so much more closely since my albums themselves were first produced. I felt it was crucial that I perform everything live and raw this time.

Nothing was pre-recorded, and there was no lip-syncing, because I wanted it to be an authentic reflection of what I was feeling at the time. And it was.

**Figures 51a and 51b.** . praCh performing live at the 8th Annual Cambodia Town Film Festival, September 2019.
Photos: Christine Su (above), Silong Chhun (below)

In September 2020, because of the COVID-19 pandemic, we held our first-ever virtual CTFF. I have to say, it was crazy putting that together, but it turned out really well! We screened 40 films, hosted interviews and panels with directors and producers, had a cooking demonstration, and even designed a coloring book for the kids! Having virtual events can be awkward, but I am proud to say that almost everything went off without a hitch. And with donations from the community, we were able to provide meals and supplies to struggling families during the pandemic/lockdown.

## What's Next for Me

I have several projects going on. I have written some screenplays and more music. I've also gotten involved in producing other Khmer artists under my label, Mujestic Records, like *The 2^nd Language* group. I worked as part of a group with the City of Long Beach to have April declared Cambodian American Heritage Month, and in April 2021 we supported [California State Assemblymember] Patrick O'Donnell in introducing a bill declaring April 11–17 as Cambodian Genocide Memorial Week. I am starting work on a project with the Smithsonian in Washington, D.C. As long as I am able, I will support my community however I can.

And speaking about things "coming full circle," I'm also working on writing a book about my brother and his experiences. Some of my early talks with him inspired my music. Now, I am learning more as I interview him and write, and I can't wait for the final result.

## My Story: Laura Tevary Mam

**Figure 52.** Laura Tevary Mam.
Photo courtesy of Baramey Production

I was born and raised in San Jose, California, but Cambodia has always tugged at my heart. Since I was a child, I have always been curious about my parents' homeland. I visited for the first time when I was 12, and I was so taken with it--the people, the landscape, the food, the temples, everything--I loved it. I used to travel back and forth between the U.S. and Cambodia, but I now live in Cambodia full-time.

My mom and dad both survived the Khmer Rouge regime in Cambodia and came to the United States as refugees. Because they had endured such hardship and grief during that time, they really wanted my brother and me to embrace American life as much as possible. So we spoke mostly English at home, attended local schools, and hung out with American friends.

My father never spoke with me about Cambodia; I believe it was too painful for him, as he lost most of his family under the regime. My mother shared some things about Cambodia but preferred to talk about life there before the Khmer Rouge.

She was born in Phnom Penh into an upper-class family (her father was a government official), and she and her sisters attended elite French- and English-language schools and were living happy and comfortable lives until the KR took over.

But seeing my parents' pain and tears whenever Khmer Rouge memories invaded their dreams (nightmares), or when they thought about family members they had lost, led me to want to know more about what had happened, not less. And I wanted to know *how* and *why* this happened: how could Cambodia be taken over by this radical ideology that led to such violence and suffering?

The people who sponsored our family to come to the U.S. wrote a book called *To Destroy You is No Loss*, and it was from reading this book that I learned the details about what had happened to my mom and dad.[45] The author wrote it in collaboration with my mom, actually. I have read and reread this book again and again, and it moves me every time.

When I attended college at the University of California, Berkeley (Go Bears!), I started to delve into Southeast Asian and Cambodian history. I majored in anthropology, and I really thought I would become an archaeologist! In fact, after I graduated, I worked for a nongovernmental organization focused on conservation and preservation of World Heritage Sites, including some of the ancient monuments in Cambodia.

Even though music had always been important to me, I had no idea that it would soon become the focus of my life and work. I had always been writing and singing, and I taught myself how to play the guitar, which my mom bought for me when I was 12. Music was one of the ways I dealt with feelings of sadness and isolation and general teenage angst when I was in high school.

For me, creating music was kind of like writing in a journal: it gave me space to express myself, to work through struggles, to discover more about myself. It helped me immensely, and once I went to college, I started sharing my music at open mic events and on YouTube, which helped connect me with other young musicians and diasporic Cambodians. It also became a way to connect more closely with my mom and dad.

## Music as a Connector and Healer

Both of my parents love music. My father is a great singer, and he taught himself how to play the guitar and the drums. My mother loved the modern music of the late 1960s and 70s--Baksey Cham Krong, Pen Ron, Yol Aularong--the rock-n-roll, garage band style that Cambodian youth embraced.

And I learned from my grandmother that my grandfather (my mother's father) was also a self-taught musician who played the *tro* and drums, and encouraged my mom to listen to music, sing, and dance.[46] He would even take her and her siblings to the Royal Ballet. He was taken away from his family (and likely executed) at the beginning of the Khmer Rouge regime, but my grandmother would sometimes call me by his name, albeit decades later and in the U.S. I am a Buddhist and believe in reincarnation, and that perhaps the spirit of my grandfather is reincarnated in me.

The thread that connects us all, my mother, my father, my grandfather, my grandmother, my brother, and me is music.

The connection that can be formed through music is what started me on the path to where I am today, as not only a performer but also the CEO of a music production company. In 2009, some friends and I formed a band called the Like Me's. We were three Southeast Asian women (2 Cambodians, 1 Filipina) just starting out in San Jose. We soon added a fourth (another Filipina) and played a lot of local gigs.

In 2010, we produced a new recording and video of "Sva Rom Monkiss" ("Monkey Dance Monkey"), a hit song performed by Pen Ron in the 1960s. In addition to the playful song, the video features a modern-day mother and daughter preparing to go to Khmer New Year. The mother at first chides her daughter for what she is wearing, feeling it inappropriate. One of the mother's friends' comments that back in the day, the mother herself would wear short skirts and go to parties and dance at New Year time. The video then flashes back to a scene from New Year 1966, when she indeed meets a young man and dances to "Sva Rom Monkiss." Later, her daughter dances to the same song in the present day, with her mother watching and smiling. The story is based upon the true story of my aunt and my cousin. The common love of music and dance connects them. The video addresses the gap and misunderstandings that have transpired between older and younger Cambodians (especially refugees and their children in the U.S.) and offers music as a means of bridging that gap.

Our goal was to spark interest among Khmer youth in pre-Khmer Rouge music, and in so doing, to create a space for broader dialogue between the generations. We wanted young Cambodians to be able to speak with their parents and older relatives about something other than the Khmer Rouge, and for the parents to have some common ground upon which to build, and then continue talking about other things--anything. The most important step for connection and healing is opening up opportunities for communication and conversation.

Music helped to foster an individual connection between my mother and me as well. While I was visiting home after I had graduated from UC Berkeley, I was playing my guitar and writing music. I had actually been writing some lyrics in English, and I went to my mom and asked if she would be able to write the lyrics in Khmer. She had never written lyrics before, but because Khmer is such a nuanced language--that is, there are certain ways of saying (or singing) things that native speakers would know, whereas a native English speaker translating them might not--and I wanted to hear how she would phrase things.

It took some back-and-forth and rewriting, but the result was a song called "*Pka Proheam Rik Popreay*," which means "Morning Flower Blossoms Beautifully." A month or so later I recorded the song and uploaded it to YouTube, thinking that people might enjoy it. The next morning, the video had more than 75,000 views from all over the world: the U.S., Cambodia, France, Australia, Canada.[47]

Moreover, people were commenting how wonderful it was to hear "original" Cambodian music.

After the Khmer Rouge regime, there were few artists left to create new music. As a result, much of the "Cambodian music" of the 1980s and 1990s was either imported, primarily from Thailand, China, Korea, Vietnam, or the U.S., or hastily produced karaoke covers of foreign songs recorded on bootlegged CDs and VCDs, sold en masse in the markets.

Those who had heard *"Pka Proheam Rik Popreay"* commented that they were longing for more "original" music, not karaoke covers. This planted the seed for me to want to encourage a broader original music movement in Cambodia.

## The Original Music Movement in Cambodia

In 2011, the Like Me's went on tour in Cambodia and performed throughout the country, joining forces with organizations like Friends International and Cambodian Living Arts to raise funds toward improving the lives of Cambodia's children. As part of our performances, we spoke to kids about the importance of art and artists in Cambodia, about taking pride in Cambodian culture and its rich history of creativity and skill, and about empowering themselves to move Cambodia toward a better future.

I absolutely feel that art can heal. Our band's byline was "Healing through Expression, Interpreting Adversity, and Celebrating Adventure." We wanted Cambodians of all generations to connect and heal through art, through music, through song, through dance.

In 2013, I embarked on a solo career, but continued my advocacy on behalf of Cambodian original music. And the more I got to know Cambodia, the more I realized that an independent music scene was already burgeoning among the youth.

**Figures 53 and 54**. Laura Tevary Mam.
Photos courtesy of Baramey Production

New bands were forming, writing, and singing their own songs, and they were not only developing, but tackling contemporary issues as well: the generation gap, domestic violence, depression, materialism, and other challenging topics. I soon realized that the industry involved in copying and selling karaoke music did not want original music to become popular as it really threatened their business model.

However, this gave me the passion I needed to disrupt a system that I felt was not working anymore. It motivated me to write more songs and collaborate more closely with my mom on the lyrics.

And so with this goal in mind, in 2016 my mom and I founded Baramey, a production company dedicated to promoting original artists. We help with financing, event production, marketing and most importantly, brand partnership. We're also working on building a legal framework for copyrighting music and protecting intellectual property, something that didn't exist in the music industry in Cambodia. We are helping Cambodian artists to create a new narrative, based on original compositions and designs rather than illegal imitations, which we knew were a source of shame.

We are selective about who we represent because we want to support creativity and ingenuity. We want artists who can sing, of course, but we also want artists who can create (i.e., write their own music and lyrics and choreograph their own dances, and conceptualize their own videos) and are willing to try new things, including partnerships with other artists. Baramey represents a continuum of genres and sounds, from R & B to pop to hip-hop.

The first band we signed was *Kmeng Khmer* (Khmer Youth), a pop/rap group that now has more than 600,000 followers on YouTube. We also signed a pioneering rap artist named VannDa, who later would completely revolutionize the Cambodian market with his production abilities.

## Coming Full Circle

In 2018, I gave a TEDx talk about the "revolution" of the original music movement in Cambodia. I talked about the necessity of moving away from reproduction or imitation of others' work toward creating original music. Today, in 2021, I can say that there is no longer a need to push for a movement. The music being produced in Cambodia now *is* original--we artists *are* the movement! We have changed the narrative.

In addition to creating original music, we have changed its structure, encouraging collaboration and combining ancient and modern. When rap first became popular, for example, artists used sampling; that is, they took existing audio recordings and repurposed them in their work. There is absolutely nothing wrong with sampling. When artists wanted to use traditional Khmer music played on traditional Khmer instruments, sampling was necessary because there were no post-Khmer Rouge recordings of these works. For the most part, neither the instruments nor the players were available.

However, now we know there are survivors--masters like Kong Nay--and these survivors are not only playing again, but they have inspired a new generation of Khmer youth to learn. We have young Cambodians studying traditional instruments and song forms. They want to learn not only western instruments, but to master the *tro*, the *roneak ek*, the *chapei*, to learn how to chant *smot* as well. The momentum is slow, as the economic return for Khmer classical musicians is nominal, but as contemporary musicians increasingly embrace ancient forms and practices, we will witness a renaissance of interest in traditional music. "Time to Rise" was groundbreaking because it was a new composition that combined both modern and traditional styles (rap and *ayai*), and paid respect to *Lok Kru* Kong Nay, a true master of Cambodian music.

In June 2021, the song broke the record as the most streamed song on YouTube in Cambodian history with 60 million views worldwide. Many have been inspired knowing that an original Cambodian song went viral across Southeast Asia. It was a matter of making the impossible possible, and I hope to support many more of these collaborations. We now have seven artists with Baramey, not including myself.

**Figure 55.** Laura Mam in concert. Photo courtesy of Baramey Production

I believe we have and will continue to reclaim what the Khmer Rouge stole, innovate a new narrative, and unlock Cambodia's vast potential.

After all, this is Cambodia's time to rise.

# Chapter 5

# Fashion Design

# ម៉ូតរចនា

Visit a Buddhist temple in mid-April in California, Minnesota, Illinois, Maryland, or anywhere else in the U.S. where Khmer Americans gather, and you will likely see women dressed in white blouses and colorful silk *sampot* (a length of rectangular cloth, folded or tied in different ways depending upon the desired outcome). Men may wear high-necked shirts created from the same types of silk, and some of the older men might even wear *sampot chang kben*.[48] Dancers wear beautiful *sampot* as well as beaded *sbai* (sashes), elaborate headpieces, jewelry, and belts, ready to perform ceremonial blessings and tell mythic stories through dance during the celebration. Khmer New Year, held in mid-April, is the occasion for wearing festive Khmer clothing. Khmer textiles, and especially certain types of silk, made with specific wefts and patterns and worn in certain ways, equate emphatically with Cambodia and Khmer culture.[49]

## The Significance of Silk

Broadly, there are two categories of traditional Cambodian silk weaving. The first is *sampot hol*, in which the weaver creates the design for the finished piece by dyeing the patterns into the yarn before weaving. *Hol* requires great skill to produce, as a given piece usually has exquisite repeating floral or animal motifs or geometric patterns. Khmer *hol* patterns have been likened to the *ikat* of Indonesia and the *patola* of India, and it is likely different kingdoms traded and shared both goods and techniques with each other. The second is *sampot phamoung*, which is silk created using a twill weave, usually in just one of more than 50 colors, but more than 20 needles are used to create the fabric, which has a distinctive iridescent sheen.[50]

**Figure 56** (left). *Sampot hol.* Photo courtesy of Darachan Ros and Richard Thiounn

**Figure 57** (right). *Sampot phamoung.* Photo courtesy of Darachan Ros and Richard Thiounn

In addition to clothing, the Khmer used silk textiles in royal regalia, such as banners and flags displayed by warrior kings as they went into battle, and parasols to protect royalty and elites from the sun. Lengths of *sampot* were very valuable and monarchs presented them as gifts to rulers of other territories or kingdoms. Brides gave them to prospective grooms prior to marriage. Furthermore, decorative silks called *pidan* with scenes from the life of the Buddha or Buddhist cosmology woven into them often hung in temples. The *pidan* were usually created using the *hol* weft technique and thus are sometimes referred to as *hol pidan*.

Prior to the Khmer Rouge regime, Cambodia produced an estimated 300 thousand pounds of silk per year. Regrettably, the Khmer Rouge detested anything associated with previous regimes or indicative of differences in class status, including ornate or expensive fabrics, so they banned silk-making, silk-weaving, and silk-wearing. The Khmer Rouge destroyed thousands of hectares of mulberry trees, whose leaves are the sole source of nutrition for the silkworms needed to generate the golden cocoons which in turn produce the silk thread. As a result, silk production plummeted; like other arts that were decimated during the regime, silk weaving is only now starting to recover in Cambodia.

Cambodians in the U.S. cherish silk as well; however, other than for Khmer holidays and holy days, such as *pchum ben* (festival of the ancestors) or special occasions such as engagements, weddings, or graduations, they do not wear silk ensembles on an everyday basis.

There are many reasons for this shift away from traditional silk attire, ranging from peer pressure to convenience to cost. For work and school, most Khmer Americans wear less ornate, less expensive, and admittedly for some more comfortable clothing. However, many Cambodian American households have lengths of silk hidden away: some are family heirlooms, some are gifts: some they keep because they are stunning or rare, or perhaps their guardians are just waiting for the proper occasion to present them.

## Cotton Comfort

In addition to silk, Cambodians have used items made from cotton (*kabbas*) for centuries. Cotton grows well during the dry season, and at the beginning of the twentieth century, Cambodia produced and exported cotton in great quantities.[51]

**Figure 58.** The cotton *krama*, recognizable by its checkered pattern, is a staple of Cambodian clothing. Photo: Christine Su

The *krama* (scarf) is one such item made from cotton. One often hears the phrase, "Every Cambodian has a *krama*," and indeed, they are ubiquitous, especially in the countryside.

There are of course beautiful silk *krama*, worn on special occasions, but for everyday use, Cambodians prefer the cotton *krama* because of its versatility. In larger sizes, it functions as a head covering, a towel, a bag, a baby sling, a hammock, and even as a weapon in Khmer martial arts, among dozens of other uses. Because Cambodians use their *krama* so frequently and in so many ways, it must be durable. It must resist tears and holes and last through multiple washings.

It is not uncommon for someone to have and use a *krama* for many years, and as such, the methods for creating cotton *krama* are as important as those for making silk. As with silk, Cambodians weave cotton on large wooden looms, usually kept under people's homes, into scarfs with the recognizable checkered pattern. Nowadays, they vary greatly in colors and lengths.

## Preserving Traditional Textile Creation

Natural disasters and economic pressures have taken a toll on the preservation of weaving traditions. In some cases, flooding has damaged or ruined looms, mulberry trees are becoming scarcer, and caring for the silkworms in various stages proves challenging and time-consuming. Increasingly, importing white silk from Vietnam or China is cheaper than cultivating silkworms or growing cotton in Cambodia; the same logic applies to ready-made chemical rather than natural dyes. Many items are now made by machine, and sellers in the markets may pass off inferior reproductions as authentic pieces.

Because some consumers (tourists and locals alike) are content to buy less expensive products, the weavers themselves find less demand for the time- and skill-intensive textiles produced on a hand loom, and their children and grandchildren prefer to find jobs with higher pay rather than learning and practicing the techniques required to make a quality handmade piece.

One of the ways in which traditional Khmer clothing can be made more appealing to modern lives is by upholding and respecting the elegance and quality of Khmer textiles while also bringing the clothing design into the 21st century. In the U.S., Rajana Threads has dedicated itself to this project. Rajana Threads' creations are based on traditional designs, but the clothing produced is more accessible and suitable for wearing to work, school, etc. Ratha Chuon Kim, the founder and designer for Rajana Threads, shares her story in this section.

## Artist Encounters

I first met Ratha years ago when we both attended a Southeast Asian American advocacy summit in Washington, D.C. Our paths continued to cross at conferences and cultural events over the years, and I often saw her assisting dancers to dress for performances. I am delighted to see that she has brought her vision of "traditional textile meets modern wear" to life.

Another artist in her own right is Krystalyna (Krystal) Chuon, Ratha's youngest sister, whom I met after moving to the San Francisco Bay Area. Krystal assisted with the research and preparation process for Rajana Threads, but also had her own ideas about bringing Khmer fashion into the modern era.

More specifically, Krystal has channeled her creative talent into the Mealea Collection, a line of earrings that combines Khmer imagery drawn from the bas-reliefs of ancient Angkor or inspired by the beauty of the Cambodian landscape with modern materials (e.g. acrylic, mirror). A writer and researcher as well, she draws upon her education in women's and gender studies in designing her pieces.                                    *-C.S.*

**Figure 59**. Krystal Chuon, Facebook post, June 6, 2021.
https://www.facebook.com/photo?fbid=1355979541447825&set=a.1259782
31114635. Accessed 05 July 2021.

## My Story: Ratha Chuon Kim

**Figure 60.** Ratha Chuon Kim, wearing one of her own *ikat* designs. Photo courtesy of Rajana Threads

I was born in Khao-I-Dang refugee camp, on the border between Cambodia and Thailand in 1980, the year after the Khmer Rouge were overthrown. I am the third of eight children, and the last to be born outside of the U.S. My younger siblings are all U.S.-born.

Because I was born in the camp, I don't have any first-hand memories of life under the Khmer Rouge, but I have heard many stories from my parents. My mom has told me, for example, that during the Khmer Rouge regime, she up at dawn to work in the fields. If you didn't know how to farm, you had to pretend you did, because the Khmer Rouge believed that those who did not know were elites or wealthy. Oddly enough, my mother came from a farming family but never learned to farm. Her father had been the sole farmer and with his work the family was able to earn more than enough to live, so the kids didn't have to farm at all. As a result, when forced to grow and harvest rice under the Khmer Rouge, my mother was one of the slowest workers, and one day, a soldier took notice. Fortunately, when the other women in her group saw that, they helped her to meet the daily quota.

She will never forget these women, she told me, although after the war they lost touch and she is unsure whether any of them is still alive.

Furthermore, my mother was light-complexioned, and feared the Khmer Rouge would think she was Sino-Cambodian. Ethnic Chinese were among those targeted for execution. She feared for her life every day.

I learned a little about my father's belief system through his story of life under Pol Pot. In particular, he told me that at one point a Khmer Rouge soldier recognized him as a member of the Lon Nol army, and consequently seized and shackled him. He was destined for execution. He told me that years before, as a child, he lived with Buddhist monks and had been educated in the temple, where he learned many *sel* (sacred chants). After he was captured, he began to chant these *sel* over and over while trying to loosen the shackles. Fortunately, before the Khmer Rouge soldier came back, the shackles came loose, and he was able to escape. He ran and searched for my mother and other family members and once he found them, started the long, arduous trek to Thailand, eventually arriving in the refugee camp, where as I mentioned I was born. It took some time and shuttling through five different countries (Thailand, the Philippines, Germany, England, and Egypt), but we eventually resettled in Boston, Massachusetts in 1981.

## Moving to the Bay Area

In the mid-1980s, we ended up relocating to San Francisco, for several reasons. First, as Cambodians we were not accustomed to the cold Boston weather! My mother became very ill, and at one point my father slipped on the ice and injured his back. Their doctors recommended that they try to move to a warmer climate to improve their overall health. Second, when we had lived in Boston for several years, my father learned that some of his Lon Nol army colleagues had also survived and were living in San Francisco. He was understandably eager to reconnect with them. So, it was decided that we were moving. I was devastated to be leaving my life in Boston--my friends, my school, and a cousin to whom I was especially close--but my father felt it would be best for the family.

My father initially planned to sell our car so we could fly to San Francisco. Someone offered to buy his car and my father was going to meet him, but then he found himself in a nearly unbelievable situation: the person who had contacted him about purchasing the car turned out to be *the same Khmer Rouge solider* who had held him captive during the Pol Pot regime! How he got to the U.S., we do not know. But when he asked to meet privately to buy the car, my father was terrified--who knows what could have awaited him at that meeting!

Instead of meeting him, he loaded all of us (my mother, two older siblings, me, and one younger sibling) into the car and we drove to San Francisco. The cross-country trip took seven days, and remember, we did not have GPS in cars at that time (this is 1985), so we used a paper map. But he had escaped the Khmer Rouge once again.

We landed in the Tenderloin area of San Francisco, where many Cambodians lived at the time. At first, we stayed in the apartment of my father's friend, but there just wasn't enough room for all of us, so my mother, my brother and I moved temporarily to the Woodward/Mission area. Eventually, we found our own small place back in the Tenderloin. There were many Khmer businesses and cultural activities there, which helped us to acclimate to our new home. However, life in San Francisco was very, very challenging. My family, which had increased to eight by this time, lived all together in a studio apartment. We slept like egg rolls. There was only one small bathroom. The Tenderloin itself was crime-infested and riddled with gangs and turf wars, which was particularly difficult for my brother.

We decided to move from the Tenderloin to Bayview-Hunter's Point, which allowed us more space but not more peace. There were few Asians there, and even fewer Cambodians! My classmates and neighbors were mostly African American, and I didn't have much interaction with White people from elementary through high school years, apart from school staff or teachers. I remember my surprise when I went to college at San Francisco State and realized that there were so many White people on the campus. I had never been in this environment and didn't even know how to act!

However, growing up among communities of color shaped me into who I am today. I believe it helped me to understand the value of tolerance, of patience, of cultural differences.

While we were not in an economically affluent neighborhood, our family stuck by each other in the Bayview and we maintained our Khmer culture through language (I am fluent in Khmer), music, food, and yes, Khmer clothing. Even though money was scarce, my mother insisted that all of us kids have at least one Khmer silk outfit appropriate for special occasions.

A few months before Khmer New Year, she would take us to a local seamstress to have an outfit made. I would get so excited, because I got to pick out the fabric and describe the type of outfit I wanted. I loved seeing all the different patterns and cuts, and spending time with my mother during this process. I think this is where my love of design, and especially Khmer-style design was born. My love of Cambodian textiles got stronger each time I saw someone in traditional attire.

**Finding myself**

I have been sketching since I was a young girl and dreamed of doing something professionally with Khmer textiles and fashion. For many years, however, this remained a dream. By the time I was a teenager, our family had eight children--it was chaos! My parents' time had to be divided among us, with most of the burden falling on my mom.

Like many teenagers, I felt misunderstood and I began to act out. My older sister was very well-behaved and was more of a traditional Khmer girl: that is, she stayed home rather than going out, she knew how to cook, etc. I was more rebellious, and I recall arguing with my parents frequently. I would go out a lot, hanging out at bonfires on the beach late into the night. Once, when my cousin from Boston was visiting, I stayed out all night, and wow, was there hell to pay when I got home. My father was so, so angry. I know now that his anger came from a place of fear and worry, but at the time, it was hard to deal with. I began to distance myself from my parents for a while. Looking back, sometimes I feel sad, because I don't feel like I had as close a relationship with my family as I could have while I was growing up.

I found my escape, believe it or not, in school. I loved school, especially my art and drawing classes. I became really involved in and passionate about sketching, drawing, painting, sculpting. When I sketch, I can lose track of time. Even now I sometimes wake up in the middle of the night with an idea and feel compelled to get it on paper.

I also loved singing, dancing, and acting. I loved being able to express myself through these mediums. I was fascinated by Khmer dance. I loved the costumes, the movements, and the music of both classical and folk dance. Most Khmer dancers start to train at a very early age, but when I was in high school, a group of friends and I went to the temple to ask if we could join or form a dance group.

We did, and I danced for a few years, which filled my spirit. I didn't see myself becoming a professional dancer (as I mentioned most dancers have years and years of training from a young age), but it helped me connect to my community and I continued to support Khmer arts by teaching my friends the dances that I had learned. At this time also, I began volunteering with local organizations.

## Honing my design skills

After college I became the executive director of what at the time was one of the only Cambodian non-profit community organizations in the Bay Area. There I continued my work with Khmer arts. I hired dance teachers to start a dance program because I knew I wanted to continue to support Khmer dance in some way. I often assisted the teachers in helping to dress the dancers in preparation for their performances. I started to familiarize myself with the appropriate costumes for different characters and stories and learned how to make sure the dancers were fitted properly (sometimes we even had to sew the dancers into their costumes!). The details of the beautiful fabrics and designs worn by the dancers enthralled me, and I continued doing this for years. I also organized numerous cultural events. Outside of work, I was often asked to dress people for weddings, holidays, and events, and happily did so, all on a volunteer basis, for more than 10 years.

When I was at work or at these events, I myself wore clothes with Khmer elements and touches, mostly of my own design, and people complimented me on them. I began to experiment, incorporating traditional patterns and fabrics into more contemporary styles. People then began asking me where they could buy the pieces I wore. The idea of opening a business centered around Khmer clothing was starting to stir in me again, but at the time, life didn't allow for it to become anything more than an idea.

I spent years working in different positions, both corporate and nonprofit, starting a family, going to school (I completed my Bachelor's degree in Asian American Studies and my Masters of Public Administration, or MPA degree), and supporting the community. To relieve my stress, I would sketch, and dream about running my own fashion/design business someday. But not until 2019 was I able to bring my dreams into reality.

## Rajana Threads: Meeting Prospective Partners

I embarked on this project very, very thoughtfully. With the help of some family members, I researched to find out what the landscape of Khmer weavers was at that time--that is, who was already (or still) creating textiles in Cambodia? Cambodia changes so quickly! We wanted to find out what organizations for Khmer women (especially women-owned) already existed and hoped to partner with one that was both dedicated to authentic methods and employed local Khmer women. This was an arduous (though very worthwhile!) process.

Because Rajana Threads was a brand-new entity and unknown, either stateside or in Cambodia, artists in Cambodia understandably found it difficult to trust us. We started with electronic inquiries (Facebook, Instagram, WhatsApp, Messenger, email, etc.) for the initial outreach to many different organizations. Some expressed interest, while others didn't; and of course, some didn't respond at all.

However, we were able to narrow down our list to a few to speak with by phone/Skype/ZOOM. In those initial conversations, we had to make our intentions very clear, and later, it was very important that we met in person with prospective partners before anything officially moved forward. In addition to them trusting us, we had to trust them: we had to know that the working conditions in the organization were safe and fair, and that their "why" matched with ours. That is, why did this organization come into being? What is its mission and vision?

It's really important to me that we support Khmer women, especially those from vulnerable backgrounds. I want to help empower them by helping them earn a steady income. In addition, I want to support local artisans by promoting authentic handwoven textiles. So much faux fabric has saturated our markets which has damaged the indigenous weaving industry. If we can get people to see the value in investing in an authentic piece, this will help our weaving culture to thrive.

It took us more than a year to finally come to agreement with several organizations: one in Phnom Penh, one in Siem Reap, and one in Takeo. We had to work the kinks out, as working internationally can be tricky.

There are many things to think about: time differences, cultural differences (I am Khmer, but I found out I am more Khmer American than I thought), language nuances (who knew there were so many words for "thread"?), upfront costs and profit-sharing, and dozens of other things we learned as we went along. Finally, in 2019, we were able to officially open Rajana Threads!

**Figure 61**. Rajana Threads logo, ©2019, which incorporates designs used in Khmer textiles. Image courtesy of Ratha Chuon Kim and Rajana Threads

### Traditional Textile Meets Modern Wear

One of the ways in which Rajana Threads aims to make Khmer clothing more appealing to modern consumers is by bringing the design into the 21st century. Our byline reads: "traditional textile meets modern wear."

I have been honing this concept for years. As I mentioned I used to wear Khmer clothes to my workplace, but these weren't always full-on traditional Khmer New Year outfits. Rather, I would wear a top with Khmer accents with a pair of modern work pants, for example, or a Khmer scarf with a modern dress. I feel like this is a good introduction for people who don't know anything about Cambodian or Khmer clothes, or who feel it would be too big a jump to just start wearing complete Khmer outfits, to transition. You don't have to go from wearing jeans and t-shirts directly to a *sampot chang kben* or a long skirt with a gold embroidered *sbai*!

Admittedly, this is a break from convention, but young people are more likely to embrace Khmer textiles (and keep Khmer culture alive) if they fit into their current lifestyle. Many of us have had the experience of wearing a fitted Khmer silk skirt to go to the temple and then sitting on the floor in a very warm space for a long period of time, quite uncomfortably. We may be able to do this on special occasions or for religious ceremonies, but otherwise, that skirt will stay in the closet.

With Rajana Threads, I have designed pieces that you can wear in the 21$^{st}$ century, for everyday activities. One of my very first designs was the *Monyda*. The reception has been great!

Another product we have introduced with our pieces is *seung*. *Seung* is a strong, beautiful cotton blend, but it hasn't received the same attention as Khmer silk. *Seung* is very appropriate and can help to support traditional Khmer design because it can be woven like silk *hol* or *phamoung*, but it is less costly and easier to produce. The *seung* is woven, cut, and sewn in Cambodia by Khmer women, but the structure, length, and cut of the garments themselves, designed by Rajana Threads, are more modern. The types of clothing we make using *seung*, like the *Monyda*, are more accessible to younger audiences and suitable for wearing to work or school.

Furthermore, *seung* "breathes" better than silk. One of my favorite pieces is our "Soriya" *seung* pants.

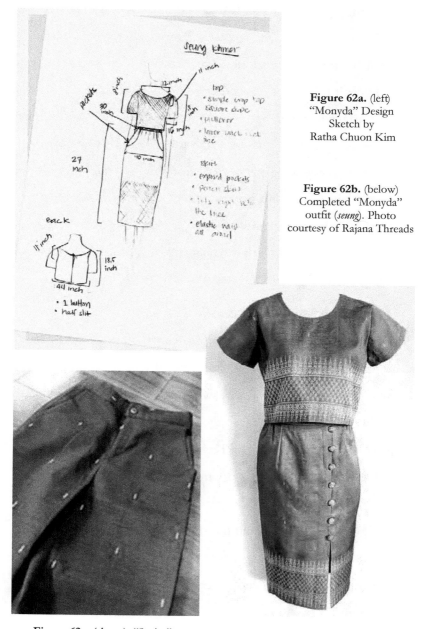

**Figure 62a.** (left) "Monyda" Design Sketch by Ratha Chuon Kim

**Figure 62b.** (below) Completed "Monyda" outfit (*seung*). Photo courtesy of Rajana Threads

**Figure 62c.** (above). "Soriya" pants crafted using *seung*. Photos courtesy of Rajana Threads

In the U.S., women wear pants or jeans to work a lot of the time. We wear skirts, too, but it's nice to have the option of wearing pants that also reflect Cambodian culture. They are made from *seung*, but also have distinctive *phamoung* patterns. It might be more of a jump to wear pants with a *hol* pattern, but we haven't ruled that out yet!

And we haven't abandoned the use of silk. We would love to create with silk, but until acceptance of Khmer styles in general is more widespread, it is not economically feasible to work solely in silk. Our hope is that once we build the business and people become familiar with our brand, we will be able to afford to make and sell high-quality silk items as well. So Rajana Threads is a longer-term investment.

## Developing My Unique Style

If I had to choose a piece that represents me and my style, it would be the *Pailin*. I called this piece the Pailin because I was inspired by the Kola minority, whom we believe migrated from Burma (Myanmar) centuries ago to what is now Pailin province in western Cambodia. The Kola women would wear blouses with brocade and buttons down the front, which I included in my design.

But I also modernized the outfit. Rather than a straight or tube skirt, for example, ours is a mini skirt with an "A" line. The top is sleeveless, reminiscent of the 1960s or 70s--that's my style.

**Figure 63a.** (right)
"Pailin" top and skirt
Sketch by
Ratha Chuon Kim

**Figure 63b.** (left)
The artist wearing a sample
of her own design, the
"Pailin." Photo courtesy of
Rajana Threads

### *What's Next?* for Rajana Threads and for Me

During the pandemic, my husband unfortunately lost his job for a while. If there was a silver lining to the situation, however, it was that he has been wonderful in helping Rajana Threads get off of the ground. He helped with mailing items and taking photos for our social media and website, and never complained about all of the inventory in our home. For me, working from home, I no longer had an hour commute, so I had that time to think, to create, to focus on my family and the business.

Still, given the pandemic, during which many have chosen or have been asked to work from home, there is less demand for office-appropriate work wear. As a result, our business has waned. But we will persevere. We know that this situation is temporary, and that people will go back to offices and classrooms eventually. This is the realization of my dream, and we are just getting started. It's definitely a labor of love!

We recently launched a jewelry line called *jeevit*, which means "life." The pieces are made from reclaimed bullet casings, crafted into our original designs by Khmer women. Each individual piece is a work of art, but from a broader perspective, these creations very much embody the spirit and resilience of Khmer people, especially Khmer women.

Out of dire situations, Khmer women have been able to create beauty. From the sadness and grief felt by those in the refugee camps, for example, women began to bring back the elegance of Khmer dance. Those who could remember how to dance transformed uncertainty into opportunity by teaching youth. Similarly, in these pieces, the bullet casings, clearly symbols of violence and killing, are transformed into art pieces with Khmer script, reading *sontapheap* (peace), *songkheum* (hope), or *sereipheap* (freedom).

My hope is that Rajana Threads can both contribute to a lasting legacy in the arts and help Khmer women become self-sufficient. To me, Rajana Threads is much more than a clothing brand. It is a source of cultural pride.

**Figure 64.** Bracelets from the *Jeevit* jewelry line. Photo courtesy of Ratha Chuon Kim & Rajana Threads

**Figure 65.** Metal bullet casings before they are transformed into jewelry. Photos courtesy of Ratha Chuon Kim & Rajana Threads

## My Story: Krystal M. Chuon

I was born in San Francisco, California in 1993, and am the youngest (*koun poeuv*) of 8 children--5 girls and 3 boys. Being the youngest affords me a unique perspective on being Cambodian, because my parents and several older siblings were born and raised in Cambodia; one was born in the refugee camps before

**Figure 66.** Krystal M. Chuon holding a copy of her chapbook, *Follow the Mekong Home.* Photo: Christine Su

moving to the U.S.; and the rest, including me, were born and raised in the U.S. These different backgrounds and histories shape how we each experience and react to given situations and to each other. It is as if there are three generations of Chuons: the 1.0, the 1.5, and the 2.0.

I grew up hearing stories about my parents' lives in Cambodia under the Khmer Rouge. It was normal to hear at least one story a day. They constantly reminded my siblings and me how hard their lives had been, working the fields in the hot sun, exhausted, frightened, and anxious, never knowing what the next day might bring or whether they would survive to find out. Curiously, these stories were often told in a joking manner, which I believe was a coping mechanism they used to distance themselves from the harsh realities they endured. Other times, they were told as stern lessons, reminding us how privileged and lucky we were to grow up and live in America. While I hadn't experienced life under Khmer Rouge myself, the vividness of these family accounts instilled in me both horror for the atrocities and respect for the resilience required to move beyond them. There is great power in these stories, and relatedly, I feel a great responsibility to make sure they are never forgotten.

## I am Khmer

I have always known that I am Cambodian, even though exactly what that meant wasn't always clear, especially to others. I remember a conversation I had with another student in the third grade, for example. My family had just moved to the suburbs, and I was the new student in my school. At lunch time I sat down next to some of my classmates, who identified themselves as Filipino and were part of the small group of Asians at the school. One of them heard I was the new girl and asked me if I was Filipino, too.

"No," I replied. "I'm Cambodian," to which she responded with another question: "What's that?"

I can't recall what I replied in turn, but thinking back, I feel that this moment (and similar moments in which my identity was questioned) pushed me to identify constantly and unremittingly as Cambodian to anyone who asked.

I chose to embark on a personal mission to immerse myself in the community and center (almost) everything I did around my Khmer identity. In my youth and adulthood, I volunteered with my sisters, Ratha and Samantha, throughout the Bay Area at various events within Cambodian communities. In school, I both delved into Cambodian history and researched current issues, producing essays on topics ranging from the importance of classical dance in Cambodian American communities to the problem of sex trafficking in Cambodia. Being active in the Cambodian and Southeast Asian community and intentional with my work allowed me to further understand myself and identity.

I have often heard and read stories by first- and second-generation Cambodians about struggling to fit in with the mainstream or wishing they were White, but I was always proud of my culture, even if those around me couldn't understand it. While Cambodia (and thus being Cambodian) was imperfect, I loved my "Khmerness" and have made it my lifelong mission to explore all that entails.

## (Re)turning "home"

I first visited Cambodia in 2005 when I was 12 years old. As a child, I had been adamant about emphasizing that I was Cambodian, but the trip made me aware of how American I really was. The feeling of not fitting in others had described suddenly made sense. I remember feeling so disconnected from my relatives, especially when some continually asked me if I knew how to speak the Khmer language.

Although I had learned Khmer growing up in a bilingual household, I wasn't speaking it consistently at home as I got older, and in U.S. schools we of course spoke and wrote in English. So I understood what people in Cambodia were saying much of the time, but felt too intimidated to speak Khmer myself because I didn't want to flounder over my words and look foolish. I usually stayed quiet around my relatives, choosing to save myself from embarrassment.

Upon my return to the U.S., however, I was even more determined to learn about my heritage and culture, and to find peace as a second-generation Cambodian/American. I made a second trip to Cambodia four years later when I was 16 years old, feeling more prepared mentally, emotionally, and physically. As a result, my experience was different; I felt more comfortable, more at home. The environment felt more familiar than the first trip. However, when it came to speaking in Khmer, I still felt uncomfortable, like when I was 12.

There is one particular incident that's still a running family joke and a blatant reminder that our (meaning Cambodian American) identities will always be questioned in Cambodia. As a family we course wanted to see the beautiful temples in the northern part of the country. I didn't know that by the time of the second trip, visitors had to pay to see Angkor Wat and other temples within the Angkor Archaeological Park. During the first trip, I was unaware about having to pay for an entrance pass as my parents took care of anything regarding that, so I assumed we could freely walk around.

Without that knowledge, once when we stopped the car at a sizable temple, I was one of the first to get out, along with my eldest sister. I headed toward it excitedly. Before I had taken more than a few steps up the stone stairs, a man with a walkie-talkie came up to us, shouting in Khmer. I couldn't understand him at first due to the distance, nor did my eldest sister hear him clearly, so she continued climbing, not realizing I had been delayed. Suddenly, I felt panicked. I didn't know what to do. Was he some kind of security guard? Was I in trouble? A part of me wanted to continue walking up and into the temple to be with my sister, a native Khmer speaker, but I was frozen in place, afraid I had done something wrong and would face repercussions if I avoided him.

Still confused, I stepped down toward the guard. He asked me if I was Khmer. In my mind, I thought well, of course I am! But the words couldn't come out. I was too shaken up to respond, especially in Khmer, and if I responded in English, he would likely doubt my identity and block me and my family from exploring the temple. Then one of my other sisters, Ratha, and her husband exited the car and the guard questioned them too. They stated that they were Khmer (in the Khmer language) in an assertive tone. With them by my side, I worked up the courage to respond in kind, but the guard wouldn't budge for any of us. There was some more discussion, but the situation by that point was so frustrating for me that I gave up and just headed back to the car. The guard eventually let my sister, her husband,

and my younger nephews, who had come out of the car, too but weren't questioned, pass through.

I had heard about the whole "speak Khmer to get a discount/free entrance" concept, but it hadn't occurred to me in that moment because I was unaware of the park entrance pass requirement, and I still felt uncomfortable speaking Khmer at the time. This questioning of my identity at the temple continued to bother me over the years. I felt "not Khmer enough" and othered, having to prove my identity only through language and not by other parameters, such as by way of my parents, my lineage.

I later learned I could have bypassed the questioning by showing my K Visa, given to foreign nationals who are ethnically Cambodian. It was like a golden ticket. All we had to do was present it to the guards (if they asked for an entrance pass) and they'd let us in. I made sure to carry my passport (with the K visa in it) with me during my subsequent trips to avoid similar incidents.

During my fourth trip to Cambodia, when I was 23, my family visited Siem Reap again. As we ascended toward the main entrance of Angkor Wat, one of the guards approached me first and asked for my entrance pass. I replied, without hesitation, "*Kyom koun Khmer, Pu*," and he nodded and apologized, noting that he thought we were of another ethnicity. It was a small win, but a win nonetheless, and I didn't even have to take out my K Visa! I was better prepared, armed with knowledge, and much more comfortable speaking Khmer than during previous trips.

**Figure 67**. Sample "K" visa issued by the Cambodian embassy for foreign nationals of Cambodian ethnicity or descent. Source: https://www.embassyofcambodiadc.org/khmer-visa.html,

Reflecting on this made me realize how trapped I felt by language and being judged for my non-fluent Khmer-speaking skills. While I still struggle, I try my best to speak Khmer when I can, even if my sentences don't always come out right!

**Becoming an Artist**

While I stumbled in Khmer, I am a skilled writer in English, and love to put my thoughts on paper. I started reading Khmer writers like Bunkong Tuon and Monica Sok whose works confront different ideas about race, ethnicity, gender, and class in the U.S., and relatedly, about racism, ethnocentrism, gender bias, and classism. They also address dual identity, family dynamics, and the influence of our ancestors on our contemporary lives. I am definitely drawn to poetry, both theirs and my own. I love the nuances of words and the intensity of emotions they can produce, and the depth of expression I can achieve in writing poetry.

In my adulthood, I learned more about the fact that part of my family is *Khmer Krom* (on my mother's side): that is, they are ethnic Khmer and live in the Mekong Delta in what is today Vietnam but used to be part of the Khmer Empire centuries ago. They are forced to live as a minority on their ancestral lands. I found myself searching for a way to reconcile these feelings of dual identity, displacement, and the threat of erasure of certain elements of Khmer history, turning to poetry to do so. I collected some of these thoughts in a chapbook I published, called *Follow the Mekong Home* (my first ever published book), in which I also explore the fluctuating definitions and unpredictable changes to the concept of "home" and my lifelong search for it.

One of the interesting things about being second-generation and a young person in the U.S. is that I grew up in a digital-forward environment. That is, my classmates and I learned about the value of the Internet and the potential of web design early on, and navigating them became part of our skill set, things we were pretty comfortable using. I dabbled a bit in online platforms and media in middle and high school but didn't truly use these skills to help me develop as an artist until after college, when I had more free time.

At that time, I started drawing and painting more, and shared my work online where I discovered a big art community and began to connect more with other Cambodians.

I developed a substantial Instagram following over time, and my Cambodian followers encouraged me to share my art with a wider audience, which I did. This led to selling prints of my artwork, a big accomplishment for me. I then realized that I could combine my love of traditional art forms (e.g., drawing and painting), my desire to learn and incorporate more about my history and culture in my work, and my skills in digital media to create innovative and unique designs. This realization ultimately led to the creation of the Mealea Collection.

## The Mealea Collection

ម្ហាលា / *mielie/*
*n. lei, wreath, garland, braid made of flowers*
*n. row, line, series, succession, set*
*n. hat (usage: royal)* ETY: *Sanskrit, Pali māla*

Excerpted from
www.mealeacollection.com

The *Mealea* Collection encompasses my passions in art, history, and women's/gender studies, emphasizing Khmer-inspired contemporary earrings that represent my commitment to cultural preservation in my own special way. Earrings have been part of Khmer regalia and fashion since ancient times. One can find dozens of different types of earrings and other jewelry depicted on the walls of the Angkor temples, for example, and archaeologists have uncovered extraordinary centuries-old physical pieces, cast in bronze and at one time attached to the stone sculptures themselves.

I learned in my research that midwives would often pierce a female baby's ears as part of the naming ceremony, so it's safe to say that earrings definitely played a major role in Cambodians' body decoration from early in their lives. I remember that my grandmother used to wear a type of earring called *kao dong trong*, an oblong shape that was thicker at one end than the other with a round flat top that, in some iterations, may be accented by a jewel. The thicker end was pushed through the pierced ear and would hang below with the flat part resting above on the lobe so that the earring would not fall out. As a child, I was always fascinated by her earrings and how they reminded me of flathead nails.

There is a wonderful book called *Khmer Costumes and Ornaments of the Devatas of Angkor Wat* by Sappho Marchal that features her drawings of *apsara* and *devata*, including intricate details of their clothing, jewelry, and headdresses. I draw a lot of my inspiration from her sketches of these ancient accessories! I also apply the knowledge that I gained from my college major in women's and gender studies. I feel I provide unique perspectives as a 2nd-generation Khmer woman and reflect that in my creative endeavors, representing and celebrating Khmer culture to the fullest.

It would be challenging to re-cast these ancient earrings today as accurately as they were made in centuries past. The earrings were quite heavy, evident by the stretched earlobes depicted on the sculptures, and would not be comfortable to wear today. More ornamental styles were likely worn only by royalty or elite women.

Yet the *Mealea* Collection earring series embodies the spirit of these ancient designs--*kbach*, floral motifs, *apsara*--in modern forms that all can wear, using lightweight acrylic materials made with cutting-edge technology.

I conduct research for each design, and each piece has its own story. The *Phka Botum* ផ្កាបុទុម design, for example, takes inspiration from the lotus bud-shaped towers of Angkor Wat and other lotus imagery throughout the temple complex. The rose-gold color of this piece represents the pink color of the lotus, while the curved lines represent the waters in which the buds will rise and bloom into a beautiful flower.

The *Romdoul* រំដួល earrings are part of the *"Kyom Khmer"* ("I am Khmer") series. The *romdoul* is the national flower of Cambodia, beloved for its light-yellow color and fragrant blooms. The earrings are created using a lightweight, shimmery gold acrylic, and wearing them exhibits pride in being a child of the Kingdom of Cambodia (*koun Khmer*).

## What's Next for Me

The Covid-19 pandemic did affect my mental health and I needed much of 2020 to adjust to this new way of living. However, I channeled any anxiety, fears, or feelings of isolation into creating. I opened a new online shop to sell my art prints, stickers, 'zines, and book in the spring of 2020 which morphed into the Mealea Collection. I had to believe that the pandemic shouldn't hinder my progress and overall determination to continue creating, writing, and sharing knowledge with others.

Keeping busy with these endeavors not only improved my mental health but enabled me to step out of my comfort zone and explore other creative art forms as well. Turning my ideas and drawings into something accessible in the 21$^{st}$ century is a beautiful, fulfilling creative process. I especially enjoy seeing others wearing my designs.

**Figure 68.** *Phka Botum* earrings, from the Flouresence Series. Photo: Krystal M. Chuon.

**Figure 69.** *Romdoul* earrings, from the *Kyom Khmer* (I am Khmer) Series. Photo: Krystal M. Chuon.

If I could go back in time and speak with a younger version of myself, I would tell myself to continue pursuing art, writing, and creating, because doing so will sustain you through the darkest of times.

*This Body of Mine* by Krystal M. Chuon

my body has carried me up holy mountains
through lush californian wilds
and crowded concrete jungles
i like the way it pushes on when my mind says, "i can't"
the way it twists and folds and bends
but not the way it betrays me
when my nerves wreak havoc
waiting for imminent doom that doesn't arrive
or in my dreams
when i can't run away fast enough
and when i fall
sending shockwaves along my bones
my body carries the laughter and joy of a thousand ancestors
over oceans, time, and space
forever fluid
flowing
and free[52]

# Chapter 6

## Culinary Arts
## ចម្អិនអាហារ

In writing about Cambodian food in the U.S., many so-called "foodies" make almost-immediate comparisons to Thai or Vietnamese food. But doing so does Cambodia and Khmer cooks an injustice, because while it reflects influences from its geographic neighbors, as well as other global tastes, Khmer cuisine is much more complex than a "kind of like [Thai/Vietnamese/Chinese] food" descriptor.

Khmer food and flavors stand on their own, even if less recognizable to Western-trained palates. Because of the relative lack of visibility of Cambodian cooking, especially in the U.S., some writers have as gone as far to say that Khmer cuisine needs to be "saved from extinction." This is not entirely accurate; if there are Cambodians, there will be Cambodian food.

What is more accurate is to say that following the Khmer Rouge regime, much of the knowledge about specific Cambodian recipes and cooking methods died as Cambodians with that knowledge themselves died. Furthermore, during the regime Cambodians were given very little food--oftentimes only tiny portions of watery rice porridge--and after the regime fell, food was something necessary to survive, perhaps with understandably less attention to culinary techniques or exact ingredients than to availability. Consequently, recipes may have been recreated, modified, or adapted to different circumstances and environments.

For numerous reasons, Khmer food has not crossed over into American eateries as quickly as have other Asian cuisines.

As mentioned above, in the aftermath of the Khmer Rouge and refugee camps, Cambodians were focused on survival. Few would have had the financial resources or business know-how to open restaurants. One might also maintain that the American palate was not yet ready for some of the unfamiliar flavors (sour tamarind or fermented fish, for example) intrinsic to Khmer cooking--at least, not on a large scale that warranted the risk of a restaurant venture.

Staples in Cambodian cooking like galangal, lemongrass, kaffir lime leaves and palm sugar were not always readily available in their new cities or neighborhoods, and it would have been challenging to purchase the bulk amounts needed to cook for large numbers of people. Further, eating Khmer food is associated with family. Prior to the Khmer Rouge regime, Cambodians would often leave work and return home for lunch to eat shared plates with their families, even in the cities. One of the methods used by the Khmer Rouge to break down the family unit was forcing Cambodians to eat silently sitting in communal dining halls in large groups with other workers. A return to eating food served at home represented a return to normalcy and life before the Khmer Rouge.

This is not to say that Cambodians in the U.S. are not entrepreneurial; on the contrary, they have been quite successful in opening independent businesses, such as donut shops, particularly in California.

The Cambodian "donut dream" began with Ted Ngoy, who came to the U.S. in 1975 and, with no background in business (or donut making), entered a manager's training program with Winchell's Donuts. Ngoy learned not only how to make donuts (while there are similar sweet items in Cambodia, donuts are an American creation), but all of the aspects of managing a store as well. Not long thereafter, he opened his own donut shop, and when more Cambodian refugees started to come to the U.S., Ngoy subsequently helped them, first providing jobs and then teaching them how to run their own donut businesses. As a result, hundreds of Cambodian donut shops were launched in the 1980s.

In recent years there has been more interest in Cambodian food and cooking, especially by members of the 1.5 and 2.0 generations of Cambodian Americans. They have begun to conduct research into pre-war and regional cuisine, writing down recipes theretofore passed down only through oral tradition or hands-on experience.

The third issue of *The Stilt House*, for example, a magazine published by the Cambodian American Literary Arts Association (CALAA) in 2021, focuses on food--both literal meal creation and the metaphorical meanings of Khmer food in contemporary Cambodian American culture.[53] Food is sustenance, both physical and emotional. Food is connection, memory, love, family, identity.

At a gathering of young Khmer American women several years ago, I brought out a copy of *Nhum: Recipes from a Cambodian Kitchen* (2019), then a just-published book by Rotanak Ros, also known as "Chef Nak." The women excitedly asked, "'Where did you get that?" and "Can I borrow this?" and proceeded to pour through the book's beautiful pages, taking snapshots of some recipes with their phone cameras. Their comments in reaction to unexpectedly discovering this book at a party revealed just how much Cambodian food meant to them, how it symbolized connection to family, culture, and history. Their feelings mirrored the sentiments of Chef Nak herself, who wrote in her introduction, "These dishes are our legacy – a legacy that was nearly lost and is now saved for future generations."[54]

**Artist Encounters**

This section explores the stories of two Cambodian American chefs: Visoth Tarak Ouk (aka "Chef T"), whose elevated Cambodian fusion fare was born of both struggle and success, and Mercredi Uy, whose experiences range from donut entrepreneur to food educator to personal chef.

I first encountered "Chef T" at a Khmer Student Coalition Conference hosted by Cal State Long Beach in 2016. Chef T was one of the opening speakers. I hadn't yet met him, but it was clear that he was well-known in the Long Beach community.

He started his speech with jokes to warm up the crowd, but his words quickly turned more solemn. He spoke of how remarkable it was to see the Khmer community come together for such an event, supporting each other. That kind of support, he remarked, wasn't easy to come by when he was the age of most of the students in the audience. He spoke about getting involved with the wrong crowd, doing things he regrets, and falling into the deepest trench imaginable.

But, he noted, he believed in second chances, which meant he needed to believe in himself, and so he changed his life. Cooking was the artistic medium that enabled him to do that. His story was so heartfelt, I knew that someday when I wrote this book (it was in my mind even then), I wanted to include him in it.

The second individual featured in this chapter is Mercredi Uy. I encountered Mercredi when I decided to search for donuts without eggs. This is an arbitrary detail, but I am allergic to eggs. Donuts, which as mentioned have been a part of Cambodian entrepreneurship in California since the 1980s, are almost always made with eggs, and I felt disappointed that I couldn't eat them. I had seen a documentary about Ted Ngoy, the "donut king," and was daydreaming about donuts.[55] I felt compelled to find out if there were any (Cambodian) donuts made without eggs. I started researching and asking around, and I happened upon a newspaper story about Mercredi, who at the time was working for a vegan, organic donut shop. Paradise found.

I reached out to Mercredi to find out more about vegan donuts and how he got involved with this shop, and the more I learned about him, the more I knew his story needed to be shared as well.                                                    -C.S.

## My Story: Visoth Tarak Ouk ("Chef T")

My parents came as refugees to the United States from Khao-I-Dang refugee camp on the Thai border, where I was born. They landed first in Oakland, CA.

In our house in Oakland, I remember watching my mother and grandmother cook, and was fascinated with

**Figure 70.** Chef T.
Photo courtesy of Tarak Ouk

everything: the smells, the activity, the conversations between them, from the time I was a toddler. I wanted to cook too, and when I was about four, I was *daam baay* (cooking) myself, making eggs and searing steak, especially when my mom and grandmother were out of the house. I think I'm lucky I didn't burn the house down!

I started to learn about the different Khmer tastes--that is, there are spices and spice combinations that are uniquely Khmer, and you really have to learn them from someone who knows how to create and use them. At that time (1980s), some of the ingredients were pretty difficult to find, like lemongrass, galangal, and tamarind.

They weren't in a regular market, but we had to have them for Cambodian cooking. You could say I developed that *kroeung* ប្រគ្រឿង flavor profile very early on and have carried it with me throughout my life.[56]

When I was eight, we moved and resettled in Long Beach. Nowadays, when people think of Long Beach, maybe they think of sand and sun, but back in the day, it was far from paradise. Our parents were traumatized by the Khmer Rouge regime and its aftermath and were focused on survival, which sometimes meant working several jobs at all hours of the day and night to support us kids (I'm one of 10!). We were put into schools where we faced cultural and sometimes language barriers and bullying.

In the face of discrimination, fear, and isolation, many in my generation, especially young men, looked for support elsewhere, leading to the formation of gangs. Gangs were created by Cambodians not only as support systems, but also, to protect themselves from other groups--Mexicans, Blacks, and others--who had their own gangs and would harass us. There were no mentors or positive male role models in my life, so I turned to my "street family" when I needed advice or guidance. I was living amongst racism, poverty, violence, and crime, and fell into that lifestyle.

Still, even in the midst of all that chaos, I loved cooking. Over the years I became pretty adept at cooking, and I loved it so much! I told myself, when I grow up, I want to be a chef. As a teenager I started to work in restaurants, first at a

Cambodian-owned donut shop, then in fast-food restaurants, in Chinese restaurants--you name it. I started training formally in the culinary arts program at Long Beach City College in 2002. I loved the classes but was still caught up in street life and was spiraling out of control.

## The Turning Point

In 2009, my sister, who had always been a good person, respectful of our elders and our culture, and like a golden child--very smart and hardworking in school--died unexpectedly, three weeks short of completing her master's degree in business communication at Cal State Fullerton. She was 26 years old. Her death was definitely a pivotal moment for me. After she died, I began to think about the fragility of life, and how someone's life can be over in the blink of an eye.

I started to ask myself what my purpose was, and I saw that I was pretty aimless at that point. What was I going to do with my life? So I returned to what I loved, cooking, which gave my life direction. I started to get serious about my LBCC classes. Sometimes it took me 3 hours to walk from my house to school, and at first, I didn't have money for books, but I was determined. I asked my classmates to photocopy chapters from their books so I could do the assignments, and often, I really would have rather slept than study, but I had a vision: I was going to succeed as a chef. This was a really challenging time, too. Unfortunately, not everyone was as pumped about my pursuit of cooking as I was, and there were many naysayers. But when you are following your passion, you just keep going.

## The Rising Phoenix

I call myself the Rising Phoenix, because when I fell, I fell so hard and landed in a bad, dark place. I hit rock bottom. But like the Phoenix, I was determined to rise up. Even when others told me I wouldn't succeed, I pushed harder. Their doubt fueled my dreams.

In 2011, I graduated with two associates degrees, one in culinary arts and one in restaurant management. In my journey to get to where I am today, I think I have worked in every type of restaurant, from donut shops to fast food to gastro pubs, and in every position, from dishwasher to executive chef. I have run a catering business, helped others to open restaurants, created entire menus – you name it, I have done it. That's what it means to give 100 percent.

In 2017, I was one of several chefs to cook for the United Cambodian Community's 40th anniversary gala. We created a multi-course fine-dining Cambodian dinner for more than 500 people. This was the first time I have seen Cambodian food served as part of a fine-dining experience. It was a very proud moment for me. And that was just a little preview of where we can go from here. Because I know that we can put Cambodian food on the map, not by turning away from traditional *kroeung*, but by being willing to experiment with new combinations and fusions and offer conventional things in a more modern way. Still, maintaining the connection to being Cambodian is really important to me, so what I cook, whether it is *samlaw* or sliders or pizza, always has some Khmer ingredients or elements.

# One Night in Battambang
# មួយរាត្រីនៅបាត់ដំបង

**Twah Koh Fried Rice**
chili butter langoustine, lemon pepper kafir lime sauce

**Lemongrass Kreung Linguini**
prawns, clam, coconut cream pesto

**Cambodian BBQ Roast Beef**
phanang potato puree

**Hunny Durian Bread Pudding**
whipped cream, chocolate ganache, coconut wafer

#ChefT #TheRisingPhoenix #DjHhunny #TheAdvocate
#Nüddlehaüs #GoodTuesdays

**Figure 71.** (left): Menu from an event in Long Beach, CA, October 2017. Image courtesy of Chef T

**Figure 72.** (right): Menu from "Sinn Sisamouth Night #2," Chef T's Special Menu, Long Beach, CA, March 2018. Photo courtesy of Chef T

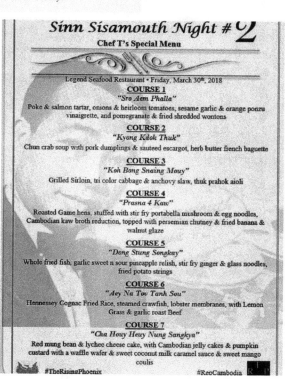

*Sinn Sisamouth Night # 2*

**Chef T's Special Menu**

Legend Seafood Restaurant • Friday, March 30th, 2018

**COURSE 1**
*"Sro Aem Phalla"*
Poke & salmon tartar, onions & heirloom tomatoes, sesame garlic & orange ponzu vinaigrette, and pomegranate & fried shredded wontons

**COURSE 2**
*"Kyong Kdok Thuk"*
Chun crab soup with pork dumplings & sauteed escargot, herb butter french baguette

**COURSE 3**
*"Koh Bong Snaing Mouy"*
Grilled Sirloin, tri color cabbage & anchovy slaw, thuk prahok aioli

**COURSE 4**
*"Prasna 4 Kaw"*
Roasted Game hens, stuffed with stir fry portabella mushroom & egg noodles, Cambodian kaw broth reduction, topped with persemian chutney & fried banana & walnut glaze

**COURSE 5**
*"Dong Stung Songkuy"*
Whole fried fish, garlic sweet n sour pineapple relish, stir fry ginger & glass noodles, fried potato strings

**COURSE 6**
*"Aey Na Tov Tanh Sou"*
Hennessey Cognac Fried Rice, steamed crawfish, lobster membranes, with Lemon Grass & garlic roast Beef

**COURSE 7**
*"Cha Houy Heuy Nung Sangkya"*
Red mung bean & lychee cheese cake, with Cambodian jelly cakes & pumpkin custard with a waffle wafer & sweet coconut milk caramel sauce & sweet mango coulis

#TheRisingPhoenix                    #ReoCambodia

I like to infuse Cambodian flavors in whatever I cook. I come up with things like *twah koh* (Cambodian sausage) fried rice with kafir lime, or lemongrass *kroeung* linguini. I love both creating and cooking and then seeing the reactions on people's faces when they experience these fusions.

I once created a series of special menus for an event honoring the famous and beloved Cambodian singer, Sinn Sisamouth, held at a local restaurant. Sinn Sisamouth is definitely an icon in the Khmer community, especially in Long Beach, so I was very thoughtful in developing the menu items. Each dish had meaning and connection and was named after one of Sisamouth's classic songs. The dishes featured modern twists on Khmer classics, sometimes playing on the song lyrics.

As one example, "Kyong Kdok Thuk" (Course 2 on the menu on the previous page) was named after the classic song, "Kyong Kdok Thuk Chun," which is about the sound a snail makes when the tide comes in. So the dish featured escargot in a soup. The song title is a metaphor of course, but it made sense to make the dish with snails and "water" [soup].

## Vision for the Future

I once posted on my Instagram: "As a kid from the streets of the LBC of the 90s, I didn't think I would live to see 40. Yet here I am." Sometimes you have to really put yourself out there, even if you might fail.

At one point I was invited to be part of a cooking competition on television--you know, where they put you up against other chefs and you have to use certain ingredients in your dishes. I did really well in the first two rounds, but in the dessert round, one of the ingredients was wasabi. For a dessert! I decided to make a donut, because even though donuts aren't really a Cambodian food, they are certainly part of the Cambodian American experience, so I thought it would be appropriate and fun.

I ended up making a wasabi donut, and it was a beautiful presentation, but unfortunately, it tasted terrible. I didn't win the competition, but it was definitely fun to stretch myself.

I have a tattoo of a phoenix as a reminder that I was able to rise up from the darkest place and reemerge as Chef T. In 2019, I named my first-born son Phoenix. My wife and son are everything to me--what I do I do not only for myself, but also for them.

**Figure 73.** *Chef T,* graphite on pink donut box, 25" x 30.5," 2019-2020. Chef T. featured as part of a billboard art exhibit, Los Angeles, April 2021. Artwork by and courtesy of Phung Huynh. Billboard exhibit by The Billboard Creative

I am grateful for this diverse country of USA, but I am also Cambodian. I'm fluent in Khmer language, and even have some knowledge of Pali and Sanskrit. I want my son to know his language, to understand it, read it, write it, and love it; to love the arts, music, and people, like I do.

To never forget who he is.

**Figure 74.** (left) Chef T (Tarak Ouk), age 2, juxtaposed with his son, Phoenix Ouk, age 2. Photos courtesy of Chef T.

**Figure 75.** (below) Chef T with son Phoenix, 2021 Photo: Becky Sar

In 2020 and 2021, Long Beach City College administrators asked me to speak at their upcoming commencement ceremonies. I accepted because I want others to know my story. Who would have thought that the student who had to walk three hours to LBCC would one day be the one to offer advice to the Classes of 2020 and 2021?

I want to continue to improve not only my life, but the lives of Cambodians and others in Long Beach and beyond.

What matters to me most is
FAMILY & Loved ones.

What I care deeply for is my
COMMUNITY.

What I'm most passionate about is
COOKING....

I love to cook.

I started to cook when I was 4 yrs old.

Went on to Donuts, Chinese food, fast food, bars, booths & eventually Culinary School Program.

Graduated from LBCC with 2 degrees, in Culinary and in Management.

All I know is the kitchen.
The fire, the food and the art.

With everything in life that you go through & with what's going on in the world & community, I find peace every time I cook.

**Figure 76.** Munchy Munch, Facebook post.
August 1, 2018.

# Lemongrass Beef Tacos by Chef T.

*Ingredients:*

**Beef:** 1 pound ribeye, cut into bite-sized pieces

## Marinade:

4 stalks of lemongrass
1 cup soy sauce
3 tbsp sugar
2 tbsp palm sugar
2 tbsp fish sauce
1 tbsp sesame oil
½ tbsp Kampot black pepper
2 tsp Chinese five-spice

## Sriracha mayo:

Japanese kewpie mayonnaise & Sriracha hot chili sauce

## Garnishes:

Chopped onions & chopped cilantro

*Recipe:*

1. Marinate ribeye in combined marinade ingredients for 12 hours.
2. Grill ribeye on flat top or in a pan until fully cooked.
3. Serve with flour tortillas (preferably 4-inch size) and sriracha mayo (mix mayo and sriracha to taste).
4. Top with fresh chopped onions and cilantro.

**Figure 77.** Lemongrass Beef Tacos recipe by Chef T.

**My Story: Mercredi Uy**

I was born in Chonburi in a refugee camp on the border between Cambodian and Thailand in 1981. When I was 10 months old, my mother, my father, my two older sisters and I relocated to the United States.

**Figure 78.** Mercredi Uy, owner of OC Crafted Donuts. Photo courtesy of Mercredi Uy

We landed in Fort Worth, northcentral Texas. Texas in general received a lot of refugees during the 1980s, mostly from Vietnam, but also Laos and Cambodia. My father found work in a leather factory where other refugees were employed and we lived in a house with several other Khmer families; however, we still felt quite isolated, and only lived in Fort Worth for about nine months before we moved to California. My mother would cook for the other families in our house to make extra money, and eventually, she was able to scrape together enough to buy a car (for $700) to move us. My mother really felt we needed to be part of a larger Khmer community where there were more cultural resources to connect with and participate in. So we moved to Echo Park in Los Angeles. Here, we were able to gather with other Cambodians and get involved in community activities.

For me, one of these activities was Khmer dance. As a teenager, I really wanted to become a professional Cambodian dancer, but I was plagued by self-doubt. Khmer dance is very strenuous, requires an enormous amount of flexibility, demands most of your time, and even with the utmost dedication, there is no guarantee of success. Also, at the time, nearly all of the roles, both male and female, were danced by women. Things are changing now, and there is more gender fluidity in dance, but when I was a teenager, men would dance the monkey role, and not much else. Finally, I wasn't sure that I could financially support myself as a Khmer dancer in the U.S., and I knew that being able to pay rent and bills were real concerns, so I decided to pursue another avenue.

If I could go back and advise my younger self, I would say, "Trust your gut. You are more powerful than you know. Don't waste your talents – share them with the world." And perhaps I would have become a Khmer dancer after all.

In fact, in my life I have done a lot of dancing, just not Khmer dance (unless you count the *romvong* everyone dances at parties). I was captain of our high school drill team and choreographed many of our dance routines. I also loved Latin ballroom dance, and even competed in high-level competitions and won dozens of medals. I guess you could say I channeled my love of Khmer dance into activities that were more readily accessible to me (i.e., in school) or more available within the larger Los Angeles community at the time.

## Becoming a Chef

One of the other things I loved to do was cook. Growing up, I spent a lot of time in the kitchen with my mother, who is a great cook. She is originally from Kampong Chhnang, and the Tonle Sap River pretty much dissects Kampong Chhnang, so not surprisingly we cooked a lot of fish. Cooking is an art as much as it is a science, and I love being creative with food, trying new or tweaking recipes, and making a dish my own-- that is, created with my own special take or flavor. So it was natural that I would pursue cooking as a profession.

I attended Le Cordon Bleu College of Culinary Arts in Pasadena, where I trained in classical techniques, developing flavor profiles, plate presentation, wine pairing, you name it. It was very intense. You have to have a true passion for cooking to get through the curriculum. But the first time I tried on a chef's coat, it just felt right, and I knew that I wanted to become a great chef.

After I finished my schooling I became a personal chef, which is very satisfying. I get to cook whatever my clients are in the mood for, within their dietary restrictions, allergies, or things they don't like. I let the market dictate the menu; that is, I like to use fruits and vegetables that are in season. I rely a lot on my training and intuition: whatever looks and smells good, I will cook.

In 2007, my mother decided to get into the donut business, and bought a donut shop in Santa Monica.

You probably know that in the 1990s, nearly all the independent donut shops in California (especially southern California) were owned and managed by Cambodians. There was a Cambodian entrepreneur, Ted Ngoy, who started the trend. He went through a training program at Winchell's Donuts, and then started opening his own chain of shops called Christy's Donuts, hiring Cambodians and teaching them about the business.

Even though donuts aren't a traditional Cambodian food, making and selling donuts in the U.S. became a way for Cambodians to succeed. Given that there were language barriers as well as discrimination against Asian refugees during this time, the donut business was a reliable venture. But rest assured, running a donut business is not easy.

The hours are very long; most bakers start in the early hours of the morning to have everything ready for the store opening at 5 or 6am, and even with machinery, making donuts is hard work. Many Cambodian-owned donut shops rely on family members to keep the business afloat, so when my mom bought a donut shop, I came on board to help. I was already employed as a private chef, but I wanted the family shop to succeed. I had never made donuts before.[57] I ended up taking a two-day crash course with Ted Ngoy on how to make donuts, and *voilà*: I added a new specialty to my culinary repertoire. And in addition to making donuts, I also helped to manage my mom's business.

**Figure 79.** Chef Mercredi Uy creating in the kitchen.
Photo courtesy of Mercredi Uy

**Figure 80.** Some of the delectable creations available at OC Crafted Donuts.
Photo courtesy of Mercredi Uy

**Exploring My Roots**

In 2012, after several years as a baker/manager at the donut shop, my mother and I realized that it was becoming too difficult to make ends meet by selling $1 donuts. I loved what I did, but after five years of grueling hours and decreasing profits, I decided to take a break and explore some of my other options. I wanted to do some traveling, and I wanted to visit Thailand and Cambodia.

This was my first trip back to the homeland, and I really didn't know what to expect. It was important to me to see and experience my home country in person, as a grown man. While I am a U.S. citizen, I will always be Khmer.

My initial trip to Cambodia was eye-opening, to say the least. Phnom Penh was overwhelming. There was so much traffic, and even though I lived in LA, I wasn't used to the noise or the congestion. I remember seeing entire families riding together on one motorbike and thinking WOW. It was so dangerous! But then again, they were doing what they had to do to get where they needed to go. I was also surprised by the markets, teeming with people trying to sell me things and bartering. I wasn't accustomed to that. It wasn't a negative experience, but it was different. And I loved it.

I also felt this yearning to come back and help. I saw so much poverty, and I knew that many people, especially kids, didn't have access to education or stable jobs. My first trip was just for a few weeks, and I knew I had to come back. I wasn't sure what I would do when I returned, but that was secondary to my desire to come back and give back.

During my second trip to Phnom Penh, on vacation with my best friend, I happened to meet a woman (Fiona) working with an NGO that strived to stop human trafficking. We talked about her work and my work, and she mentioned *Mith Samlanh* (Friends), a Cambodian-led non-governmental organization (NGO) that aims to improve the lives of marginalized and impoverished children by providing training in various trades that can lead to jobs. They were looking for a Khmer chef who knew how to cook "Western" food! She thought I would be perfect to take on the role of Head Chef, who would not only cook but also teach others how to cook food that could be served in the Friends' restaurants. What were the chances that I would meet someone who happened to know about a chef position in Cambodia that would also allow me to give back? Doing something I loved?

### *Mith Samlanh* (Friends)

After I returned to LA, I couldn't stop thinking about the organization and the position, and how this was an opportunity

**Figure 81.**
*Mith Samlanh* (Friends) logo

to help Khmer youth to learn something I was very passionate about myself. I got back in touch with Fiona, and she helped to set up meetings for me to talk with the Friends' administrators. The next thing I knew, I was back in Phnom Penh for a final interview with the Friends team![58]

Ultimately, I was hired as the Head Chef and cooking instructor there for about one year. The restaurants are real businesses serving real customers, so we worked hard to recreate the menu, which hadn't been updated for years. In the U.S., I had been working as a private chef, and I pretty much decided what I was going to cook within my clients' parameters, so being part of a large organization where decisions are made more collectively was challenging, but also fulfilling. Sometimes I went back and forth discussing the menu and specials with members of the Friends team for weeks. I learned a lot about teamwork and cooperation. And it was hard work. The electricity often went out (right in the middle of a meal service, of course), and it was hectic and hot and humid.

There are two different restaurants: *Romdeng*, which focuses on Cambodian cooking, and *Friends the Restaurant*, which features both Asian and Western cooking, so there's always something going on. It was a life-changing experience. I was also able to start to reflect on my own identity. Here I was, a Khmer American, working in Cambodia, cooking Western food! Being in Cambodia allowed me to explore my own history and culture and reflect upon how they influenced my own life.

Teaching, too, was a very fulfilling experience. I taught the students about combining and layering flavors, maintaining a hygienic workspace, appropriate food preparation and storage, and presentation as well as purchasing, scheduling, customer service, and other aspects of hospitality management. I really enjoyed knowing that was I was doing was making a difference in the lives of these kids. I had been given so many opportunities growing up in the U.S., and I wanted to give similar opportunities to kids in Cambodia. And I ended up meeting my future husband while I was working there, so that changed the course of my life for the better as well.

## Returning to the U.S.

In 2015, I got married and my husband Bee and I returned to live in the U.S. I went back to my livelihood as a personal chef, and in 2016, I also got a job as a baker for a donut shop in Los Angeles. That was an interesting experience because the donuts were vegan and organic. I am not sure we could ever call donuts a health food, but the donuts I made during this time were definitely made with wholesome, plant-based ingredients. I made everything from scratch and created my own dough using a sourdough "mother" instead of traditional yeast. I got to experiment with different flavor combinations and really refine my technique and create some unique products.

Eventually, however, I started to get the itch to venture out on my own. I continued my work as a private chef while my husband and I finalized plans to open our own donut shop in Orange County. Fortunately, both of us had been working in the culinary industry for most of our lives, so we felt ready to take the leap.

We were so excited to launch OC Crafted Donuts in 2019, and we are really enjoying what we are doing. Our donut menu features some distinct flavors, like blueberry cream cheese and pistachio green tea, and we've been experimenting with fun designs and decorations. We offer custom donuts that can be personalized, like those baked in the shapes of different letters to spell out a name, for example.

My creative process, whether for one meal or for a full menu, is pretty simple: I pull out a blank sheet of paper and just start writing down any ideas that come to mind that are remotely related to the theme or focus of the menu. Good ideas, bad ideas, doesn't matter; I just write them down, and then I edit, edit, edit. Sometimes a dish takes me 10 minutes to conceptualize and write down, and sometimes it takes a couple of days. I like to let the ideas flow, no matter how crazy they may seem at first. Cooking truly is an art as much as it is a science and I believe that when you make something from scratch and follow the basic principles of cooking, as long as you use high-quality ingredients, the magic all comes together.

With donuts, I just create things I would like to eat! Donuts are definitely very "American," with flavors like Boston Cream, Banana Cream Pie, Oreo. Only now am I starting to learn more about Southeast Asian flavors. My husband cooks a lot of Asian food at home: rice, sour soups, grilled meat. Who knows? As I learn more, I may start to create items using Southeast Asian seasonings.

Running our own business has been both exciting and exhausting, but we love it. We are hoping to open additional stores in the not-too-distant future.

**What's Next for Me**

It has been a busy few years! We have been fortunate in that Bee and I managed to stay employed during the COVID-19 pandemic, and both of us are in good health. We just moved into a new house, and we are going to spend time settling in, decorating it, and then filling it with good memories. We are very blessed.

**Figure 82**. Mercredi and Bee in their shop, OC Crafted Donuts
Photo courtesy of Mercredi Uy

# Chapter 7

## Film and Theatre Arts
## ខ្សែភាពយន្តនិងសិល្បៈល្ខោន

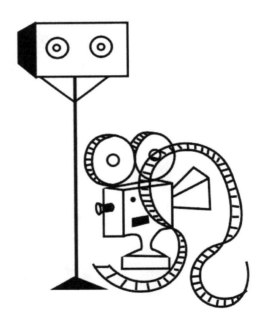

After achieving independence in 1953, Cambodia enjoyed relative peace and prosperity and Prince Sihanouk, who abdicated from his position as King in 1955 to become Head of State, encouraged the development of a vibrant arts and culture scene. He opened Cambodia to outside influences in architecture, fashion, music, and film. Cambodia began to see an influx of French, Indian, Chinese, Thai, U.S., and even Cuban and Russian films, and to develop a local film industry.

Between 1960 and 1975, more than 400 films were produced in Cambodia. The popularity of film spread, especially (but not exclusively) in Phnom Penh, which in the late 1960s hosted several international film festivals. Theatres sprang up and Cambodians flocked to them, eager to see love stories, Cambodian legends, and fantasy narratives in film.

Filmmaking essentially came to a halt when the Khmer Rouge took over the country in 1975. In addition to executing known artists, including filmmakers, the Khmer Rouge deliberately destroyed theatres and film archives. Decades passed before the film industry began to rebuild. When the universities reopened in the 1980s, neither the Royal University of Fine Arts nor the Royal University of Phnom Penh established a film department, nor did an independent film school exist; as such, there simply was no domestic mechanism for producing film directors or cinematographers.

Cambodians both in Cambodia and in diaspora were focused on surviving in their new realities, recovering from the devastation of the Khmer Rouge regime and reclaiming their lives. If they had time to watch television or movies at all,

Cambodian refugees often clung to the invented worlds presented in Thai, Chinese, and when they could be found, pre-Khmer Rouge films that appeared on bootlegged VCR tapes and DVDs and played on repeat in their homes. Filmmaking itself seemed frivolous (and certainly not something one would consider as a career), and moreover, most Cambodians interested in making films after the war simply did not have the capital to do so.

Still, slowly filmmaking is resurfacing. Renowned writer and filmmaker Rithy Panh, who fled to France after the fall of the Khmer Rouge, produced and continues to make numerous films in and about Cambodia. He founded the Bophana Center in Phnom Penh in 2006 with the dual goals of both collecting and archiving any surviving films from the past and training young Cambodians in cinematography and production techniques. The Ministry of Culture and Fine Arts established the Cambodia Film Commission in 2009 to promote Cambodia as a prime location for filmmakers and facilitate the permitting, casting, and production processes. Cambodia once again hosts several international film festivals, including CamboFest, launched in 2007, and the Cambodian International Film Festival, launched in 2010.

More recently, famed American actor Angelina Jolie, whose son is Khmer, directed the film version of *First They Killed My Father*, based on the book of the same name written by Loung Ung. Released in 2017, the film thrust Cambodia into the spotlight for the international community in a way it arguably hadn't been since the 1984 release of Roland Joffe's *The Killing Fields*. In early 2017, HRH King Sihanmoni and HRH the Queen Mother Norodom Monineath Sihanouk attended the *First They Killed My Father* premiere screened at the Terrace of the Elephants at Angkor, as did Angelina Jolie, Loung Ung, and Rithy Panh.

Interestingly, in the U.S., the development of Cambodian American film and filmmakers has occurred in parallel with the rebuilding of the film industry and training of filmmakers in Cambodia. That is, young creatives in both the U.S. and Cambodia have had to learn about filmmaking from scratch, with few Cambodian mentors, in a world in which technical equipment and the knowledge required to use it effectively changes at light-speed. Innovative Cambodian American artists have (re)turned to Cambodia as the literal and figurative backdrop for their films, whose themes speak to the challenges and aspirations of a new generation. While the Khmer Rouge period certainly informs their experiences, their stories often begin rather than end with a family's physical departure from Cambodia and relocation to the U.S.

As such, their work ventures into new territory: acculturation, isolation, discrimination, racism, inter-generational conflict, and longing to (re)connect with their Cambodian heritage. Moreover, young filmmakers have learned the value of collaboration. They may live thousands of miles apart, but with the assistance of technology may work collectively.

## Artist Encounters

The first artist featured in this section is filmmaker Caylee So, a 1.5 generation Cambodian American whose film *In the Life of Music* (2018) won numerous awards, and the Cambodia Oscar Selection Committee chose to enter it for the Best International Feature Film category for the 2020 Academy Awards.

*In the Life of Music* is one of the films that moved me in ways I cannot explain. I was the moderator for the Q&A session after the film screened at Cambodia Town Film Festival 2019, and as I saw Caylee and the others involved in making the film seated on the stage, for the first few moments I was so emotional I could barely speak. I finally managed to start the discussion with, "This is the film I have been waiting to see my entire life." Indeed, I had always looked for but had never found a film that explored the intergenerational issues faced by Cambodians and Cambodian Americans until this remarkable work by this remarkable individual.

Sokuntary Svay comments that in creative works by Cambodian Americans, "the 1.5 stories simultaneously look forward and back, with characters searching for guidance from the past and yet finding the search at odds with present-day desires in their current life in America," and many who watch this film will recognize themselves and their family members in the cast of characters, and their personal and collective experiences in the three storylines.[59]

Caylee shares her fascinating journey in this chapter.

The second individual introduced in this section is Kalean Ung, the creator of *Letters from Home (LFH)*, a solo show based on her experiences growing up in the U.S. as the biracial daughter of a Khmer father and European American mother. I was drawn to Kalean and *LFH* because I rarely meet another person like myself--that is, one with a Khmer father and White/European American mother, and who grew up not speaking Khmer. I see myself reflected in her poignant work, yet her story is unique and extraordinary, as is she.

I include Kalean's story in this chapter because of her career as an actor and teacher. The majority of her work is in live theater, and while theater and film acting are distinct from each other and unique, the techniques, skills, and experiences garnered as an actor in one medium can certainly translate into the other. While the execution of the acting may differ in each, both require intense preparation, research, and individual analysis of given characters.

Moreover, I like the juxtaposition of Caylee and Kalean in this book, as Cambodian Americans representing artists both behind and in front of the camera.     -C.S.

*Author's note: On October 5, 2021, renowned Cambodian filmmaker Ly Bun Yim passed away at the age of 79. Ly Bun Yim was prolific, having produced more than 20 films between 1960 and 1975. This chapter is dedicated to Ly Bun Yim with appreciation and respect for his talent, dedication, and the joy he brought to others through his work.*

## My Story: Caylee So

I was born in Khao-I-Dang, a refugee camp on the Thailand-Cambodia border, on September 17th, 1981, soon after my parents escaped from the Khmer Rouge regime. Then when I was just three years old, my family left Khao-I-Dang and immigrated to

**Figure 83.** Caylee So, aka Mom Chamrong. Photo taken at Khao-I-Dang refugee camp. Photo courtesy of Caylee So

the U.S., to Virginia, where I spent most of my youth.

I grew up in a family like most of the Cambodian American families I knew in Northern Virginia. We were low-income, and Mom and Dad worked two to three jobs. We roamed our small corner of the Culmore (Falls Church) apartment complexes. We were shuttled to "The Church of Jesus Christ of Latter-Day Saints" on Sundays, and on Mondays we would light an incense for Buddha and his teachings. We were a dual language household, with dual religions. We'd celebrate American New Year in January, Chinese New Year in February, Cambodian New Year in April.

When I was 18 years old and to the complete surprise of my parents, I joined the U.S. Army National Guard.

In 2002, when I was 21, I received a singular phone call that changed the course of my life forever. At the time I was a part-time soldier while also a student pursuing a business degree at Northern Virginia Community College. In that phone call, I learned that my mother, who at 50 years old was still a spirited and seemingly healthy woman, had suffered a brain aneurysm. She fell into a coma, and two days later, we lost her.

In the months that followed, as I scrambled in my grief to collect pieces and memories of her life, I discovered that she, a Cambodian refugee who had created her own business in the U.S. as a cleaning contractor, appeared in very few photos. Jumping from job to job, contract to contract, she was occupied with the daily struggles of a low-income household and rarely found time to take photos, nor had she written down a single word of her own thoughts. What remained of her were rare fading snapshots taken over random decades, scant physical evidence of her existence.

In mourning her death, I was saddened not only about the loss of my "Ma," but also by the absence of her story. When she was alive, it never occurred to me to ask about her life before us, her life in Cambodia. From my perspective, I was an American: my identity had no hyphenation, and I hadn't given much consideration to my Cambodian heritage.

## Searching for My (Mother's) History

When my family and I buried my mother, her gravestone was engraved with the dates April 10, 1952 – November 22, 2002.

**Figure 84.** A rare photo from my childhood of me with my
mother, circa 1992. Photo courtesy of Caylee So

In the months afterwards, my family members and I began debating about whether 1952 was her real birth year. And in the U.S., we knew she used the name Sophally Mom, but we were unsure whether or not that was her true birth name. Oftentimes refugees changed their information, fearing the Khmer Rouge might find them later.

Confused by my father's recollection and my siblings' doubt in the accuracy of what I had believed was the truth, I became fixated on my own Cambodian (hyphen) American narrative. Who was I? Where did I come from?

What did it mean to be born in a refugee camp after the time of "Pol Pot," when most of my aunts, uncles, grandparents, had been murdered? What was the Khmer

Rouge genocide and why did my parents barely speak of it? And why did it never matter to me before?

My thoughts returned to a memory from years before. While I was in high school, just months before the tragedy of 9/11, I signed up to join the U.S. military. I hadn't told my mother I was going to do so. When she found out, she looked at me with a sadness I will never forget. I didn't understand why at the time, because for me, this represented a commendable path I was choosing for myself as an American. To my mother, however, me joining the military meant deliberately putting myself in danger and embracing war, something she had left everything she knew in order to escape. My parents' silence about their lives under the Khmer Rouge kept me very far removed from Cambodia's history. I hadn't understood the extensive loss the genocide had on our family. Collectively we lost more than 20 family members, but we also lost our home, our sense of connection to a place and a people.

Now that my mother was gone, I felt the weight of her sacrifices, and felt compelled to piece together her history as a way to somehow keep her alive.

## (Re)discovering Myself

I began writing, trying to fill the holes within my soul her absence had left. I transferred to George Mason University and traded in business for an English (creative writing) degree.

Numbers and charts were objective and concrete, and no longer bore any interest for me. Stories were subjective mysteries I wanted to understand, and I sought to write my own stories into existence.

In 2005, I was deployed with the U.S. Army to Iraq. The war and the country itself were riddled with so many complexities that decades later, I'm still trying to deconstruct my own feelings about being inside that conflict. How could I feel proud of my service for my country amidst the stinging awareness that my uniform made me the villain in someone else's narrative? But it was there, on the streets of Iraq, in between combat missions that I found myself at a bootleg stand purchasing a copy of the newly released movie, *Million Dollar Baby*. Later that evening in the MWR (morale, welfare, and recreation) tent, I pressed play on the DVD player and took a seat in a dark room full of soldiers in uniform, all of us trying to escape from our realities for two hours. And sure enough, right until the end credits rolled, we forgot where we were. We were transported to another world, immersed in the story. That experience sparked my interest in film and its ability to captivate people in a way that could cause them to forget their own circumstances. I wasn't sure how, but I knew then that film would play a major part in my life.

## Becoming Caylee So, Film Director

In 2009, after completing two Army tours in Iraq, I decided to pursue a master's degree in Film Directing at Chapman University's Dodge College of Film and Media Arts in California. I had almost no film production knowledge or experience, but I felt confident that this was my path to pave. As part of my application for the program, I submitted my first feature-length script, entitled *The Ashes of Home*.

*The Ashes of Home* tells the story of Hope, a 2<sup>nd</sup>-generation Cambodian American daughter who decides to steal the ashes of her deceased mother from her estranged sister, so that she can take the ashes back to Cambodia. For years thereafter, the character of Hope followed me. Haunted me.

She was not me, but in her I saw a reflection of a version of myself--the "me" who had lost my mother, who had longed to return home but was never able to do so while she was alive. This is not only my story, but that of many of the 1.5 and 2.0 generations, caught in the hyphen between Cambodian and American.

**Figure 85**. Caylee behind the camera.
Photo: Sothearos Kiep

At Chapman, I committed every waking moment to the ambition of learning. I loved studying the art of filmmaking, but the real excitement began when I started production of my own films.

My directorial debut, *Testigo Illegal* (2011), recounts the story of an illegal immigrant (Oscar) who witnessed a murderous crime, but because of his illegal status, was too afraid to report it to the police; but by staying silent, he became wracked with guilt, and found himself torn between serving justice and protecting his family. That year, I was awarded the *Zonta's Women in Film* grant for Most Promising Young Filmmaker, and I finally started to believe that this--filmmaking--was where I belonged. Being involved in this creative work was painful, but inspiring. I began to truly understand the power of story.

In 2012, I directed *Rupture*, a short film which relates an episode in the story of a pregnant woman in a small village in Burkina Faso. The young woman is in labor and as it progresses, it becomes clear that this will not be an easy birth. As viewers, we agonize over what could happen-- what will become of the young woman, and if she does not survive, what will become of the baby? With this film, I was exploring the idea of inherited circumstances--that is, how as children we inherit heavy burdens of those who came before us and live in the shadows of hard losses. The question is, how do we free ourselves from this? Can the cycle be broken?

*Paulina* (2012) was my first foray into Cambodian American stories. In a way, I was terrified. On one hand, I wanted to give a voice to our community and our stories, most of which have remained hidden for decades. On the other hand, I knew I was taking a risk because *Paulina* broaches sensitive issues: one, gambling and addiction in the Cambodian American community, and two, the complicated relationship between Cambodian refugee parents and their U.S.-raised Cambodian American children. While Paulina's specific experiences were not mine, I find pieces of myself in it, because I too was the U.S.-raised child of refugee parents, and I, too, had observed things in my community that I did not understand but felt powerless to change. There is a dialogue in the film in which a police car drives by the gambling house. This could ostensibly lead to trouble, but one character, a one-armed genocide survivor, remarks, "Don't worry. We're the invisible people."

In many ways, the stories of Cambodians in the U.S. have been rendered invisible. When we arrived, many families were placed in some of the most isolated neighborhoods, forced to speak a language not their own and expected to somehow forget that they had endured unimaginable trauma. We were supposed to blend into the so-called American melting pot and leave the past and our stories behind.

For this film, which was also my master's thesis, I was recognized by the Director's Guild of America as Best Female Student Director, and that year I completed my Master of Fine Arts degree in Film Production.

## Sharing Stories: The Cambodia Town Film Festival

In 2012, right before my graduation from Chapman, praCh Ly, a Cambodian American rapper who had also produced some documentaries, approached me with an idea for a film festival to be held in Cambodia Town, Long Beach, California. He asked if I would be on a selection committee that would decide what films would be screened.

**Figure 86**. Promotional Posters from the 8th Annual Cambodia Town Film Festival, Virtual Edition (2020). Images courtesy of CTFF

I was excited about the prospect of viewing films spotlighting and giving a platform to Cambodian voices. I was "in" immediately.

Months later, as discussions and ideas continued, both of us, as a partnership, began laying the groundwork for making the festival a reality. Through our extensive research and planning, naturally, we became co-directors.

Our original idea was to host something small. I didn't know how many Cambodia-related films were out there nor how many people would submit films for consideration, but I figured that as long as we had five films we could screen, we could make some kind of magic happen. We ended up screening more than 20 films that first year including documentaries, classics, and shorts. Over the years (we are in our 9th year of CTFF) our programming has become more inspired, more ambitious, and more exciting as the number of films has increased alongside the rising number of talented brave new storytellers.

### In the Life of Music

My graduate school idea for *Ashes of Home* never materialized into an actual film, but the theme of the daughter of a Cambodian refugee taking her mother's ashes back to Cambodia stuck with me. Once I had training in filmmaking, I started to think about creating a film with a similar story, one that would address the intergenerational issues faced by the 1.5 and 2.0 generations.

Then, in 2014, I saw a film called *Don't Think I've Forgotten: Cambodia's Lost Rock 'n Roll* (2014), a documentary directed by John Pirozzi about the amazing rock and roll musicians of 1960s and 70s Cambodia. The film had a powerful effect on members of the Cambodian community, and on me. I realized how important music had been to them, and how when musicians were killed and recordings destroyed by the Khmer Rouge, that part of their history and story had been taken away.

The songs and singers, Sinn Sisamouth, Ros Sereysothea, Pen Ron, and others in the film stayed with me, in my heart, and they followed me to Cambodia later that year.

**Figure 87.** Promotional image for *In the Life of Music*.
Image courtesy of Innovision Pictures

Then someone pitched a short film idea, to me, and in turn I pitched a feature-length story that wrapped itself around one of my favorite Sinn Sisamouth songs, "Champa Battambang," a song so full of love and longing that I had always felt a connection to it.

This idea metamorphosed into *In the Life of Music*, my first feature film, released in 2018. Initially, *ITLOM* was supposed to be three different stories told over three decades, directed by three different directors, but it became something else. It became one complex and extended narrative of a family connected by a singular song. The song, too, had a life.

There are three time periods represented in the film: 1968, the Song of Love; 1976, the Song of Death; and 2007, the Song of Birth; and the way in which "Champa Battambang" functions is different in each decade.

First, 1968 represents the "golden era" of Khmer music, of Sinn Sisamouth and the Bayon Band, prior to the time when war began to engulf the country. Here, "Champa Battambang" is happiness, going out and enjoying each other's company, celebration, and falling in love. Second, 1976 takes place in the middle of the Khmer Rouge regime (1975-1979), during which the characters have seen their lives upended, their joyfulness and exuberance replaced by silence and sorrow. Here, the song is doleful and anguished.

Finally, 2007 is the year that many Cambodians in diaspora began to travel to Cambodia--some returning, some experiencing it for the first time. As such, here the song represents hope, and the possibility of finding (or reconnecting to) their identity.

I feel like the story willed itself into existence and kept organically changing into what it ultimately wanted to be: a love story. A war story. A coming home story. A story full of hope...of family. It is a flawed but beautiful story, full of heart...it is our love song to our parents, their legacy, and our shared history.

I'm thankful to my co-director Sok Visal, my creative partner Neardey Trinh, and the entire production crew of this film. To say everything was a challenge would be an understatement, but collectively, the team of producers, cast, and crew just believed in it and we pulled every string we had to make this film happen.

**Figure 88.** On the set of *In the Life of Music*.
Image courtesy of Innovision Pictures.

## What's Next for Me

In the wake of the COVID-19 pandemic, which has isolated us from each other in many ways, I find that *my telling Asian stories is more important than ever*. Stories connect us. I have a point of view when telling stories and it's uniquely mine, but there are themes and refrains within them that help us to find our way back to each other.

I want to keep making more films, keep telling more stories, keep building foundations that can make space for my community. There's still a lot of work to do; still a lot of stories to explore; and a lot of community building and unity that needs to happen. I think if we collaborate and support each other, we can do amazing things.

## My Story: Kalean Ung

**Figure 89.** Kalean Ung, actor.
Photo courtesy of Joshua Lipton

I was born in Philadelphia, but I did not grow up there. When I was just an infant my father got a job teaching music composition at Arizona State University, so we moved to Phoenix, and I spent the first part of my childhood there.

We lived in a White, middle-class neighborhood, where I was one of probably two Asian kids, other than my sister. I remember there was only one other (East) Asian girl in my class. But we lived up against the mountains, and there was always a wonderful energy in the desert that I miss.

Just before I started 7th grade, we relocated to California to join my father, who was teaching at University of California, San Diego. San Diego is indeed beautiful, but it was a rough transition for me. I was surprised because our new community in San Diego was much more diverse. But still, you know how everyone has a group in school? I didn't have a group. I had to figure out where I fit in, especially because I was mixed.

## Family, Culture, Music

As I mentioned, there weren't other Khmer in my neighborhood in Arizona, but there was a Cambodian family that lived not too far away from us, and I remember that they ran a hot wing restaurant. They also had a Pac-Man machine and other arcade games in the restaurant, which was exciting for a young kid. I really felt a lot of love from them: the females in the family would braid my hair (they were older than me), for example, and they were very kind. My dad's brother also lived in Arizona and we visited with him, but there wasn't a lot of emphasis on "Khmer culture" in my childhood. That is, the things we were doing were not necessarily unique to Khmer culture. They were just regular things that we just happened to do with Khmer relatives or friends. All except for eating. Obviously, there was always a lot of eating that was happening!

On the East Coast we did have my Khmer grandma and aunties, but even with them the culture and language weren't taught to us directly. I understand that the 1980s were complicated, and I was born in the middle of them (1986). I think Cambodians in the U.S. were focused on survival, and my mom doesn't speak Khmer, so there wasn't a "need" to speak Khmer to communicate as a family. I think my dad does feel some regret that he didn't teach us Khmer, but I also know that he was doing his best. These were extraordinary circumstances. I think every parent feels the same way: that is, *I'm going to give my children what I didn't have*, and they gave us so much!

In San Diego, one of my Great Aunt's (Auntie Sisophan) daughters owned a donut shop. After we moved to San Diego, we spent time with her and her family, and I remember hearing whispers about the war from them, but I don't recall anything directly stated or expanded upon. I think I knew there was a genocide, but I didn't know much beyond that; we were shielded from that pain. Occasionally, I would meet people who were connected to my family in some way, like people who had lived in our house for a while, or whom my mom and dad had sponsored. That "transition" had kind of ended by the time I was born, and my family (at least my sister and I) were disconnected from most of it. It is odd that I wasn't privy to any of this information. But you know that even if it's not talked about, children are so intuitive and they know something is going on, even if it isn't made explicit.

My maternal grandmother is Sicilian, and both of my grandparents were painters. Indeed, ours is a family of artists. My Mom was a viola major at Northern Illinois University when she met my Dad in January, 1978. He had accepted his very first teaching job there, hired as a one-year replacement for someone on sabbatical. They were both active in an experimental improvisation group that combined instruments from multiple cultures with electronics.

Although my parents have collaborated as musicians throughout their relationship, in the last decade and a half or so (since my sister and I have been out of the house), my mom has been performing pieces my dad has written for her which requires her to sing and play the viola in a very advanced way.

This has been both incredible and as you can imagine, intense at times!

My sister, Sonika, played the violin as a child, and continued some music training as an undergraduate, but majored in psychology and now is a clinical psychologist. We are very close. We talk all the time. I think that we are both doing the same thing (exploring trauma, identity, healing), just in different ways.

## Becoming an Actor

I was very clear that I wanted to pursue higher education to study voice. I knew when I performed as a singer that it felt "right." My parents are both accomplished musicians, but it is interesting--they never pushed me in any particular direction. I danced, I sang, and played a little bit of piano, but I was never forced. In hindsight, my inclination toward music was more about the embodiment and the transformation involved in the creative process.

Even in high school, I was very clear about what I wanted to do and made a lot of decisions for myself. I had decided I was going to major in voice and go to auditions, and my parents were supportive of that. I had a plan for how I was going to do things, and once I started the process, my dad took me to visit schools so I could make my decision about where to pursue my studies. Ultimately, I completed my undergraduate education at the University of California at Santa Cruz (UCSC). I remember that the practice rooms were in a building overlooking the ocean. It was beautiful.

UCSC had an amazing music program that was structured like a conservatory. I earned my Bachelor of Music degree, and I feel that I received an excellent education there.

I remember having a pivotal conversation with my UCSC voice teacher, Patrice Maginnis. When you are a music major, you have the benefit of private lessons every week, and you develop a closeness with your mentor that you might not have as a student in other disciplines. I was very lucky to have this teacher who saw me and recognized my strengths. In my final year of school, she asked me,

"Kalean, do you want to be an opera singer?"

I loved singing and would have been happy to pursue that path, but my teacher encouraged me to take an acting class. She saw something in me that was unexplored. The idea intrigued me, so the day after I graduated from UCSC I moved to San Francisco and started an acting workshop at American Conservatory Theatre (ACT). After the four weeks of that workshop, I called my teacher in tears and said,

"I LOVE acting! But I just finished my degree in music."

"You know, Kalean," she responded, "just because you love acting doesn't mean that you lose everything you have with music. You take that with you." I was so fortunate to have her as a mentor.

I then spoke with my acting teachers at ACT about pursuing acting, and they were very supportive and encouraged me to apply for graduate school.

That was a turning point for me. I auditioned for schools but ultimately chose to attend the California Institute of the Arts (CalArts) in Valencia.

Throughout the audition/admissions process, it became clear to me that at some of the schools, I was going to be appreciated in large part because of the diversity that *I* would bring to the school. At CalArts this wasn't the case; I could see that the graduate program I would be joining was already diverse. I felt that the faculty there really saw *me*, as an individual and an actor. CalArts is also an interdisciplinary school, so I felt that faculty would lean-in to the fact that I was also a singer. And they did. They gave me many opportunities that helped mold me into who I am, rooted in that identity.

CalArts has a fantastic curriculum, and incidentally, it is how I met Marina McClure, who was a directing student there, and who is also my collaborator and director for my solo play, *Letters from Home (LFH)*. During your first year, the training includes forming yourself as an artist, rather than just acting technique. The longevity, the thread of who you are, if you have done the foundational work in school--you'll have that forever. I had a wonderful mentor, Marissa Chibás, and she is still there for me. I give her so much love and appreciation because I know that if I have flown away from myself, from the core of who I am as an artist, she can always tether me back. In fact, she was the first to tell me that I needed to write a solo play about my experiences, which became *LFH*.

During graduate school I was in a production of *Camino Real* by Tennessee Williams at Boston Court Pasadena directed by Artistic Director, Jessica Kubzansky (also a CalArts graduate). Because it was a co-production, the cast was a mix of professionals and CalArts students. This opportunity led me to being seen and provided me with many future opportunities. *Camino Real* had a long run, so I had many weeks of performing and learning how to sustain a role. In school, productions generally have a much shorter run time. I was in school full time (8 hours a day) and rehearsing and performing in the play at night, so I learned that I needed to balance my time and energy.

I completed my Master of Fine Arts in Acting, which is the terminal degree in the field. I also met my husband, Sam, at CalArts. He was a year ahead of me in the acting program. He is American but grew up in Geneva. He came back to the United States for his undergraduate studies, returned to Switzerland where he worked for a while, and then came back for graduate study at CalArts.

## Experiences That Molded Me

I have nurtured my creativity in so many ways. One of my favorite performance memories took place during the first summer I acted with the Independent Shakespeare Company. We presented *Twelfth Night* at Griffith Park in LA. Every summer, their plays take place near the Old Zoo and people come with their families and have picnics while watching the shows. By the end of that particular season, there were about

3000 people at the park every night. It is so magical! The audience is a true reflection of what Los Angeles really looks like, which is so cool. There was a comedic part in the play where my character, Viola (who is in disguise as Cesario) and Sir Andrew engage in a duel, and we staged it as a very funny scene. People would laugh so hard, and I remember one night there was so much laughter that I could literally *feel* their laughter on my chest. I could actually feel the vibrations; I was in a vibration of laughter. I will never forget that feeling. It was wonderful.

**Figure 90.**
Kalean and Sam on their wedding day, in 2016 .
Photo courtesy of Hannah Arista

I've also formed relationships with people who come to see the shows. I have watched children who come every summer grow from year to year. It's a beautiful community vibe. There's a weird stardom that happens when performing in a community venue; for example, people in my neighborhood will recognize me when I'm sitting out in my yard or walking in the neighborhood, and there is this real sense of connection to my city in this way.

During the last decade of professional work, I've gotten a myriad of performance opportunities that have included classical theatre, experimental theatre, new opera, or somewhere in between. Straddling many worlds where I can do interdisciplinary work is exactly what I want to do and working with companies like Four Larks Theatre, CalArts Center for New Performance, and the opera company, The Industry, have been so transformative in that way. I've been able to act in wonderful classical theatre roles playing characters like Lady Macbeth, Desdemona, Queen Margaret, and Isabella while also getting to do experimental theatre and performance art with gigantic puppets with Gawdafful National Theater.

I also love teaching and have been doing a lot of it simultaneously while acting. Teaching allows you the ability to look outside of yourself, which is so important for me as an artist. It not only keeps you sharp, but also for me serves as a completion of the artistic cycle of giving and receiving. I think about the significance and power of being both vulnerable and strong as an actor when I am teaching now.

If I can create a space in the classroom in which my students feel they are and can be vulnerable to explore and even fail, I feel that I have succeeded. I know I was given that space and privilege to do this and I hope to bring the same to the next generation of artists, especially for my students of color. Some students have come up to me and said, "I want to write a solo play, too," and knowing that I inspired that, like my mentor inspired me, is amazing. I can't wait to see what emerges.

### *Letters from Home*

In 2009, Marissa Chibás had suggested that I write my story. I knew it would be a profound undertaking, so I let the idea sit for a few years and to be honest I wasn't ready. It wasn't until 2016, when the refugee crisis was escalating and the election was intensifying, that I put serious thought into developing it. I was horrified by what was occurring in our world, especially in the United States, knowing that I come from a family of refugees.

I approached my father and told him that I was considering writing a play about his and my stories, about his journey to the United States, about what had happened in Cambodia, about my experiences growing up here. He mentioned he had some letters he could show me. They were letters from family and friends, written in Khmer, hidden in a drawer in his study. They related some of what had transpired in Cambodia after he left, in particular in the 1970s under the Khmer Rouge regime. Many of those who wrote were then living in desperate circumstances in refugee camps and hoped my father could help them to escape, to come to the United States.

My knowledge of the existence of these letters served as the catalyst to truly begin the process of exploring my father's history, my history.

I felt an enormous sense of responsibility to tell these stories to the world. At the time, I was performing in a production with the Independent Shakespeare Company (ISC) when Artistic Director Melissa Chalsma let me know about a "New Works" opportunity coming up in February 2017 and hearing a little bit about the story I knew I needed to write, she encouraged me to submit something. That gave me a deadline for what had been a daunting aspiration. And so I started to write and I couldn't stop! This was the beginning of a new artistic chapter for me of learning to voice my family stories and learning to collaborate with people to bring my artistic visions to life.

I performed the first, staged workshop version of LFH at ISC and at my father's 75th birthday celebration at UCSD in 2017. The next iteration came in 2018 at the Cambodia Town Film Festival in Long Beach, then a longer, full production of the play at ISC in 2018, and then on to many subsequent opportunities at Willamette University, Mission College, and University of California at Irvine, which also gave me the opportunity to co-curate a companion exhibit at the Southeast Asian Archive at UCI called "Music, Letters, Home." During the COVID-19 pandemic, I also adapted a four-camera multimedia livestream of the play that took place remotely in my home office. The current version is 13 chapters, a journey back and forth in time in which I explore themes of family, sacrifice, and hope. The play blends my research with my father's original music and Marina McClure's visionary direction.

**Excerpt from *Letters from Home*:**

> KALEAN
>
> Dad, I am writing a play.
>
> You must write the music.
>
> Please dad, we need the letters!

*She sees him pause and take a breath. As she watches she tells her confidants—*

Within a couple of days he scans and transcribes them for me.

He comes back with the translations. His eyes are deep and hollow.

> DAD
>
> I began transcribing the letters and the ghosts came back. Now they are here in my office. I cannot shut my eyes without seeing them.
>
> KALEAN
>
> Oh. I'm sorry dad. I didn't know.
>
> DAD
>
> I am only a composer. You are an actress. I don't know how to work with words, but you do.[60]

Writing *Letters from Home* was so emotional and so empowering because it is my story. There is no category for me. Even in acting, there is no category for me, no one who looks like me or is me. I used to shrink because of that. But with *LFH*, I realized that I can't wait for someone to write for me or a character of me. I have to do this myself.

This is my path to being seen; someone will see my work and recognize that oh, there *is* someone like Kalean and that Kalean can and must be a part of this or that project. But until then, I just have to keep going, and hope that people catch up.

## What's Next for Me

I have been extremely busy for an extended period of time. I am now taking a break to reflect on all my experiences. I have had to say no to many projects to give myself space to think about how I want to spend my time, about what I truly want to do next. It's easy to just say yes and then watch the months and years go by!

There are so many things I want to do, but I, Kalean, can't do all of them at the same time. There is a part of me that wants to write new things, and a part of me wants to ensure that *Letters from Home* has a bigger life. And my dad and I have a five-year-goal: to write an opera. I don't really know what that entails yet. We wrote a grant to support this goal, and while we didn't get the grant, we received some great feedback from one of the reviewers who encouraged us to move forward with it. I will take some time to think about who I want to be a part of that project. As prolific as he is, my dad has never written an opera before, but we learned so much from *LFH* upon which we can expand, and we will explore this new work together. I am so excited about it.

One of the things I think about is that I have never had a Cambodian acting student. Where are the Cambodian actors? There aren't that many of us, so as a teacher I haven't had the opportunity to teach Khmer students, yet I hope to find those that are interested in acting and mentor them.

I am interested in exploring how to heal intergenerational trauma, in all ways, whether internally in my family or more broadly through my art. I think the reason I started writing was because I had to--I needed to do it. I will work in whatever artistic form necessary toward my healing. I'm still searching.

I think I will always be searching.

**Figure 91.** Kalean Ung in a performance of *Letters From Home,*
Independent Shakespeare Company, 2018.
Photo courtesy of Grettel Cortes

# Chapter Vignettes

The opening page of each chapter features an illustration representative of the genre or art form discussed within. Created by artist Seoun Som, these unpretentious yet exquisite vignettes reflect the striking diversity and creativity of Khmer arts, past and present. I am truly thankful for Seoun's willingness to introduce our chapters so beautifully.

I met Seoun in Athens, Ohio. At the beginning of this book, I noted that when I first arrived in Athens, where Ohio University is located, to my knowledge I was the only Khmer there (exclusive of international students from Cambodia). During the third year of my position at Ohio, I noticed someone perusing the bulletin board outside of my office. Seconds later he knocked on my door, and subsequently I met one of the most fascinating individuals I have ever encountered--and he was Khmer! Brilliant and extraordinarily talented yet soft-spoken and humble, Seoun has been a dear friend for nearly a decade. I am thrilled to be able to highlight his work in this book.

## My Story: Seoun Som

**Figure 92**. Seoun Som,
refugee visa photo.
Photo courtesy of Seoun Som.

I was born in a refugee camp in Serak Keo, Thailand and am of Cambodian descent. I grew up in Adelaide, Australia, but have spent a substantial amount of time living in the U.S.

Using various mediums, my work speaks to both the personal and the universal, forming metaphorical conn-ections between my lived experiences as a Cambodian in the West and a nostalgic ancestral land. My photos, sculptures, and installations address the conflict inherent in being stuck between two worlds, yet also reflect the limitless possibilities inherent in hybridity.

I received a BFA from Youngstown State University in Ohio and a MFA from the University of North Carolina at Chapel Hill. I have taught courses in both traditional and digital photography.

## Artist's Statement

In my work, I use personal iconography as a starting point. I strip my history as well as the art materials down to crucial elements, allowing for a greater, more universal understanding of my work without losing the integrity of personal and historical reference.

Figure 93. Seoun Som, artist. Photo: Seoun Som.

As a transient, I switch between cultures and identities. In a way, I am a hybrid of many cultures and identities. This hybridity is reflected in my work, which addresses the connectivity between transients and those that are acclimated to a specific cultural identity. I use the notion of connectivity to refer to the exchange of ideologies between my perspectives against that of a dominating culture.

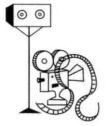

# CONCLUSION

While this book chronicles the experiences of more than a dozen artists, I found it difficult to stop writing. Each time I read through the chapters, I wanted to ask more questions, hear more histories, and write more descriptions and interpretations.

In the Acknowledgements section at the beginning of this work, I noted that I wish I had this book to read when I was growing up. I feel even more strongly about that now, because for me, through this book stories replace the silence--of not knowing, of not understanding, of not belonging. How I longed for these stories as a child, a student, a Cambodian, an American--as a human being.

Most U.S. history textbooks, if they include Southeast Asian Americans at all, lump them together, usually at the very end of the book. They inform the reader in a few paragraphs that there was war in "Indochina" in the 1960s and 70s which resulted in thousands of refugees relocating to the U.S. beginning in the 1980s. And while this is true, a cursory mention certainly does not reflect the diversity of experiences of these communities, or the individuals within these different communities.

Even within the discipline of Asian American studies, the curricula have rarely or barely included the experiences of Southeast Asian Americans, especially Cambodian Americans. And yet here we are. My hope is that this book can shed light on some of these collective experiences and individual journeys and inspire us to share more.

The American poet Muriel Rukeyser wrote, "The universe is made of stories, not of atoms."[61] Certainly, it is through stories that we truly engage with life and through which we find meaning. This book of stories reminds us that war is not something abstract. Scholars can intellectualize and develop theories about why war happens and how to interpret its causes and effects. First-hand stories, however, remind us that war is not just a series of military maneuvers or policy decisions. It is a bomb which destroys a village, a wounded child caught in the crossfire, a family torn apart. It is an earthquake whose aftershocks continue to be felt, and whose damage must be confronted, sorted through, rebuilt, and healed.

In 2017, I launched the Khmer Generations Project, a digital stories project to document the stories of the Cambodian experience. Because many of those who have first-hand knowledge about what happened during the Khmer Rouge regime are in their 60s, 70s, and older, I established the project hoping to gather the stories of our elders while we still can. But as I began to interview people, I realized that the stories of younger Khmer are also vital. I now hope to also capture narratives that reflect how the 1.5, 2.0, and even 3.0 generations negotiate their relationships with their elders, acknowledge their Khmer heritage and history, and reconcile their Cambodian and American identities.

The project stalled due to the pandemic, but I hope to begin again with renewed energy and appreciation for the importance of these stories. Moreover, our expanded goal with the Khmer Generations Project is to include not only digital stories, but original creative works as well: drawings, paintings, poems, fiction, nonfiction, music, films, dance, designs, and other artistic endeavors by members of the Khmer community. Through these arts, we can continue the conversations about Cambodian diasporic histories and identities.

To this end, we hope others will join us, share their artistry with us--and with our future generations--and contribute to the dynamic narrative of "Khmerness" in the United States.

## Connect with us

If you would like to know more about the artists and their work or about the Khmer Generations Project, connect with us on social media.

| Vannak Pen/Lok Kru Kirihingsa |
| --- |
| @kirihingsa2021 |

| Tanaka Nhong |
| --- |
| @naka.xcvi |

| Reaksmey (Mea) Lath/Khmer Arts Academy |
| --- |
| www.khmerarts.org/ |
| /khmerartsacademy |
| @khmerarts |

| Heidi Hou |
| --- |
| www.eventsbythecea.net/heidi |
| @eventsbythecea |

| Sayon Syprasoeuth/Sayon Arts |
| --- |
| www.sayonart.com |
| /sayonart |
| @sayonart |

| Alan Khum/Alan Khum Art |
| --- |
| www.alankhum.com |
| /alankhumart |
| @juturnal |

| praCh Ly/Cambodia Town Film Festival |
| --- |
| www.prachly.com/ www.cambodiatownfilmfestival.com |
| /CambodiaTownFilmFestival |
| @cambodiatownfilmfestival |

| Laura Tevary Mam/Baramey Production |
| --- |
| www.baramey.com/ |
| /barameyofficial |
| @barameyofficial |

| **Ratha Chuon Kim/Rajana Threads** |
|---|
| 🌐 www.rajanathreads.square.site |
| 🄵 /rajanathreads |
| 📷 @rajanathreads |

| **Krystal M. Chuon/The Mealea Collection** |
|---|
| 🌐 www.mealeacollection.com/ |
| 📷 @themealeacollection |

| **Visoth Tarak Ouk/Chef T** |
|---|
| 📷 @ therisingphoenixlbc562 |

| **Mercredi Uy/OC Crafted Donuts** |
|---|
| 🌐 www.occrafteddonuts.com |
| 🄵 /occrafteddonuts |
| 📷 @OC Crafteddonuts |

| **Caylee So/BeNorth Films/In the Life of Music** |
|---|
| 🌐 www.benorthfilms.com/ www.inthelifeofmusic.com |
| 🄵 /inthelifeofmusic |
| 📷 @cayleenorthmusic/@inthelifeofmusic |

| **Kalean Ung/Letters from Home** |
|---|
| 🌐 www.kaleanung.com/ |
| 🄵 /kalean.ung |
| 📷 @cambocombo |

| **Christine Su/Khmer Generations Project** |
|---|
| 🌐 www.khmergenerations.org/ |
| 🄵 /khmergenerations |
| 📷 @khmergenerations |

If you are interested in obtaining an accompanying study guide for this book, or if you are interested in sharing your story in Dr. Su's next book, please send an email to *christine@khmergenerations.org.*

# Notes

## Introduction

[1]In the late 1960s, sociologist Ruben Rumbaut used the term "one and a half generation" to describe Cuban American child immigrants, commenting that they were "stuck between cultures" as their experiences differed from those who were fully first-generation (adult immigrants or refugees) or fully second-generation (children of immigrants or refugees born in the U.S.). He later revised the term to "1.5 generation" in describing Southeast Asian American youth in the 1980s. Some scholars, including Rumbaut, eventually ascribed to a 1.5-generation scale. That is, they identify sub-categories according to age of arrival: those who arrived in the U.S. between ages six and 12 are the truest "1.5s." Those who came at age five or younger are "1.75s," their experiences closer to those of the second generation, with little or no memory of their native country. He designates older youths, who arrived in the U.S. between the ages of 13 and 17 as "1.25s," more likely to have an outlook similar to the first generation. For purposes of this book, the 1.5 generation refers to all those born outside of the U.S. (e.g., in Cambodia or in the refugee camps on the Thai-Cambodia border, or in interim centers in the Philippines), who then relocated to and grew up in the U.S., and the 2.0 generation refers to those Cambodians born in the U.S.

[2]Southeast Asia Resource Action Center (SEARAC, 2020), Policy brief: *The Right to Heal: Southeast Asian Mental Health in California*, p. 11.

[3]Khmer Girls in Action, *Step Into Long Beach: Exposing How Cambodian American Youth are Under Resourced, Over Policed, and Fighting Back for their Wellness!* Long Beach, CA: Khmer Girls in Action, 2011.

[4]Sokunthary Svay, "Cambodia Film Version 1.5: New Narratives for Khmers in America." *Hyphen Magazine: Asian America Unabridged.* Issue 8, Fall 2014. Accessed 25 May 2021 via https://hyphenmagazine.com/magazine/issue-28-revolution-issue-fall-2014/cambodian-film-version-15

## Chapter 1: Ancient Khmer Martial Arts

[5]Originally constructed as a Hindu monument by King Suryavarman II (r. 1113-1150), Angkor Wat became a Buddhist temple under the reign of King Jayavarman VII (r. 1181-1218).

[6]The *Reamker* is the Khmer adaption of the *Ramayana*, an ancient Indian (Sanskrit) epic which follows Prince Rama's quest to rescue his beloved wife Sita from the clutches of Ravana, his nemesis, with the help of an army of monkeys.

[7]Grappling refers to the technique of seizing, gripping, or otherwise gaining physical advantage over an opponent in order to force him or her into a submissive position. Grappling moves include takedowns, throws, and holds.

[8]*Pradal serey* is believed to be the precursor of *Muay Thai*, although there is disagreement about which came first. There are definite similarities and undeniable connections between the two. *Pradal serey* was originally fought bare-handed and bare-footed in the open air, but during the colonial period, the French mandated that boxing gloves be used and a defined space be crafted (this became the "boxing ring") in which matches would take place.

[9]A brief sample of *pradal serey* music can be found here: https://wiki2.org/en/Pradal_serey

[10]As *bokator* has become more popular, some have begun to use *bokator* as an umbrella term but in this work, I use *kbach kun boran Khmer*, of which *bokator* is considered one style.

[11]Some scholars and practitioners assert that the term *bokator* combines the terms *bok*, meaning "to pound," and *tor*, meaning "lion"; thus, *bokator* = "to pound a lion," a reference to the strength and courage required of those who practice it. However, this interpretation is the subject of spirited debate in the *kbach kun boran* community.

[12]*Surviving Bokator* (2018), a film by Mark Boschler and Sandra Leuba, chronicles the story of Grand Master San Kim Sean, a martial arts master who is working to revive *bokator* in Cambodia. For additional information about the film, see https://bokatorfilm.com/

[13]Some sources state that there are 8, rather than 12 *tvear* in *kbach kun boran*. Because this chapter focuses on the story of *Lok Kru* Kirihingsa, who asserts there are 12, we will use this number.

[14]Because Cambodians are subsumed within the aggregated "Asian American" category, believed to have fared well in terms of economic and educational success compared to other persons of color, issues faced by Cambodians in the U.S. (poverty, lack of access to resources, etc.) are often overlooked.

[15]*Kun Khmer* - ក្បាច់គុនបុរាណខ្មែរ Khmer Martial Arts Facebook page, posting from September 16, 2015. Accessed 15 May 2021 via https://www.facebook.com/photo?fbid=10153595455354304&set=a.10 150174988914304.314962.183993594303

## Chapter 2: Classical Dance

[16]As defined by Khmer Arts on their homepage, https://khmerarts.org. Accessed 28 April 21.

[17]Art historians and scholars note that technically *apsara* are the dancing figures who come out of the Churning of the Sea of Milk, whereas the other, standing figures who appear throughout the temples are *devatas*. In casual conversation (and in many guidebooks), most of the female figures carved into the temple walls may be referred to as *apsara*.

[18]Queen Kossamak choreographed the *Robam Apsara* in 1962, with the lead role first performed by Princess Bopha Devi in 1964 at an event in honor of Charles de Gaulle, then-President of France.

[19]During the *Sangkum Reastr Niyum* (1955-1970) under Norodom Sihanouk, classical dance became more accessible to "ordinary" people; that is, those outside of the royal family or high nobility.

[20]Suppya Helene Nut, "The Legend of Apsara Mera: Princess Norodom Buppha Devi's Choreography for the Royal Ballet of Cambodia." *Asian Theatre Journal*, Vol. 31, No. 1 (SPRING 2014), pp. 279-289. Accessed via https://www.jstor.org/stable/43187297 on 28 April 2021.

[21]Norodom Sihanouk had relinquished his title as King to become Head of State in 1955.

[22]The United Nations Transitional Authority in Cambodia (UNTAC) was a peacekeeping operation brought in to facilitate elections in 1993.

[23]The primary instrumental ensemble that accompanies classical dance is the *pin peat*. Instruments played in *pin peat* include the *sralai* (oboe), *roneak ek* (xylophone), *roneak dek* (high-pitched metallophone, *korn thom/touch* (large/small gongs), *chhing* (cymbals), *sampho* (small double-barrel drum) and *skor thom* (large double-barrel drum).

[24]As described on the Khmer Arts website, "Artistic Director Sophiline Cheam Shapiro has been expanding the dance's possibilities through works that push against the form's boundaries by enlarging the movement and gestural vocabularies, introducing new narrative devices, originating movement patterns, and experimenting with musical accompaniment, setting and costuming [. . .] Today, her students and others working outside of official institutions are making dances from a deeply personal perspective, defining for themselves how classical dance will respond to its contemporary context." Khmer Arts homepage: https://khmerarts.org. Accessed 28 April 2021.

[25]There are hundreds if not thousands of different gestures and body postures. For comprehensive accounts of various gestures, postures, etc. and their meanings, see *Earth in Flower: The Divine Mystery of the Cambodian Dance Drama* by Paul Cravath (2008), *Dance and the Spirit of Cambodia* by Toni Shapiro (1994), and other studies of the art of Khmer dance.

[26]There are both narrative and non-narrative dances in the classical repertoire, as well as many folk dances that incorporate aspects of village life (e.g., fishing, farming, etc.). Folk dances generally have less elaborate (yet no less charismatic) costumes.

## Chapter 3: Fine Arts

[27]Ingrid Muan, *Citing Angkor: "Cambodian Arts" in the Age of Restoration, 1918-2000*. Doctoral Dissertation, Columbia University, 2001, p. 2.

[28]See also Penny Edwards' *Cambodge: The Cultivation of a Nation, 1860–1945*, University of Hawai`i Press, 2007, an outstanding, nuanced analysis of how Cambodian nationalism and identity (Khmerness) was constructed by several different influences rather than the French alone: colonial administrators, Khmer intellectuals, Buddhist reformers, savants, and other elites.

[29]Henri Mouhot, *Travels in Siam, Cambodia and Laos 1858 - 1860*. Originally printed in London, John Murray, 1864; reprinted in Singapore, Oxford University Press, 1992, pp. 278-279.

[30] For an excellent analysis of French influence in shaping the narrative of "Cambodia" as a nation and the role of Angkor in that narrative, see Penny Edwards' seminal work, *Cambodge: The Cultivation of a Nation, 1860-1945*. Honolulu, University of Hawai`i Press, 2007.

[31]Ly Daravuth and Ingrid Muan, *Cultures of Independence: An Introduction to Cambodian Arts and Culture in the 1950s and 1960s*. Reyum Publishing, 2001, p. 244.

[32]Ingrid Muan, *Citing Angkor*, p. 130

[33]*Cultures of Independence*, p. 254.

[34]Ingrid Muan, *Citing Angkor*, p. 480.

[35]In March 2021, an elderly Asian woman named Xiao Zhen Xie was violently attacked on Market Street in San Francisco. This incident was one of a surge of harassment and escalating attacks on Asians in the Bay Area after the outbreak of COVID-19 (coronavirus), which many felt was "caused" by China and by association (albeit erroneous) Asian Americans. Asian Americans Advancing Justice has published a report on anti-Asian violence across the U.S., in which they state, "The latest wave of hate is the result of years of attacks on immigrant communities by the Trump Administration and racist rhetoric by other elected officials related to the COVID-19 pandemic. But racism against Asian is not a new phenomenon. It is part of the deep structural racism that has long impacted communities of color." For the full report, visit  https://www.advancingjustice-aajc.org/publication/faq-reporting-anti-asian-hate .
[36]On October 17, 1989, a 6.9 magnitude earthquake hit the San Francisco Bay Area, killing 67 people and causing more than $5 billion in damages. Many Cambodians (and others) left San Francisco after that event.

[37]Alan Khum, "Obscure Origins." Solo Exhibition at SOMArts Ramp Gallery, San Francisco, August 2016.

## Chapter 4: Contemporary Music

[38]See "Time to Rise" by VannDa ft. Master Kong Nay on YouTube here: https://www.youtube.com/watch?v=rvje5oblrLw

[39]See video of Master Kong Nay's PSA on COVID-19 here: https://www.youtube.com/watch?v=lOsZZUmrjt0

[40]After the fall of the Khmer Rouge, the subsequent Vietnamese-controlled administration, known as the "People's Republic of Kampuchea" (PRK, 1979 - 1991) did include lessons about the Khmer Rouge, but their inclusion was propagandistic and included graphic images of torture and death. Not until 1991, after the Paris Peace Accords, when Cambodia agreed to hold free and fair elections for a new government, did the curriculum change. In a strange turn of events, however, the new curriculum barely mentioned the Khmer Rouge at all. Claiming that the absence of the Khmer Rouge from inclusion in history curricula was necessary for national reconciliation, the government directed teachers not to mention this period in their classrooms. See Khamboly Dy, "Challenges of Teaching Genocide in Secondary Schools," in *Policy and Practice: Pedagogy about the Holocaust and Genocide Papers,* 2013, paper #4. www.commons.clarku.edu/pedagogy2013/4. Not until the publication of *A History of Democratic Kampuchea, 1975 – 1979* (Dy, 2007) was published in 2007 by the Documentation Center of Cambodia was there any material available that offered an overview of this time period.

[41]*DALAMA* is, according to praCh, a combination of the words *drama, dilemma,* and *trauma.*

[42]For a fascinating in-depth exploration of praCh's music, especially the second album in the *DALAMA* trilogy, read Cathy Schlund-Vials' piece entitled, "A Transnational Hip Hop Nation: praCh, Cambodia, and Memorialising the Killing Fields," in *Life Writing,* 5:1 (2008), pp. 11-27.

[43]praCh as told by Kong Nay." *Words Without Borders*. Soundcloud, October 30, 2015. Accessed 01 July 2021.

[44] See https://prachly.com/archives/tag/cambodia-town-film-festival and James Chow, "PraCh Ly Performs 'Dalama,' Perhaps for the Last Time" *Long Beach Post*, September 16, 2019. https://lbpost.com/hi-lo/prach-ly-performs-dalama-perhaps-for-the-last-time. Accessed 07 July 2021.

[45] *To Destroy You is No Loss: The Odyssey of a Cambodian Family*, written by JoAn D Criddle. (San Jose, CA: East/West Bridge Publishing House, 1992/2nd edition, 1998).

[46] The *tro* is a traditional Cambodian stringed instrument, with a sound box at one end and strings that connect to tuning pegs at the other. The *tro* is played with a bow.

[47] The video can be accessed via https://youtu.be/qdae6kAP02M

## Chapter 5: Fashion Design

[48]*Sampot chong kben* refers to a long piece of fabric that is wrapped around the waist, with part of the fabric extended in front and then rolled into a knot, pulled between the legs, and secured in the back (often with a belt), providing the appearance of pants.

[49]Khmer silk dates to the early centuries of the Khmer Empire, and patterned silk textiles can even be seen in the carvings on the walls of the temples of Angkor. Silk was one of the commodities that was imported into and exported out of Cambodia. The Angkorian sculptures reflect these economic and cultural exchanges as well; analysis by scholars has found patterns similar to those of Indian textiles and designs reflective of Chinese influence, and there are also great similarities between Khmer and Indonesian *ikat* [a resist-dyeing technique in which the yarn or thread is dyed prior to being woven into cloth.]

[50]There are dozens of variations within the broader categories of *hol* and *pamoung*, each created or used for unique occasions or ceremonial functions, including but not limited to *sampot tep apsara, sampot charabap, sampot sang, sampot samloy*, and more. For detailed descriptions of the appearance and purpose of the many types, see the work of the late Morimoto Kikuo, founder of the Institute of Khmer Traditional Textiles (IKTT), or Gillian Green's *Traditional Textiles of Cambodia: Cultural Threads and Material Heritage* (2003).

[51]Green, *Traditional Textiles*, p. 44.

[52]Poem by Krystal M. Chuon, excerpted from https://krystalmchuon.medium.com/this-body-of-mine-adc5259d61e6 ; accessed 18 June 2021

## Chapter 6: Culinary Arts

[53] Cambodian American Literary Arts Association (CALAA), *The Stilt House*, "Food and Identity" Issue 3, 2020, edited by C. Su. Accessed via https://www.calaalowell.org/food-and-identity on 25 May 2021.

[54] Nathaly Lee and Rotanak "Nak" Ros, *Nhum: Recipes from a Cambodian Kitchen*. Phnom Penh: Rotanak Food Media, 2019.

55 *The Donut King* (2020) is a documentary about Ted Ngoy, an immigrant from Cambodia who helped dozens of Cambodians to start donut businesses. He is credited with popularizing the pink box in which donuts from many shops in southern California are served.

56*Kroeung* គ្រឿង refers to a paste of spices that serves as the base for many Khmer dishes. There are numerous variations on *kroeung*, but most have lemongrass, garlic, galangal, kafir lime leaves, turmeric, and shallots. The spices are ground using a mortar and pestle, and the delicious paste is used in soups, stews, stir-fries, and as a marinade.

57Cambodian cuisine doesn't really have a lot of sweet baked goods. There are, however, an abundance of incredible baked goods in France, where many Cambodians who have lived or traveled, so pastries and cakes are not wholly unknown in Cambodia. Cambodian desserts are made with coconut milk, tapioca, bananas, jackfruit and such, but they are usually cooked over a fire or fried, not baked.

58For more information about *Mith Samlanh* and its programs, visit https://www.mithsamlanh.org/.

59Sokunthary Svay, ibid.

## Chapter 7: Film and Theatre Arts

60Kalean Ung, *Letters from Home: A Live-Streamed Solo play for Four Cameras* (print version), 2021, p. 16.

## Conclusion

61Muriel Rukeyser's *The Speed of Darkness*, written in 1968, offers a fascinating comment on the threat of silence, and the importance of breaking through the silence to tell one's story.

*My night awake*
*staring at the broad rough jewel*
*the copper roof across the way*
*thinking of the poet*
*yet unborn in this dark*
*who will be the throat of these hours.*
*No.     Of those hours.*
*Who will speak these days,*
*if not I,*
*if not you?*

# Works Cited

*Art Wraps for the Heart of the Tenderloin* art project. Created and conceptualized by Central City SRO Collaborative and the Tenderloin Housing Clinic. San Francisco, CA, September 2017.

AsiaLIFE. "#IAmOriginal." *AsiaLIFE Cambodia*, 1 June 2018, www.asialifemagazine.com/cambodia/iamoriginal. Accessed 01 July 2021.

Asian Americans Advancing Justice. "FAQ: Reporting on Anti-Asian Hate." *Asian Americans Advancing Justice*, 20 Apr. 2021, www.advancingjustice-aajc.org/publication/faq-reporting-anti-asian-hate. Accessed 13 June 2021.

Aymonier, Etienne, et al. *Cambodia Past: Explaining the Present*. DatASIA, Inc., 2016.

Baramey Production. "Our Evolution," 2021, baramey.com/our-evolution. Accessed 04 June 2021.

"Bokator: The Martial Art on the Edge of Extinction." *Culture Trip*, 16 Mar 2018, Available via: theculturetrip.com/asia/cambodia/articles/bokator-the-history-of-traditional-khmer-martial-arts. Accessed 3 June 2021.

Cambodian Alliance for the Arts. "Laura Mam & Her All-Female Band, 'The Like Me's.'" *Cambodian Alliance for the Arts*, 25 Oct. 2013, cambodianallianceforthearts.com/laura-mam-her-all-female-band-the-like-mes. Accessed 10 June 2021.

Cambodia Film Commission. "Filming in Cambodia." *Cambodia-Cfc.Org*, 2019, cambodia-cfc.org/filming-in-cambodia. Accessed 04 June 2021.

Cambodian American Literary Arts Association (CALAA). "Food and Identity." *The Stilt House 'Zine*, Issue 3. Lowell, MA: CALAA, 2020.

Chemburkar, Swati. "Dancing architecture at Angkor: 'Halls with dancers' in Jayavarman VII's temples." Journal of Southeast Asian Studies, 2015 (46), pp 514-536.

Chapman, William. *Ancient Sites of Southeast Asia: A Traveler's Guide through History, Ruins, and Landscapes*. Honolulu: University of Hawaii Press, 2018.

Chea, Narin, et al. *Seams of Change: Clothing and the Care of the Self in Late 19th and 20th Century Cambodia*. Edited by Ly Daravuth and Ingrid Muan. Phnom Penh: Reyum Publishing/Art Media Resources Ltd, 2003.

Chow, James. "PraCh Ly Performs 'Dalama,' Perhaps for the Last Time" *Long Beach Post*, September 16, 2019. https://lbpost.com/hi-lo/prach-ly-performs-dalama-perhaps-for-the-last-time. Accessed 07 July 2021.

Cravath, Paul. *Earth in Flower: The Divine Mystery of the Cambodian Dance Drama*. Holmes Beach, FL: DatSAIA, 2008.

Criddle, JoAn D. *To Destroy You is No Loss: The Odyssey of a Cambodian Family*, San Jose, CA: East/West Bridge Publishing House, 1992/2nd edition, 1998.

*Don't Think I've Forgotten*. [Film] Directed by John Pirozzi. Argot Pictures, 2014. Study guide (by LinDa Saphan) available.

Drutman, Kristy. "What It's like to Belong to the 1.5 Generation." *The Tab US*, Available via https://thetab.com/us/2016/07/11/what-its-like-generation-29952. Accessed 01 Feb 2021.

Dy, Khamboly. *A History of Democratic Kampuchea, 1975 – 1979*. Phnom Penh: Documentation Center of Cambodia, 2007.

Edwards, Penny. *Cambodge: The Cultivation of a Nation, 1860–1945*. Honolulu: University of Hawai`i Press, 2007

*Enemies of the People*. [Film]. Directed by Thet Sambath and Rob Lemkin. Old Street Films, 2009.

*First They Killed My Father.** Directed by Angelina Jolie. Netflix, 2017

Freeman, Michael, and Claude Jacques. *Ancient Angkor*. Reprinted. London: Thames & Hudson Ltd, 2008.

Green, Gillian. *Traditional Textiles of Cambodia: Cultural Threads and Material Heritage*. Chicago: Buppha Press, 2003.

Institute of Khmer Traditional Textiles (IKTT). Founded by Kikuo Morimoto, 1996. https://www.ikttearth.org/

*Jailbreak* [Film]. Directed by Jimmy Henderson. Kongchak Pictures, 2017.

Jameson, Narin. *Cooking the Cambodian Way: The Intertwined Story of Cooking and Culture in Cambodia*. Third edition. Phnom Penh: JSRC Printing House, November 2016.

Khmer Arts. (homepage) www.khmerarts.org. Accessed 01 May 2021.

*Kun Khmer* - ក្បាច់គុនបុរាណខ្មែរ Khmer Martial Arts Facebook page, posting from September 16, 2015. Accessed 01 July 2021.

Lisbon, Quinn. "Across Languages and Generations, One Family Is Reviving Cambodian Original Music." *NPR*, 29 Feb. 2020, choice.npr.org/index.html?origin=https://www.npr.org/2020/02/29/810155936/across-languages-and-generations-one-family-is-reviving-cambodian-original-music. Accessed 21 Dec. 2020.

Ly, Boreth. *Traces of Trauma: Cambodian Visual Culture and National Identity in the Aftermath of Genocide*. Southeast Asia: Politics, Meaning, and Memory Series, 66, edited by David Chandler and Rita Smith Kipp. Honolulu, University of Hawaii Press, 2020.

Ly, praCh. *DALAMA: The End'n is Just the Beginnin'*. Mujestic Productions, 2000.

Marchal, Sappho, and M. P. Hansen. *Khmer Costumes and Ornaments of the Devatas of Angkor Wat*. Amsterdam-Netherlands, Netherlands, Amsterdam University Press, 2005.

Mortland, Carol. *Grace after Genocide: Cambodians in the U.S.* 1st ed., New York: Berghahn Books, 2019.

Mouhot, Henri. *Travels in Siam, Cambodia and Laos 1858 - 1860*. Originally printed in London, John Murray, 1864; reprinted in Singapore, Oxford University Press, 1992.

Muan, Ingrid. *Citing Angkor: The "Cambodian Arts" in the Age of Restoration, 1918-2000*. 2001. Columbia University. Ph.D. Dissertation. Available via www.studykhmer.com/videos/muan_citingangkor.pdf. Accessed 12 January 2020.

Noren-Nilsson, Astrid. *Cambodia's Second Kingdom: Nation, Imagination, and Democracy*. 1st ed. Ithaca, NY: Cornell University Southeast Asia Program Publication, 2016.

Nut, Suppya Helene. "The Legend of Apsara Mera: Princess Norodom Buppha Devi's Choreography for the Royal Ballet of Cambodia." *Asian Theatre Journal*, Vol. 31, No. 1 (SPRING 2014), pp. 279-289. https://www.jstor.org/stable/43187297 Accessed 28 April 2021.

"Phnom Penh's Urban Artistic Renaissance." *Khmer440.Com*, www.khmer440.com/k/2015/09/phnom-penhs-urban-artistic-renaissance. Accessed 4 June 2021.

Phung, Hyunh. *Chef T*, graphite on pink donut box, 25" x 30.5," 2019-2020. Billboard located at Santa Monica NS 100ft E/O Hollywood Frwy F/W. Part of the 2021 LA Billboard Exhibition. https://www.thebillboardcreative.com/2021-show, Accessed July 5, 2021.

Reyum Institute of Arts and Culture. *Cultures of Independence: An Introduction to Cambodian Arts and Culture in the 1950's and 1960's.* First edition. Phnom Penh, Reyum Publishing, 2001.

Rojas, Leslie Bernstein. "Gen 1.5: Where an immigrant generation fits in." March 21, 2012. *Multi-American:How Immigrants are refining 'American' in Southern California.* Blog available via: https://www.scpr.org/blogs/multiamerican/2012/03/21/7963/what-is-a-1-5-where-an-immigrant-generation-fits-i/ Accessed 03 July 2021.

Ros, Ratanak and Lee, Nataly. Nhum: Recipes from a Cambodian Kitchen. Phnom Penh: Rotanak Food Media Co., 2019.

Roveda, Vittorio. *Khmer Mythology: Secrets of Angkor Wat.* Trumbull, CT: Weatherhill, 1998.

Royal University of Phnom Penh. Dept. of Media and Communication, et al. *Kon: The Cinema of Cambodia.* Phnom Penh: Konrad-Adenauer-Stiftung, 2010.

Rukeyser, Muriel. *The Speed of Darkness.* New York: Random House, 1968.

Rumbaut, Ruben G. "Ages, Life Stages, and Generational Cohorts: Decomposing the Immigrant First and Second Generations in the United States." *International Migration Review* Vol 38 (3), Fall 2004, pp. 1160-1205.

Rumbaut, Ruben G. and Ima, Kenji. *The Adaptation of Southeast Asian Refugee Youth: A Comparative Study. Final Report to the Office of Resettlement.* San Diego, CA: UC San Diego Department of Sociology, January 1988. Available via: https://eric.ed.gov/?id=ED299372 . Accessed 31 July 2021.

Schlund-Vilas, Cathy. "A Transnational Hip Hop Nation: praCh, Cambodia, and Memorialising the Killing Field." *Life Writing*, 5:1 (2008), pp. 11-27

Shapiro, Toni. *Dance and the Spirit of Cambodia.* Doctoral Dissertation. Ithaca: Cornell University, 1994.

"praCh as Told by Master Kong Nay." SoundCloud, *Words Without Borders: The Online Magazine for International Literature*. October 30, 2015. Available via: https://soundcloud.com/words-without-borders-mag/a-cambodian-rap-prach-ly-and-kong-nai. Accessed 01 July 2021.

Southeast Asia Resource Action Center (SEARAC). *The Right to Heal: Southeast Asian American Mental Health in California*. Report and policy recommendations. Washington, D.C.: SEARAC, 2021. https://www.searac.org/california/the-right-to-heal-southeast-asian-american-mental-health-in-california/. Accessed 22 July 2021

Southern California Public Radio. "Gen 1.5: Where an Immigrant Generation Fits In." *Southern California Public Radio*, 5 Jan. 2016, www.scpr.org/blogs/multiamerican/2012/03/21/7963/what-is-a-1-5-where-an-immigrant-generation-fits-i. Accessed 21 July 2021.

Srey, Cornelia Bagg. *A Pocket Guide to Cambodian Silk - Third Edition: - What It Is - Where to Find It - How to Come Home with a National Treasure*. Third Edition, Singha Books, 2017.

Su, Christine M. *In the Life of Music. Discussion and Study Guide*. Long Beach, CA: Innovision Pictures, 2021. Available from the author.

*Surviving Bokator*. Directed by Mark Bochsler. Produced by Sandra Leuba, 2018.

Svay, Sokuntary. "Cambodia Film Version 1.5: New Narratives for Khmers in America." *Hyphen Magazine: Asian America Unabridged*. Issue 8, Fall 2014. https://hyphenmagazine.com/magazine/issue-28-revolution-issue-fall-2014/cambodian-film-version-15. Accessed 4 June 2021

*The Donut King*. Dir. Alice Gu. Logan Industry Production, 2020. Film.

Ung, Kalean. *Letters from Home: A Live-Streamed Solo play for Four Cameras*. Music by Chinary Ung. Developed with and directed by Marina McClure. Los Angeles, CA, 2021.

Untitled. "Munchy Munch," Facebook, 1 Aug 2018. https://www.facebook.com/photo?fbid=1019544758230776&set=a.147702075415053. Accessed 01 July 2021.

Vannith, Touch Yin, and Chakrya Khiev. "Revitalising Ayai, Khmer Traditional Song." *Phnom Penh Post*, 2 May 2012, www.phnompenhpost.com/lift/revitalising-ayai-khmer-traditional-song. Accessed 01 June 2021.

"Will the Real Generation 1.5 Please Stand Up?" *KQED*, 27 Feb. 2013, www.kqed.org/education/4744/will-the-real-generation-1-5-please-stand-up. Accessed 01 September 2020.

Yang, Nkauj Iab and Quyen Dinh. *Intergenerational Trauma and Southeast Asian American Youth in California.* Policy Brief. Southeast Asia Resource and Action Center (SEARAC), April 2018. RISE for Boys and Men of Color. Available via: http://www.equalmeasure.org/wp-content/uploads/2018/04/Rise_YangDinh_R1.pdf. Accessed 15 July 2021.

## Selected Films by Cambodian Americans

*A River Changes Course.** Directed by Kalyanee Mam. Documentation Center of Cambodia and Migrant Films, 2012.

*Bitter Melons.* Directed by Thavary Kouch. Tiger Bear Productions, 2019.

*Daze of Justice.** Directed by Michael Siv. Little Connor Productions, 2016.

*In the Life of Music.** Directed by Caylee So and Sok Visal. Innovision Pictures, 2018.

*Lost World.* Directed by Kalyanee Mam. Produced by Emmanuel Vaughn-Lee, Adam Loften, and Kalyanee Mam. GoProject Films, 2018.

*Paulina.* Written and directed by Caylee So. Produced by praCh Ly and Perry Stallings, 2012.

*Samnang.* Directed by Asaph Polonsky. Written by Vanaira Taing. American Film Institute, 2013.

**\*Accompanying study and discussion guides available for classroom/community use**

# About the Author

Dr. Christine Su is an educator, historian, writer, and community activist based in San Francisco.

The biracial daughter of a Khmer father and a Scottish mother, Christine's research efforts focus on Cambodian diasporic history and culture, and multiracial and transcontinental identity.

Christine served as the Director of the Center for Southeast Asian Studies at Ohio University from 2010-2014, before relocating to the Bay Area. During this time, she facilitated numerous MOUs and study abroad exchanges with institutions in countries throughout Southeast Asia.

Christine serves on the board of directors of the Cambodian Americans for Rural Education (CARE) Foundation, the board of directors of the Southeast Asia Community Center (SEACC) in San Francisco, the editorial board of the *Journal of Southeast Asian American Education and Advancement*, and the advisory board of the Cambodia Town Film Festival. She is the senior editor of *The Stilt House*, a publication of the Cambodian American Literary Arts Association based in Lowell, Massachusetts.

Christine is the founder of the Khmer Generations Project (www.khmergenerations.org), a digital stories initiative that seeks to document the stories of Khmer of all generations through online oral history.

Christine earned her Ph.D. from the University of Hawai`i at Manoa, master's degree from Bowling Green State University, and bachelor's degree from the University of Notre Dame. She currently works in student services at College of San Mateo, where she is also adjunct faculty.

CPSIA information can be obtained
at www.ICGtesting.com
Printed in the USA
BVHW031140161122
651986BV00013B/1349

9 780578 955377